Cleanroom Software Engineering Practices

Shirley A. Becker
American University

James A. Whittaker
Florida Institute of Technology

IDEA GROUP PUBLISHING
Harrisburg, USA • London, UK

Senior Editor: Mehdi Khosrowpour
Managing Editor: Jan Travers
Copy Editor: Beth Green
Printed at: BookCrafters

Published in the United States of America by
Idea Group Publishing
Olde Liberty Square
4811 Jonestown Road, Suite 230
Harrisburg, PA 17109
Tel: 717-541-9150
Fax: 717-541-9159
E-mail: jtravers@idea-group.com

and in the United Kingdom by
Idea Group Publishing
3 Henrietta Street
Covent Garden
London WC2E 8LU
Tel: 071-240 0856
Fax: 071-379 0609

Library of Congress Cataloging-in-Publication Data

Becker, Shirley A., 1956-
Cleanroom software engineering practices / Shirley A. Becker, James A. Whittaker.
p. 208 cm. — (Series in software engineering management)
Includes index.
ISBN 1-878289-34-9 (softcover)
1. Software engineering. I. Whittaker, James A., 1965- II. Title. III. Series.
QA76.758.B43 1997 96-27545
005.1'068—dc20 CIP

British Cataloguing in Publication Data
A Cataloguing in Publication record for this book is available from the British Library.

Cleanroom Software Engineering Practices

Table of Contents

Preface

In a practical sense, it may be said that many aspects of Cleanroom have been well-kept secrets. The Cleanroom method has been used successfully on projects of various sizes and levels of complexity. But success stories of Cleanroom use often focus on a particular aspect of Cleanroom or on final results while providing few details on its implementation.

The purpose of this book is to bring together concepts, lessons learned and best practices resulting from Cleanroom projects with which the authors participated in the past several years. The emphasis is on practical techniques rather than mathematical theory, and it offers a fresh look at Cleanroom from a practitioner's perspective. It presents Cleanroom as a flexible and tailorable approach based on sound principles. In this way, it helps to dispel the myth that Cleanroom is rigid and orthodox. This is a book to guide the judicious use of advanced software engineering practices.

Several sections of the book are focused on organizational issues for the effective implementation of Cleanroom techniques. These concepts are primarily an outgrowth of experiences with large-scale projects that were distributed across many sites. The concepts on process improvement, information management, and team-based development provide a foundation upon which Cleanroom techniques can be introduced in an organization.

Acknowledgments

Many individuals deserve our appreciation for their contributions in making this book a reality. Geir Fagerhus and others at Q-Labs provided insight and words of encouragement throughout the production of the book. The authors' contributions are remarkable in the amount of time and effort that has gone into producing quality chapters. Michael Deck participated in more than one review and provided invaluable feedback.

It is important for us to acknowledge the pioneering work of Dr. Harlan Mills. Dr. Mills was a mentor to many of the authors. He was an innovator in advanced software engineering who respected the rights of others to use his ideas in new and different ways. We hope that he approves of our interpretation of Cleanroom.

Dedication

We would like to dedicate our efforts to Dr. Harlan Mills, the creator of the Cleanroom approach. Several of the authors have had the fortunate experience of working with him and have wonderful stories to share of his insight, humor, diplomacy, and kindness. Perhaps one of his greatest gifts was his ability to communicate formal concepts and ideas in a straightforward, practical way. As a result, many practitioners have been able to successfully use formal methods in every aspect of the development process. We would like to note that much of the authors' contributions are extensions of Dr. Mills' work.

Dr. Mills' contributions have had a major impact on the way software and systems are developed. His influence in the software engineering community will continue for many decades. One of his many contributions was the recognition that a computer program was a rule for a function. With this, mathematical rigor could be applied to the development and verification of programs.

Dr. Mills was an IBM Fellow and a full Professor of Computer Science at the University of Maryland until retirement. After his retirement in 1987, Dr. Mills founded a company called Software Engineering Technology (SET), Inc., that provided practitioners support in applying Cleanroom. His Cleanroom approach bridged the development gap between theory and practice that in the past has been a major issue for researchers and practitioners alike.

One of his colleagues and personal friends, Arnold Beckhardt, has written a few observations about Harlan Mills whom he refers to as the "Renaissance Man". We share Mr. Beckhardt's observations in a tribute to Dr. Mills.

I first met Harlan at IBM Federal Systems Headquarters in Bethesda, Maryland in the mid-sixties at the height of the Saturn/ Apollo program. At that time, I was the Operations Manager at the Federal Systems Huntsville facility where we were responsible for delivery of the Instrument Unit Stage of the Saturn Launch Vehicle. This stage was the "electronic brains" of the Saturn with among other units a guidance computer and related life critical software. We had gone to the Division Headquarters for a Program Review; the most amazing part of the review was Harlan offering succinct comments and suggestions about many different aspects of the Instrument Unit, not just on software but on hardware issues as well. From this first meeting, I always had the feeling that here was a man who could help you talk through and solve any kind of problem. In 1970, I was transferred to Division Headquarters and had the opportunity to work more closely with Harlan. Our paths crossed frequently and we talked about many subjects. It was during this time that I really began to appreciate the broad range of his interest and the many areas he had thought about in a problem solving way. Ever since those years, I have thought of Harlan as a real Renaissance man.

While our paths had separated again in 1973, when I was transferred to another IBM location, we stayed in touch. It was a happy coincidence that Harlan and I both decided to live in Vero Beach after we retired from IBM. Harlan and I got together again in 1987 when he talked to me about trying to find ways to improve the general state of the software development process. He had served on several studies both inside IBM and the Air Force and he was convinced that his ideas were a better way to "build a mousetrap" than current practices. He was always eager to share his ideas and wisdom without worrying about who got the credit for the results. When we first talked about starting up a business to act as a "technology transfer" agent, we started out with a nonprofit model; we soon realized that we would have a better opportunity to succeed in the transfer of his ideas to the marketplace if we could accept research and development contracts as a regular profit-oriented corporation as contrasted with nonprofit consulting.

While I focused primarily on the business aspects, Harlan continued to refine his ideas about software specifications, development and testing. I had spent a good part of my technical career in the system test area and we had many sessions about the best way to test both hardware and software; was there any relationship to the statistical techniques of quality control utilized in hardware testing and how did they apply to the software test problems. While we talked a great deal about the concept of "tools", Harlan never was a big advocate of "tools for software testing." His favorite saying was that the best tool for software developers was an eraser and a waste paper basket! The amazing part of being a business partner with someone like Harlan was that ...he just wanted the whole world to share his ideas.

It has been in these last seven years that I began to hear Harlan reminisce about his many projects in the past. He told a story about how as a child in Liberty City, Iowa, his parents had bought a six-volume encyclopedia for him and his brothers. Given a subject, he could usually state what page it was on. It was in this early childhood that his first interest in games developed, not only in playing them but in inventing them. He told me how he had discovered how much harder it was to invent a crossword puzzle than to work on one. His mathematical interests were developed in high school where he once found an article in the Sunday *Des Moines Tribune* about a university student who had "trisected the angle". In a class discussion of the problem, Harlan found a flaw in the college student's solution; he remembered embarrassing the teacher who hadn't caught the flaw.

So even then he was thinking of doing things "error free."

When Harlan started college in 1937, he studied everything but math. He had a great interest in art and English writing courses. He told me about how he and his roommate spent most of their time playing bridge and became the bridge champions of the university. Harlan left college after his freshman year and worked in his father's dental lab until he went off to the U.S. Army Air Corps in 1941. Harlan became a B-24 instructor pilot and established a formal training curriculum that was extensively utilized by the training command. In 1946, Harlan went to Iowa State and finished his B.S. in math in two years, his M.S. in a year, and his Ph.D. in two years.

Everybody who knew Harlan has their favorite stories about his different interests. One of my favorites was when he told me about his "play writing" experience. In 1979, when he was working for IBM and had already become an IBM Fellow known everywhere as the IBM software guru, he started to compose a play entitled, "Secrets of a Mississippi River Boat Gambler." I remember having trouble believing this until he pulled out from files copy of the script! That was another attribute of Harlan's. He had the most extensive collection of everything he had ever worked on and somehow could always find what he was looking for.

Harlan was a truly unique person to work with and he has left a legacy of work that continues to be the foundation of software engineering practices.

Arnold R. Beckhardt
Founding Organizer
SET, Inc.

CHAPTER 1

An Overview of Cleanroom Software Engineering

Shirley A. Becker
American University

James A. Whittaker
Florida Institute of Technology

This chapter presents an overview of the Cleanroom software engineering process model. The Cleanroom process is comprised of five core techniques that provide the engineering rigor and precision necessary for achieving quality results. These techniques are: (1) formal specification and design of intended behavior, (2) incremental development process model, (3) stepwise refinement of specifications to code, (4) correctness verification of developed code, and (5) statistical certification of compiled software. These techniques are applied in a team-based environment and are the basis for Cleanroom process adherence.

Cleanroom is a set of principles and practices for the specification, development and certification of software-intensive systems. It is based on the work of the late Harlan D. Mills, one of the world's foremost computer scientists and an early pioneer of what we now call "software engineering." Dr. Mills made a practice of success in software development at IBM where he achieved IBM's highest technical designation, Fellow. He did so by applying engineering rigor to the software development process. His methods are based on two principles: *that programs are rules for mathematical functions* and that *software testing is sampling*. The former principle allows specifications for software to be written in precise functional notation and provides mechanisms to prove that a developed program correctly implements its specification. The latter principle allows testing to be conducted as a scientific experiment, providing quantitative measures about the software being developed and also maintaining a framework for statistical process control.

In order to exploit the facts that programs are rules for mathematical functions and that software testing is sampling, Dr. Mills defined the techniques that he collectively named Cleanroom. The core techniques are:

1. Formal specification and design of intended behavior.
2. Incremental development process model.
3. Stepwise refinement of specifications to code.
4. Correctness verification of developed code.
5. Statistical certification of compiled software products.

Some of these techniques are not unique to Dr. Mills' methods. For example, incremental development can and is performed by many who do not use the other techniques. However, each of the above techniques was either invented by Mills and his colleagues or have a particular way of being applied that make them unique to Cleanroom.

The remainder of this chapter gives an overview of each of these techniques. Later chapters provide greater detail about the specific techniques that are being used in practice to facilitate the execution of the core techniques. It is important to note that we are describing how each method is implemented in practice today. We do not preclude the possibility that the techniques may change in the future. Indeed, Cleanroom is defined by the two principles, *programs are rules for mathematical functions*, and *testing is sampling*, and not the techniques that are currently used to implement these principles.

Formal Specification and Design of Intended Behavior

Formal specification of intended behavior is perhaps the most important step in any development methodology. The specification is the basis for many follow-on steps in the development cycle: planning and executing a design strategy, communicating with users and sponsors, and generating test cases and oracles are a few examples. In Cleanroom, the goal is to achieve a complete, consistent, and correct description of system behavior. Incorrect or incomplete specifications often result in schedule delays and major rework because the system does not meet quality and/or performance expectations.

The theoretical foundation of Cleanroom specification is that a program is a rule for a mathematical function. Mills identified three levels of abstraction for describing programs as rules for functions as shown in Figure 1 (Mills et al., 1986). These three functional views are called the *black box*, *state box*, and *clear box*, respectively. The black box is generally considered the specification of the system and the state and clear boxes are considered design. They are defined as follows:

The black box is an external view of the system using inputs, input histories (or some appropriate abstraction) and outputs. Its behavior when expressed as a mathematical function, i.e., the black box, is a mapping of input histories (all possible sequences of inputs) to a single output. Construction of the black box is the subject of Chapter 2, "Specification Practices," by Stacy Prowell. In Chapter 3, "Development Practices," by Michael Deck, a *data encapsulating* black box is presented as an alternative to the classic history-based black box.

The state box is a finite-state machine. It is an expanded description of the black box where input history is captured as *state data*. The state box is comprised of state information and an internal black box that uses the inputs and state data to generate an output and to update the state. The behavior of the state box is defined as a function whose

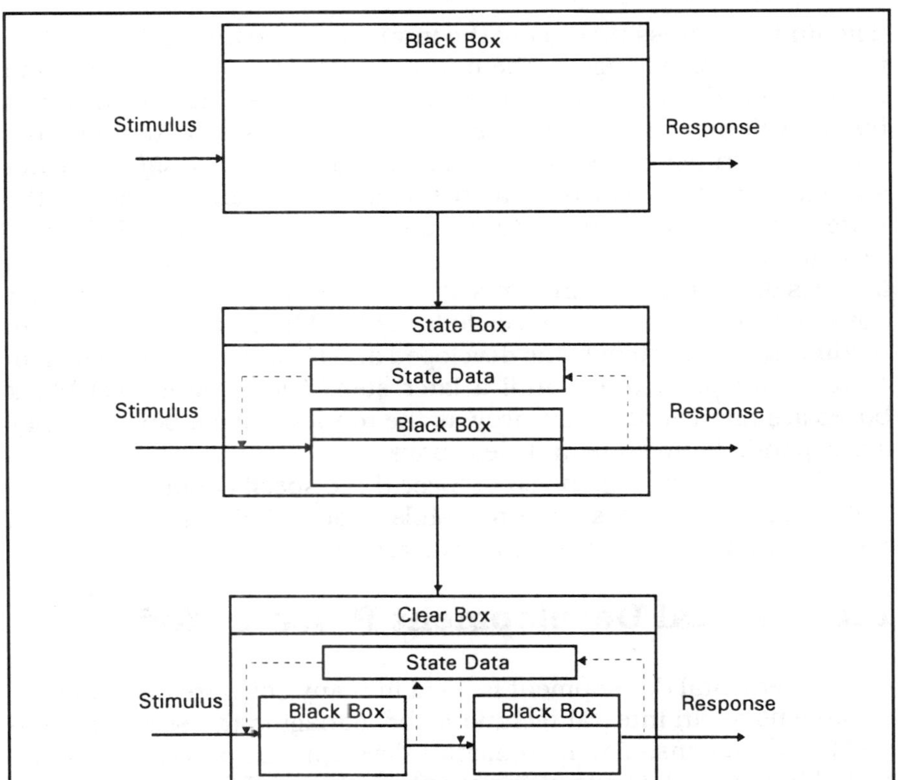

Figure 1: The Three Box Structures Views

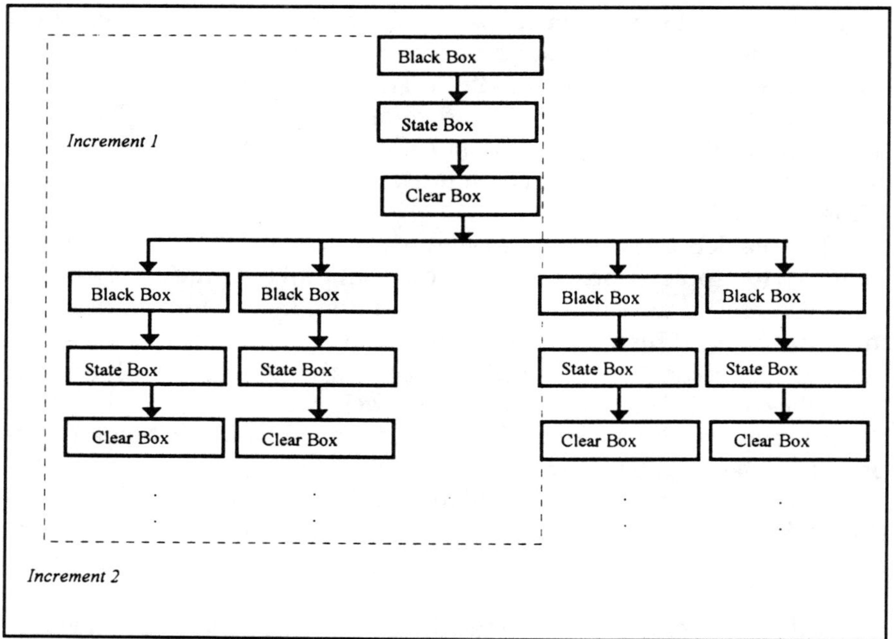

Figure 2: Box Structure Usage Hierarchy

domain is the cross product of the inputs and the internal state data items and whose range is the outputs crossed with the state data items. Thus, during state box design, developers decide how the input history will be stored by the system. Since this step constrains the possible solution space, it is generally considered design and not specification. The clear box has the same functional behavior as the state box but uses a procedural rule to describe system behavior. Essentially, the clear box is code. In practice, clear boxes can be written in a design language or in the target programming language. A clear box can also contain references to lower level black boxes in order to modularize the system being developed and to postpone the design of certain functional units until a later step. These lower-level black boxes are handled the same way as the top-level black box, i.e., they are expanded into state and clear boxes.

The usage and expansion of these three specification and design artifacts is called box structures (Mills et al., 1986) and is shown in Figure 2 in a box structure *usage hierarchy*.

Incremental Development Process Model

Incremental development is used in many software development paradigms as an integral technique for managing the size and complexity of systems. The incremental development process, as illustrated in Figure 3, is one of the core techniques of Cleanroom and is used to reduce the risk associated with managing large systems by focusing on smaller, manageable subsystems of increments that accumulate into the final system.

An increment is defined by a subset of the system's functionality. Essentially, the system is broken into parts and developed and integrated incrementally. For example, if a project has three increments then increment one will be developed and tested as a separate product. Then increment two will be developed, integrated with increment one and the combination tested. Similarly, increment three is a combination of the first two increments with new code for increment three. In all cases, testing is conducted on the accumulation of the current and all prior increments.

An increment should possess the following properties:

- It should be externally executable. This means that testers should be able to apply inputs to the increment at the system level and observe the outputs that the system generates without building additional non-product scaffolding code. Also, this allows any increment to be demonstrated or delivered to end-users should this become desirable.
- It should contain all the functionality of prior increments. Thus, the increments accumulate transparently into the final product. The last increment of a particular project represents the entire product being developed.

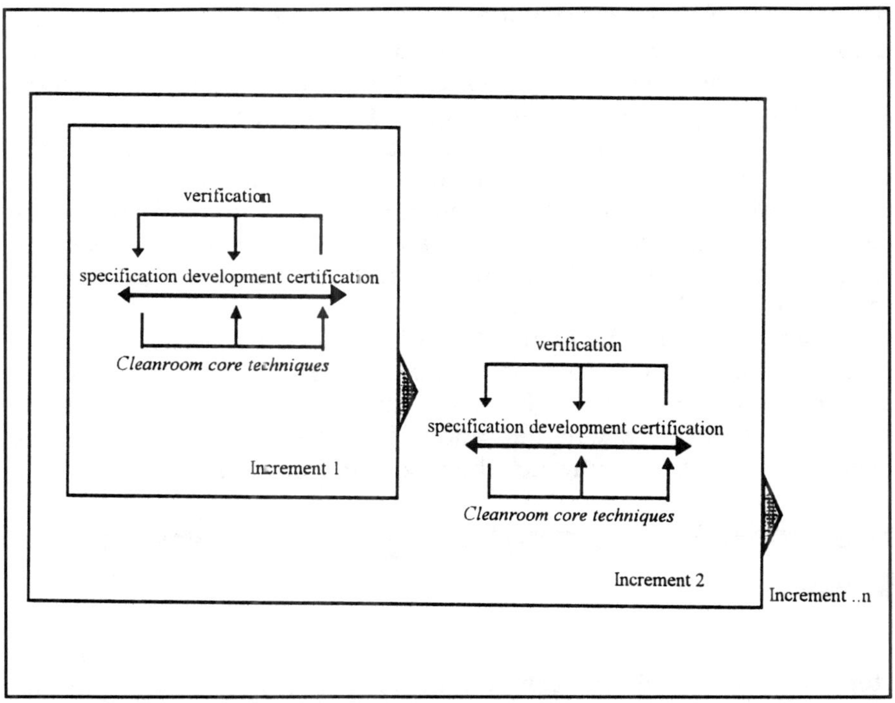

Figure 3: Incremental Development

There are several important benefits that result from the use of incremental development. These include:

- Specification, design, and certification activities may be performed as often as necessary until quality standards have been met.
- Intermediate delivery of a product is possible. Users can assess the accumulating system early; possibly resolving requirements misinterpretation earlier than otherwise.
- Timely feedback can be obtained in order to react to new or modified requirements.
- Intellectual control over a system can be maintained by decomposing it into a set of manageable increments.
- "Big-bang" integration and testing are avoided by continuous integration as increments are subsystems with accumulated functionality over previous increments.

The steps of incremental development are summarized below.

Step 1: Decompose the system into increments. Increments are extracted from the system specification and can be defined based on size, reusability, complexity, development expertise, past experience, or other factors (Cobb & Mills, 1990). There may be systems where the requirements are not fully known but even in these situations increments can be established. An increment may be modified at a later date when the requirements do become known. The increments are described in an *increment plan* that also contains information about performance, quality, and the integration strategy for all increments. This artifact includes increment-specific information such as expected start and completion dates and required resources.

Step 2: Perform the Cleanroom development and certification tasks on each increment. The Cleanroom techniques of formal specification, stepwise refinement, correctness verification, and statistical certification are applied to each increment as the system evolves into the final product. The artifacts produced from this step are described in subsequent chapters of this book.

Step 3: Assess the completion of an increment. The increment plan is updated as increments are completed in order to track the progress toward the successful completion of the system. This assessment will determine whether additional work is required on the existing increment or whether the next increment may be initiated.

Stepwise Refinement of Specifications to Code

Code for an increment is created from the specification in a stepwise manner where each step moves the design closer to actual implementation. The overall objective is to maintain intellectual control as the specification is expanded into lower level details. The specific objectives of stepwise refinement are to:

- Expand the specification into implementation via small steps where each expansion is verified against the previous step.
- Maintain intellectual control by designing data and control constructs at appropriate levels of abstraction before implementing the details.

Stepwise refinement produces a system that has been designed and verified in small, manageable components. The end result is an incrementally developed system that has been verified for correctness at each level of design refinement. This is achieved by decomposing the black box design into its respective state and clear box designs. This stepwise refinement process is performed until the lowest level box structures are compilable or can be directly translated into code. The steps of stepwise refinement of specifications to code are summarized below. A comprehensive discussion is found in Chapter 3, "Development Practices," by Michael Deck.

Step 1: Expand a clear box into lower level designs. The functionality of the clear box is expanded into lower level black box and state box designs. This is a creative design activity that defines intended functions at lower levels in the system design.

Step 2: Verify the correctness of the expanded designs. The newly created or modified designs are team reviewed for correctness. The proof of correctness is a derivation process whereby the design's functionality is compared against its intended function. If the functions are not the same, then the design must be modified and reviewed again. The verification process is described below.

Step 3: Expand low level designs into code. At the lowest level of design, the intended functions are translated into application code using a fixed set of control and data structures. These structures are limited to those that can be verified using the technique described in Chapter 3. Exceptions can be made to expand the set of allowable structures, however, verification techniques are necessarily less rigorous when this is done.

Correctness Verification of Developed Code

Once a clear box is fully refined into code, it is verified against the set of intended functions (which in turn came from the state box) from which it was developed. This step is the primary debugging process for Cleanroom and is performed to:

- Determine that the clear box correctly implements the state box.
- Remove any errors that were introduced during development.
- Completely review the code for completeness, consistency and correct-

ness.

Verification is achieved by deriving the program function of the clear box code and then comparing it to the intended function carried over from the state box. The comparison requires that the two functions operate on the same domains and that they produce the same output for each domain element.

The steps taken in verification are outlined below. Complete treatment of these steps is given in Chapter 3, "Development Practices," by Michael Deck.

Step 1: Abstract the program function of the clear box. As described above, Cleanroom programs are constructed by a stepwise refinement process using a limited set of control structures such as while-do loops and if-then-else statements (see Linger et al., 1979). In order to verify a structured program, teams start with the innermost control structure, identify its program function by determining its effect on the program data space, and then using the program function in place of the code in all future verifications.

This process is continued with the next innermost control structure, continually reducing the program by replacing larger code blocks with smaller statements of their function.

The actual function abstraction process is carried out by using *correctness conditions* for each structured code fragment. Correctness conditions reduce the verification process to a finite set of conditions that must be checked in order to verify that the program correctly implements its specification. These conditions are described in detail in Chapter 3.

Step 2: Compare the abstracted program function to the intended function. Eventually, the function abstraction process will produce a set of intended functions that can be directly compared with the state box. Technically, one must check that the state box function and the abstracted clear box function operate on the same domain and produce the same output for each domain element. In practice, the goal of Cleanroom development is to make this step as easy as possible by creating a clear, easy to understand design.

The general rule is that the verification steps should be a part of the design process and not an extra step. That is, we "write our programs with verification in mind." To this end, most Cleanroom developers will carry over state box functions into the clear box as functional commentary for the code. This means that each control structure has its intended function documented as follows:

```
[statement of intended function]
if
   p
then
   g
 fi
```

Thus, simple comparisons can be carried out during design. The goal is correctness by design, not an arduous and time consuming verification step.

Statistical Certification of Compiled Software Products

In Cleanroom each increment of compilable functionality is statistically tested in order to:

- Ensure that it meets the quality standards defined by the development organization.
- Certify a level of reliability that the product will deliver in the field.
- Provide feedback for quality control and process improvement.

This is achieved in Cleanroom by recognizing and exploiting the fact that testing is sampling. That is, since it is not possible to test all possible scenarios of use, a subset of uses is randomly selected and applied to the software under test. The use of random selection allows us to infer characteristics of the entire population of possible scenarios based on the execution results of the sample.

The steps taken in certification are outlined below. Complete treatment of these steps is given in Chapter 4, "Certification Practices," by James Whittaker.

Step 1: Plan the test. During test planning, the certification team determines how each increment will be tested. In general, the increment in question is examined for conflicting user profiles, independently operating functional units, and so forth that can or must be tested separately. This process is called *stratification of the input domain* and creates sub-populations called *strata*. Once all the strata are identified, a *sampling plan* is created that describes the amount of testing that will be conducted for each.

The artifacts produced during this step are:

- the stratification plan which describes each stratum to be developed,
- the sampling plan, and
- a description of which physical testing resources are to be devoted to each increment and each stratum, including automation, staffing, etc.

Step 2: Develop usage models required by the test plan. The population of possible uses of the system under test is described in a mathematical model called a usage model. The usage model is constructed by considering all external inputs and how they interact with the system being tested. The result of this step is that usage is modeled by what is essentially a state transition diagram depicting inputs applied and states reached as a result of applying each input.

The artifacts produced during this step are:

- usage models representing each stratum and
- documentation of the models containing an explanation and description of each model.

Step 3: Develop and validate the usage distribution. The usage model is assigned a usage distribution based on the goals of the test. Generally, the goals fall into one of the following categories:

- typical usage certification,
- critical usage certification or
- stress testing.

For typical usage certification, data is collected from the field; either in the form of real data from a working prototype or by polling potential users. This data is used as the basis to estimate transition probabilities which are then validated against the test plan and usage information.

For critical usage certification, the probabilities are assigned according to the nature of the functionality being modeled. Highly critical functions are given high probability weights and non-critical functions are given low weights.

For stress testing, i.e., testing that stresses all parts of the system, uniform probabilities are generally used.

In general, a complex system will have multiple strata. Often there are strata of each type named above for a given increment.

Step 4: Generate the test cases and certify the increment. Each increment is tested at the system level when it is delivered by the development team. The test cases are generated in advance from the usage models, applied to the increment and then measures taken that describe test progress.

If failures occur, they are reported to the development team which has the responsibility to make changes to the code, verify the changes and redeliver the code to the test team. Based on the measures, one of three possible outcomes will occur:

- The increment is certified and released.
- The increment is found to be of insufficient quality but is repaired and re-certified.
- The increment is rejected because of low quality.

The measures taken against an increment are fed back into the development and testing process as well. It is often the case that they lend insight into process-related problems that, once identified, can be fixed for future development activity. Root cause analysis of each fault uncovered by testing is necessary to determine exactly where the process failed.

An Organizational Framework for Cleanroom Support

An organizational framework, shown in Figure 4, is needed to support the effective use of the core techniques of Cleanroom in a team-based environment. This framework identifies Cleanroom process adherence by all teams as being integral to the successful engineering of high-quality software. The strict adherence to the Cleanroom core techniques establishes a basis for achieving a higher level of organizational maturity as defined by SEI's Capability Maturity Model (Humphrey, 1989). Organizational maturity and Cleanroom is discussed in Chapter 5, "Using Cleanroom to Raise Software Process Maturity," by Rick Gibson.

An organization needs high-performance teams for the successful application of the Cleanroom core techniques. In Chapter 6, "A Team-Based Organization Structure For Support of Cleanroom Development," Tove Janzon, Bengt Nilsson, and Shirley Becker identify organization improvement (OI) concepts that become the basis for

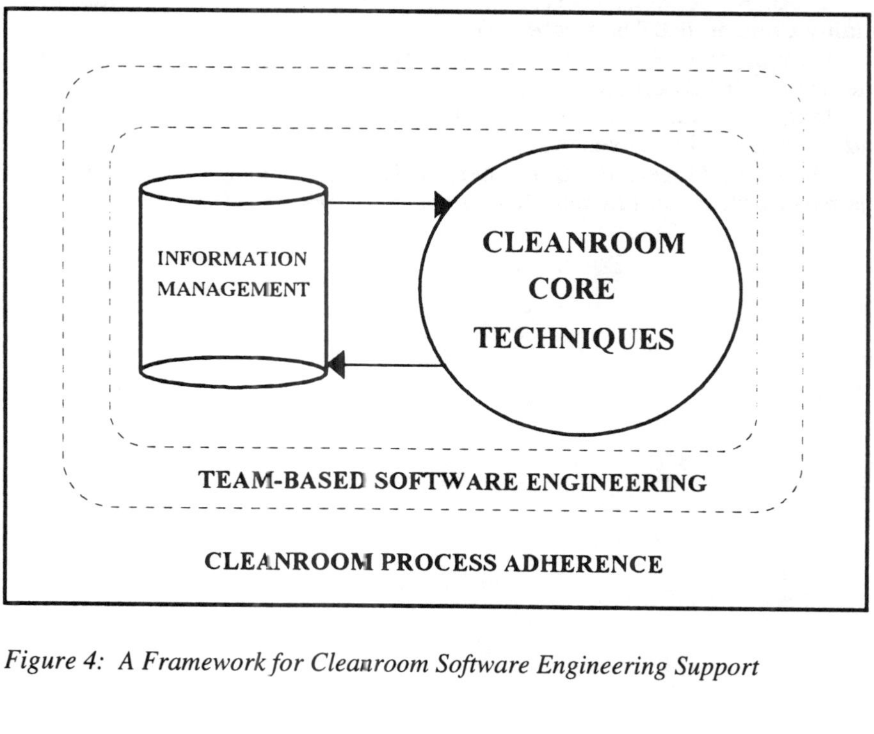

Figure 4: A Framework for Cleanroom Software Engineering Support

building high-performance teams. These OI concepts include *well-developed organization soft skills, a formal team process model, a strong commitment discipline, and process adherence to the Cleanroom core techniques.* A formal team process model called a Team Assignment Model is described that empowers teams, management, and an organization to achieve common goals. These goals are based on project teams applying the Cleanroom core techniques during the completion of team assignments.

Information management is an important component of the support framework as the organization, management, and teams need timely access to information during the application of the Cleanroom techniques. At the organization and management levels, information abstraction capabilities provide a basis for intellectual control over project development and Cleanroom process adherence. For effective teamwork, information management includes support of the team assignment, its decomposition into tasks and responsibilities, the team's plan, progress reports, and deliverables. Information management is described in Chapter 7, "Information Management For Cleanroom Support," by Shirley Becker.

These organizational concepts of process maturity, team-based organization structure, and information management provide a foundation for the successful introduction and use of the Cleanroom core techniques.

References

Cobb, R., & Mills, H. (1990). Engineering Software under Statistical Quality Control. *IEEE Software*, 7(6).

Humphrey, W.S. (1989). Characterizing the Software Process: a Maturity Framework. *IEEE Software*, 5(2).

Linger, R., Mills, H., & Witt, B. (1979). *Structured Programming: Theory and Practice*, Addison-Wesley, Inc, N.Y., N.Y.

Mills, H., Linger, R., & Hevner, A. (1986). *Principles of Information Systems Analysis and Design*, N.Y., Academic Press.

CHAPTER 2

Specification Practices

Stacy Prowell
Software Engineering Technology, Inc.

A good software specification is the central element of a Cleanroom development cycle. Initially, all the effort of the Cleanroom process is directed toward developing a good specification from the requirements. After such a specification is developed, the effort turns to developing code and usage models from the specification.

> ***Definition 1.*** A *specification* is a document that describes, in a complete, precise, verifiable manner, the characteristics of a system or component, and, often, the procedures for determining whether these provisions have been satisfied (IEEE Computer Society, 1990).

Producing a good specification is a challenging task. Under Cleanroom, specifications are as *implementation-free* as possible. That is, a specification contains information on what the software will do, but defers as much of the detail as possible about how the software will be implemented. This allows the external behavior of a system to be specified independently of any particular internal solution. As the specification is iteratively refined into code, implementation decisions are made by considering the possible solutions, and choosing the one which designers agree is the best solution.

The specification evolves through five phases.

1. The domain-specific requirements are analyzed to discover the *system boundary, users,* and *transactions.*
2. The transactions are refined to create an *interface specification,* which describes all discrete inputs and outputs, and a *natural language specification,* which describes the output generated for each input in whatever terms are most convenient (English text, mathematical formulae, graphs, etc.).
3. The interface specification and the natural language specification are refined to create a black box specification. Important properties of the *black box specification* are verified to insure it is a "good" specification.
4. State information is introduced into the black box specification to transform it into a *state box specification.* Important properties of the state box specification are verified to insure it is a "good" specification.
5. An algorithm is chosen to implement each part of the state box, transforming it into a *clear box specification,* which is then iteratively refined until the final product (compilable, executable code in some environment) is generated.

This chapter covers the first four phases. The last phase may involve additional iterations of these specification steps, as difficult or challenging parts of the clear box are refined to code. In addition, the last phase will depend, in part, on the target language. If one is using a functional language, such as ML or LISP, the approach will differ from the approach for Smalltalk, C++, or Ada. A more formal treatment of black and state box specification may be found in Prowell (1996).

Throughout this chapter we will make reference to verification and validation, so it is appropriate to define these terms now.

Definition 2. *Validation* is the process of evaluating a system or component during or at the end of the development process to determine whether it satisfies specified requirements. (IEEE Computer Society, 1990).

Definition 3. *Verification* is the process of evaluating a system or component to determine whether the products of a given development phase satisfy the conditions imposed at the start of that phase. (IEEE Computer Society, 1990).

One may think of these two terms in the following way. Validation asks if we are solving the correct problem. Verification asks if we are solving the problem correctly.

Requirements Analysis

Requirements

First, it will be helpful to say precisely what it meant by "system" and by "requirement."

> ***Definition 4.*** A *system* is a collection of components organized to accomplish a specific function or set of functions. (IEEE Computer Society, 1990).

> ***Definition 5.*** A *requirement* is a condition or capability a system must possess to satisfy a contract or standard, or needed by a user to solve a problem or achieve an objective. (IEEE Computer Society, 1990)

The above definition indicates that there may be two kinds of requirements: *user requirements*, which must be present for the software to be useful, and *contractual requirements*, which are additional requirements imposed by contracts or by standards. Contractual requirements are highly domain- and project-specific. For this reason we will deal primarily with user requirements in this section.

The specification phase typically begins after the requirements phase is complete, with some set of requirements in a domain-specific form. These requirements are usually not satisfactory for beginning construction of a formal specification; they must be refined and an initial design determined. Alternately, there may be no initial set of requirements. In this case the requirements must be discovered by considering what the user needs, and then refined as above to determine an initial design. Requirements are seldom fully known prior to development; fortunately, the specification process forces these problems into the open and allows developers to deal with them sooner rather than later (Dyer, 1992).

The discovery and definition of requirements, known as the *requirements phase*, is a domain-specific activity, and will not be covered in this chapter. We will assume here that an initial set of requirements is known. For more information on discovery and definition of requirements, one is advised to consult references (Dyer, 1992; Jacobson, 1992; Mills, et al., 1986).

System Boundary

Given the initial requirements, practitioners must choose an initial design which satisfies the requirements. The first step is to determine the system boundary.

Definition 6. A *system boundary* is a precise definition of what is internal and what is external to a system.

We must know everything that is to be included in the system (the boundary must be complete), and nothing may be both inside and outside the system (the boundary must be consistent).

Definition 7. An entity which is outside the system boundary, and which can affect the behavior of the system or whose behavior can be affected by the system is called a *user*.

People may be users when they interact with the system. Other hardware and software systems may also be users. For some embedded software, there may be no human users at all. One will have very little or no freedom when defining the system boundary for an embedded system.

Definition 8. A *stimulus* is any user-originated event which may affect the future behavior of the system. A *response* is system behavior which is observable by a user (Prowell, 1996).

That is, a stimulus is information flow across the system boundary into the system, and a response is information flow across the system boundary out of the system. One may simplify the problem by ignoring some users, and considering them to be within the system boundary. For many problems the correct choice of system boundary may not be obvious. Should some hardware or software module be included in the boundary, or excluded? The following design principle will be helpful when defining the system boundary.

Principle 1. [Predictability] If a user's responses (stimuli to our system) are completely predictable from the point of view of our system, then the user may be treated as internal to the system.

For example, an external module which performs simple arithmetic operations on its inputs may be considered internal to the system, thus eliminating the stimuli and responses associated with the module and consequently simplifying the specification. The output of a thermocouple, pitot tube, external random number source, or clock is not, however, predictable from the point of view of the software, and thus these must remain outside the system boundary. Failure to correctly specify the system boundary may lead to seemingly nondeterministic system behavior, as we will see in the section on black boxes.

Transactions

Mills defines a transaction as a sequence of stimuli and associated responses "in which all responses, but the last, are predictable by the user" (Mills, 1988). We broaden the definition here, but still keep the spirit of Mills usage. Our intent is to use the term in much the same sense as "use case" is used by Jacobson (1992).

> ***Definition 9.*** A *transaction* is a behaviorally-related series of stimuli and associated responses which accomplish a particular task.

One may thus list the transactions we wish a system to implement, and gain a high-level view of the system functionality, for use either in discovering requirements or validating requirements. For instance, the transactions for a project management software system might be:

1. create a new project record;
2. enter project schedule and milestones;
3. modify project schedule;
4. add personnel records;
5. delete personnel records, and modify project assignments accordingly;
6. assign personnel to projects;
7. produce an assignment report; and
8. mark project milestones as completed.

Each of the these transactions may involve many different stimuli and responses. Stimuli may include clicking "New" on a "Project" menu and entering a file name. Responses may include displaying a file selection dialog, displaying error dialogs, etc. Every stimulus and response should be necessary for one or more transactions, and the stimuli and responses should be sufficient to model all transactions (and handle error cases of transactions). Mills identifies this as transaction closure (Mao, 1993; Mills, et al., 1986; Mills, et al., 1987; Mills, 1988).

> ***Definition 10.*** *Transaction closure* means that the current system definition is sufficient to capture all transactions, and that all system elements are necessary for some transaction (Mills, 1988).

The term abstraction is used throughout this chapter, and it is important that it not be read as "vague."

> ***Definition 11.*** An *abstraction* is a many-to-one mapping.

An abstraction groups many things (possibly other abstractions) together by omitting details about the things. Transactions are an abstraction from sequences of stimuli. A single transaction represents a possibly-infinite collection of sequences of stimuli. Consider the many different sequences of stimuli you may use to open a file in a word processor. The details about what particular sequence of stimuli is applied are omitted, and all such sequences are grouped under the transaction "open a file." It is important to choose the correct level of abstraction when working. In some cases one may wish to deal with the transaction "open a file." In other cases, one might deal with the stimuli and responses themselves.

As we will see, box structures defines a series of abstractions. At the highest level are transactions. At the lowest level is executable code.

Prototyping

Experimentation and proof-of-concept is extremely important to the development of software systems. Prior to using a new compiler, software, or hardware module, experiments should be conducted to insure that the module performs correctly, is compatible with all other modules, and is the best choice for the problem at hand. The author once had the misfortune of being involved in a large software development project in which two commercial interface packages were chosen: one for inter-process communication, and the other for constructing user interfaces. People were trained in the use of each package, though none were trained in the use of both packages, and these people verified all code produced. During the first execution of the software, we discovered that the two interfaces were completely incompatible, and that the reasons for this incompatibility were not in any of the documentation.

Prototypes should never be confused with products. One constructs the prototype not for the code, but to learn about some aspect of the development. Consequently, one solves the prototype problem in whatever way is most expedient for discovering whatever information one requires, and not as a reliable, reusable, maintainable component of a software product (Neufelder, 1993).

The interface specification

Definition 12. The *interface specification* (IS) is an artifact which identifies the users, system boundary, stimuli, and responses. Additionally, the IS identifies any relevant standards or implementation constraints.

The IS consists of a high-level description of the system's interfaces which identifies the system boundary, followed by an enumera-

1.2 Main Window

The Main Window consists of four menus: a Project menu, with the options New, Open, Save, Save As, Import, Print, and Exit; an Edit menu with the options...

1.2.1 Select:Main.Project.Open. This stimulus is generated by selecting "Open" from the "File" menu on the Main Window.

1.2.2 Select:Main.Project.Close. This stimulus is generated by selecting "Close" from the "File" menu on the Main Window.

1.2.3 Select:Main.Project.Save. This stimulus is generated by selecting "Save" from the "File" menu on the Main Window.

...

1.6 File Selection Dialog

The file selection dialog is a standard Motif file selection dialog (see Motif Reference Manual (Ferguson, 1993)), with the "Help" button suppressed. Depending on the context in which the File Selection Dialog is invoked, the "OK" button may be re-labelled "Open," "Save As," or "Import."

1.6.1 Select:File.Open. This stimulus is generated by clicking the "OK" button on the file selection dialog.

1.6.2 Select:File.Cancel. This stimulus is generated by clicking the "Cancel" button on the file selection dialog.

Figure 1: Example Interface Specification

tion of the users. For each user, the set of stimuli originating with the user is given, along with a short description of the stimulus. When there are logically multiple parts of an interface, each part should be described separately, along with the stimuli and responses associated with that part. There will typically be only one part to the interface for another hardware or software system, and several parts for a human interface. Stimuli should be given some symbolic name. As far as interactive displays are concerned, the IS may constrain, but need not determine, the layout. An example of part of an IS is given in Figure 1.

When there are relevant standards, these should be indicated. For example, an IS might specify that the interface is intended to conform with a particular style guide, or that a controlled hardware interface is a standard RS-232C port. The interface specification should be readable by domain experts and users for validation.

The IS is developed as soon as an initial design is chosen. Prototyping should be carried out before the IS is developed to insure the concepts are sound, the tools are adequate, and the environment is well-understood.

The natural language specification

Definition 13. The *natural language specification* (NLS) is an artifact which specifies the response for every stimulus, in whatever terms are most convenient.

The NLS is developed as soon as the IS is ready. During development of the NLS, the IS may be revised as details are uncovered. The NLS is consequently organized in the same manner as the IS; a list of user interfaces is given, and all stimuli are listed for each user interface. For each stimulus, all possible responses are given, and the conditions under which each response is generated are identified. An example of part of an NLS is given in Figure 2.

1.2 Main Window

1.2.1 Select:Main.Project.Open. A. If there is currently no project open, the modal File Selection dialog is displayed with the "OK" button relabelled as "Open." [R5.4]

B. If there is currently a project open and the project has no unsaved changes, an Okay-Cancel dialog is displayed with the text "The current project will be closed." If the user clicks "OK," the Okay-Cancel dialog is dismissed and operation continues as in 1.2.1.A. If the user clicks "Cancel," the Okay-Cancel dialog is dismissed and the user is returned to the Main Window. [R5.4]

C. If there is currently a project open and the project has unsaved changes, an Yes-No-Cancel dialog is displayed with the text "The current project has unsaved changes. Save first?" If the user clicks "Yes," then the project is saved, the dialog is dismissed, and operation continues as in 1.2.1.B. If the user clicks "No," then the dialog is dismissed and operation continues as in 1.2.1.B. If the user clicks "Cancel," the dialog is dismissed and the user is returned to the Main Window. [R6.2.3]

1.2.2 Select:Main.Project.Close. A. If the current project has unsaved changes, the...

1.2.3 Select:Main.Project.Save. The current project is written to the corresponding file on disk following the format given in 1.1.A. [R4.9]
...

1.6 File Selection Dialog

1.6.1 Select:File.Open. A. If the File Selection dialog was displayed in response to a Select:Main.Project.Open, and the selected file name is a valid, unlocked project file on disk, the contents of the file are read and become the current project. [R6.2.1] ...

Figure 2: Example Natural Language Specification

The NLS serves as a communications bridge between developers and domain experts. As the software is developed and details are discovered, these should be reflected in the NLS, where they may be validated by domain experts. Additionally, the final version of the NLS will provide an excellent starting place for construction of user documentation. The NLS is a living document, and it need not be "complete" until the software itself is complete.

Requirements Traceability

> ***Principle 2.*** [Requirements Traceability] Every element of the software should have a specific reason for existing, which can be traced either to some requirement or to some documented assumption made during development.

Traceability has two purposes. First, it supports correctness validation and insures that all requirements have been considered in the design of the software. Second, it supports change of the software. If a requirement or assumption is later found to be in error, the consequences of the change may be discovered by tracing the requirement through the development documentation.

Each initial requirement should be tagged with some identifier. The tag can then be used to uniquely identify a requirement. For example, a requirement may be "If three device access time-outs occur during initialization, the software should issue an error DEVINIT and halt," and the tag for this requirement might be R1.4.1. Decisions about the interface included in the IS should also be tagged for later reference. For example, consider the following fragment from an IS. "IS7.3.1 Time-out: A connected device may signal time-out on read or write by setting bit 7 of the monitor word high and clearing bit 1 (the busy bit)."

Any reference to a tag is called a *trace* (IEEE Computer Society, 1991). For instance, given the previous two tags, one might discover the following in the NLS. "Time-out: If this is the third Time-out stimulus and there has never been a DevInit stimulus, then issue a DEVINIT error and halt. [R1.4.1, IS7.3.1]" The trace gives the reason for the behavior documented in the NLS. If domain experts discover a problem when validating the NLS, this problem can then be traced to the original requirements, which may be corrected.

Whenever tracing is not possible, and assumptions are needed, the assumptions should be documented and tagged for later reference. Each artifact of the development process should be tagged and traced to previous artifacts.

Finally, when faults are detected during system testing, developers may begin to deduce the fault in a top-down fashion, by first looking at the requirements, then at the NLS, etc., until they discover the source of the fault. All code which must be changed can then be discovered by tracing the faulty requirement or assumption.

IS/NLS validation

There is really no formal property we may verify in the IS and NLS. We can and should, however, validate them against the requirements from which they are derived. This validation should be carried out by the entire development team and at least one expert in the problem domain. The following items must be checked.

1. [Sufficiency] Every stated requirement has at least one trace in either the IS or NLS. If a requirement would not normally appear because it refers to an implementation issue, such as a constraint on the state space or algorithm, the requirement should be copied into a "Requirements Forwarded" section of the NLS and tagged as though it were part of the NLS. It is important that the artifacts at each level are sufficient to begin work on the next level. This will prevent a constant chase through an ever-growing paper trail.
2. [Necessity] Every item in the IS and NLS is justified by a trace to one or more requirements or documented assumptions.
3. [Closure] The stimuli and responses are sufficient to capture the desired behavior.

Black Box Specification

The Black Box Function

Throughout the rest of this chapter we will use the term "function" in the sense of a mathematical function, also called a "mapping."

> ***Definition 14.*** A *function* f associates with each element of a set called the *domain* a single element of another set called the *range*. If D is the domain and R is the range for function f, we write $f{:}D \rightarrow R$, and say that f *maps* D into R. Let $d \in D$ be an element of the domain, and let $r \in R$ be an element of the range. If f associates d with r, we write $f(d)=r$ and refer to d as the *argument* of f and r as the *value* of f for d (Stoll, 1979).

The black box specification is a completely external view of the software system, which hides internal details such as the state space and algorithm (see Figure 3). As such, it can only make reference to information which crosses the system boundary, i.e., stimuli and responses. The black box specification describes software behavior by assigning a response for every stimulus history. Let S be the set of all stimuli, and let R be the set of all responses. We denote the set of all

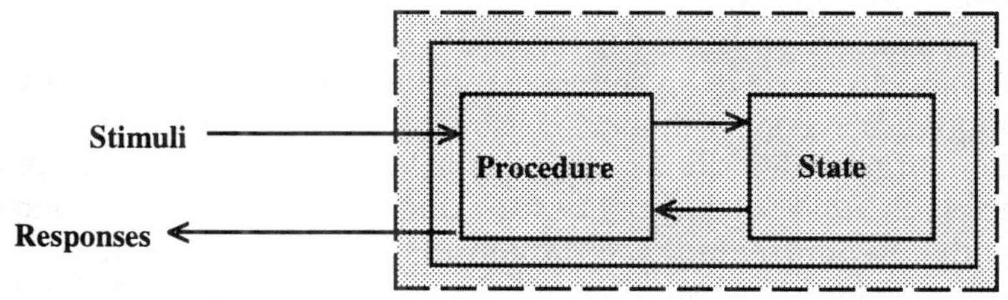

Figure 3: Black Box View

stimulus histories (sequences of stimuli) by S^*.

One can think of a black box informally as a mechanism which accepts a sequence of stimuli and, for each stimulus accepted, issues a response (Mills, et al., 1986). Since software does not necessarily issue a response for every stimulus, we include a special "response" called the *null response*. This special response simply means the software issues no response at all. Further, some stimulus histories may not be possible because of flow of processing or because of the definition of the stimuli themselves. For instance, if one models invocation as a stimulus, one would not expect to see any stimuli prior to the first invocation. All such impossible histories are called *illegal histories*, and we write "illegal" for their response. The two special responses, null and illegal, allow us to specify a response for every stimulus history in S^*.

The black box specification denotes a mathematical function BB:$S^* \rightarrow R$, called the black box function, mapping from domain S^* into range R. For any history of stimuli $s_1 s_2 \ldots s_n$, the next response (the response generated for most-recent stimulus s_n) is the value of the function for the history, or BB($s_1 s_2 \ldots s_n$). The black box function must give a response for every history, and the response must be unique.

> ***Definition 15.*** A black box is *complete* if it gives a response for every history. A black box is *consistent* if the response given is unique.

Two interesting problems arise with this functional view. The first is how to handle cases in which we do not care about the specific value of a response. For example, the software may generate a series of data fields for every stimulus. On some stimuli we only care about the first field, and will ignore the others. In this case, we do not care what value the other fields contain—they may contain any value of the correct type. We call these *don't care* situations, and note this in the response associated with a sequence by writing "don't care" for the values with which we are not concerned. The black box will still denote a function, and once we reach implementation we may assign some particular value to those fields.

The second problem concerns the level of detail included in the black box. As we develop software through the state and clear boxes, additional behavior will be added which arises from the specific implementation decisions made at each level. Therefore some behavior at the black box level may not be fully understood, and we wish to defer these details to the implementation. Also, the black box should only include "necessary details." The following rule of thumb is helpful in determining which details to include, and which to defer.

> ***Principle 3.*** [Necessary detail] If a detail does not affect either long-term behavior or external requirements, it can be deferred to the implementation.

As an example, suppose a system must load three pieces of data at invocation over a TCP connection. It may proceed by trying to read each item sequentially, or it may attempt to get all three at once. If the software cannot get any item, it waits until the item becomes available. Only when all three items have been read can the software continue. How the software obtains the initial data—whether it always performs three reads or tries to get all on a single read—does not affect the long-term behavior of the system. Further, it is reading from a well-understood interface, and the TCP software is not affected by the decision to read one-at-a-time or all-at-once. The decision thus has no effect on external requirements. This detail is not necessary at the black box level, and should be deferred until the implementation. The whole start-up sequence (read, possibly wait and read more) can be deferred to the implementation. We need only model success and failure of invocation, and we may model these as two different invocation stimuli.

Some details which arise frequently when using another vendor's software in conjunction with the system under development can be omitted altogether. For instance, under normal circumstances when using a windowing system it is not necessary to model mouse movement, keyboard focus, selection of menus, etc., because these details are handled by the windowing system. Only stimuli which actually reach the software system of interest and which pass the necessary detail test should be included in the black box.

"Don't care" situations are sometimes referred to as *non-deterministic specifications*, and handled using relations instead of functions. The term *non-deterministic* is somewhat misleading, however, since it has a specific theoretical meaning in computer science, and software executing on a real computer is deterministic. Therefore we prefer the term "don't care," which doesn't have the additional theoretical baggage.

During construction of a black box, it may appear that the

software is behaving non-deterministically. This can usually be attributed to an incorrect system boundary which results in a failure of transaction closure. For instance, assume you want to write a guessing-game program. The program will choose a random integer from one to one-hundred and then will accept guesses. For each guess, the computer will respond "higher" if the chosen number is higher than the guess, "lower" if the chosen number is lower than the guess, and "right" if the chosen number and the guess are the same. We might identify one user—the person playing the game. The stimuli are integer guesses, and the responses are "higher," "lower," and "right." We must now determine the response for a given sequence of stimuli, such as 17, 219, 42, 300, 2, 76. What will the next response be? It is impossible to tell from the given information. The problem is that the system boundary is incorrect, and the stimuli and responses are not sufficient to capture the behavior (transaction closure has failed). Either the random number source is outside the boundary, and therefore is a user with stimuli and responses, or the random number source is inside the boundary, and we know its function. If it uses a clock, again the clock will be outside the boundary.

Stimulus abstraction may also be used. Stimulus abstraction refers to replacing several stimulus histories with a single *abstract stimulus* which omits details of the specific histories. For example, we might replace the history of selecting "Open" from the "File" menu, moving around the dialog, and finally highlighting or typing a file name and clicking the "Open" button on the dialog with a single stimulus "OpenFile(*n*)," where *n* is the file name. We may allow histories replaced by abstract stimuli to overlap. For instance, we may be interested in knowing when every 1,000th clock pulse is received by the software. We then create an abstract stimulus "1000Pulses" to represent this event, and ignore the individual clock pulses. The history represented by this abstract stimulus may overlap other histories represented by other abstract stimuli. For example, clock pulses will be occurring during the OpenFile(*n*) stimulus. If a 1,000th clock pulse occurs among the stimuli of the OpenFile(*n*) but before all history conditions for the OpenFile(*n*) have been met, then we will have a 1000Pulses followed by an OpenFile(*n*) in the abstract history. This does not mean that all stimuli required for the 1000Pulses occurred before all stimuli for the OpenFile(*n*).

For every abstract stimulus used, the precise history conditions for the stimulus must be defined, and definitions for abstract stimuli must be disjoint (only one definition may be satisfied at a time).

As an example, consider a small menu system. We have four stimuli.

1. Invoke the system.
2. Move the highlight up in a list of choices.
3. Move the highlight down in a list of choices.
4. Select the highlighted entry.

The list of choices may be "Open Project," "Create Project," "Close Project," "Edit Project," "Save Changes," and "Exit." We might replace the above stimuli with the following abstract stimuli.

1. Invoke the system (no change).
2. Select "Open Project."
3. Select "Create Project."
4. Select "Close Project."
5. Select "Edit Project."
6. Select "Save Changes."
7. Select "Exit."

These abstract stimuli omit the details of cursor movement and allow us to work with simpler histories when constructing conditions for a black box. For example, we might want to know if the user has saved changes since editing. It will be hard to express such a condition using only the up, down, and select stimuli. It is very simple using the new abstract stimuli.

The remainder of this section describes how to discover and document black box behavior, as well as how to verify and validate a black box specification.

Black Box Creation

One begins creation of a black box once the IS and NLS have been validated. Recall that the black box denotes a function BB:$S^* \rightarrow R$. Every function has three components: a domain, a range, and a mapping rule which describes the value for every argument. The black box function is implicitly described by the IS and NLS. What we must do to create a black box specification is give an explicit description of the function.

Functions may be described in any number of ways. For example, here are several ways of describing the factorial of a positive integer $n>0$.

- $n! = \prod_{i=1}^{n} i$
- $\begin{cases} 1! = 1 \\ (n+1)! = (n+1)(n!) \text{ if } n>1 \end{cases}$
- $n! = 1 \times 2 \times 3 \times \ldots \times n-1 \times n$
- $n!$ = product of all positive integers m, where $(m \leq n)$

Each of these representations conveys the definition of the factorial. The factorial is defined for any integer $n > 0$ and the value $n!$ is unique. Thus the definitions are complete and consistent. As with the second definition of factorial above, functions may be specified by cases. Consider the following definition for the sign function, which takes an integer argument.

$$
\begin{aligned}
\text{sign}(n) &= -1 \text{ if } n<0 \\
&= 0 \text{ if } n = 0 \\
&= 1 \text{ if } n>0
\end{aligned}
$$

Whenever we specify a function with cases, we require that the cases be *disjoint* and that they *cover* the domain.

> ***Definition 16.*** A set of cases is *disjoint* if at most one of them can be true for any argument in the domain. A set of cases *covers* the domain D if, for every element of the domain $d \in D$, at least one case is true.

Clearly the cases in the sign function are disjoint and cover the set of all integers, since every integer must be either less than, greater than, or equal to zero.

When writing a black box, you may discover it is convenient to have functions such as the sign function or factorial function, and to use these when defining the black box function. Such component functions are called *specification functions*, and they have the domain S^*. A specification function need not use all the stimulus history; a specification function may use only the most recent stimulus, or only part of the most recent stimulus. If every stimulus consists of three integers (A,B,C), and we want to know the historical maximum of the first integers A and the factorial of the second integer B of the most recent stimulus, we might use the factorial function given previously and define another function called "max" which gives the maximum value of a series of integers.

$$
\begin{aligned}
&\max(a_1) = a_1 \\
&\max(a_1 a_2 \ldots a_n) = a_n \text{ if } a_n > \max(a_1 a_2 \ldots a_{n-1}) \text{ and } n>1 \\
&\max(a_1 a_2 \ldots a_n) = \max(a_1 a_2 \ldots a_{n-1}) \text{ if } a_n \leq \max(a_1 a_2 \ldots a_{n-1}) \text{ and } n>1
\end{aligned}
$$

We will write the black box specification as a series of tables with disjoint conditions which cover the domain of interest. This is not to preclude other ways of representing the black box function, including formal black box languages. In the author's experience, however, the tabular representation has many advantages. In particular, it does not seem to support one implementation over another. Look back at the different representations for the factorial function. The first representation may be thought of as a loop, and the second seems to imply a recursive implementation. However, the purpose of a black box is to specify behavior, not implementation. One should avoid a representation which carries explicit information about the algorithm or state space, as those items are properly discovered later in the process and the focus at this stage should be discovering and documenting external behavior.

The stimulus set can be obtained from the IS. For every stimulus in the IS, the NLS gives a list of responses and conditions. We will construct the black box in essentially the same format. A black box will have one table for every stimulus, and that table will list the responses for that stimulus and the historical conditions under which each response is produced. The following procedure can be used to create a black box from an NLS and IS.

1. Beginning with the IS, create a table for every stimulus and trace the table to the stimulus definition in the IS. Each table should have four columns: tag, response, conditions, and trace. The tag is for later reference to a row of the table, and can be any unique value.
2. Define any abstract stimuli you are going to use. Include these in a reference section prior to the black box tables.
3. For each stimulus, examine the NLS and list each response given in the response column of the table, one per row.
4. Determine conditions for the stimulus-response pairs in the table. For every response listed in a stimulus' table, determine what historical conditions (possibly in terms of abstract stimuli and specification functions) lead to generating the particular response when the given stimulus is the current stimulus. Either trace your solution to the appropriate text in the NLS or add an assumption to the NLS, tag it, and trace to the assumption.
5. Stop work when all stimulus-response pairs have conditions, and review your work with your peers. Specific points to review are discussed in the next subsection.

For example, the IS and NLS fragments given in Figures 1 and 2 lead to the black box table shown below (Table 1). Responses have been replaced with numbers to save space in the table. The specific information about each response should be listed in a reference section prior to the black box tables. We use *h* to refer explicitly to the stimulus history. "ProjectEdited(*h*)" is a specification predicate (a special case of specification function) which is true exactly when there have been changes made to a project more recently than the project has been saved, for history *h*.

Black Box Properties

If any changes are discovered in the NLS or IS, these should be validated by the development team and at least one domain expert

Tag	Response	Conditions	Trace
BB:1.1	R1	There has been a Select:Main. Project.Open which was followed by a Select:File.Open more recently than any Select:Main. Project.Close, and ProjectEdited (*h*) is true	NLS1.2.1.C
BB:1.2	R2	There has been a Select:Main. Project.Open which was followed by a Select:File.Open more recently than any Select: Main.Project.Close, and ProjectEdited(*h*) is false	NLS1.2.1.B
BB:1.3	R3	There has never been a Select: Mail.Project.Open, or there has been a Select:Main.Project.Close more recently than the most recent Select:Main.Project.Open	NLS1.2.1.A

Table 1: Stimulus Select:Project.Open (IS:1.2.1)

prior to continuing. Remember that the NLS is your opportunity for communication with domain experts and the customer. Take advantage of this whenever you can, since lower-level artifacts will not provide another such opportunity until you reach executable code.

Before proceeding to the state box, the black box should be verified and validated by the entire development team. It is not necessary to include domain experts. Verification of a black box entails checking for completeness and consistency. Validation of a black box entails checking for correctness[1]. Since the black box is simply a formal restatement of behavior in the NLS, and closure has presumably been validated for the NLS, there is no need to repeat this check for the black box.

Consistency and completeness are verified by considering each black box table, and insuring that the table is complete and consistent. For consistency, every pair of condition entries should be disjoint—if one is true, the other must be false. Proceed as follows, row by row. Assume the condition for each row is true, and the show that this implies the conditions for all other rows must be false. For example, in Table 1 the first two conditions cannot both be true, because one requires ProjectEdited(*h*) to be true, and the other requires it to be false.

For completeness, at least one row of the table must always be true. Proceed as follows. Consider each row and assume all other rows are false. Show that this implies that the chosen row must be true. Again consider Table 1. Assume the second and third rows are false. Making the third row false indicates that there has been a

Select:Main.Project.Open which was followed by a Select:File.Open more recently than any Select:Main.Project.Close. Adding the fact that the second row must also be false gives the additional information that ProjectEdited(h) = true. This is exactly the condition given in the first row.

If the set of conditions is found to be correct, but incomplete, then some sequences are illegal or possibly should be mapped to null. An additional "otherwise" condition can be added to repair this problem.

Validation of correctness requires the following steps.

1. [Sufficiency] Every item from the NLS has at least one trace in the black box. If a requirement would not normally appear because it refers to an implementation issue, such as a constraint on the state space or algorithm, the requirement should be copied into a "Requirements Forwarded" section of the black box and tagged as though it were part of the black box.
2. [Necessity] Every item in the black box is correctly justified by a trace to one or more items in the NLS and IS.

State Box Specification

A state box includes *state data* as well as stimuli and responses. This state data is introduced to eliminate stimulus history references by storing the essential parts of the history, effectively reducing the problem from one involving an infinite number of possible histories to one involving some finite state space.

State Box Function

The state box specification exposes the internal state space but keeps the algorithm hidden from view (see Figure 4). The state box denotes a mathematical function called the *state box function*, where T is the set of all possible states. In other words, the state box function

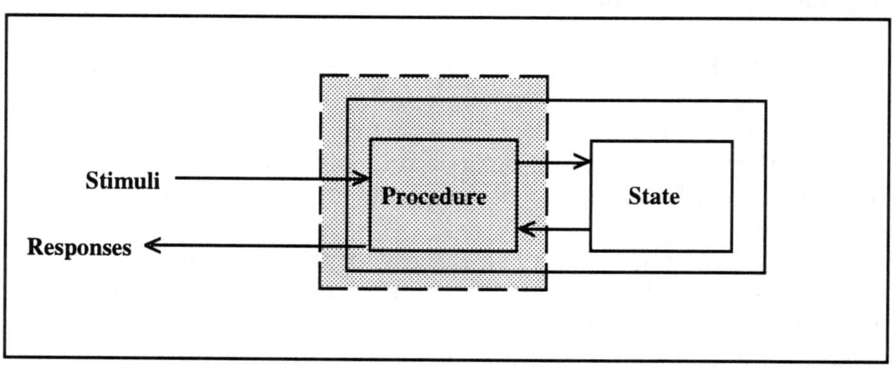

Figure 4: State Box View

takes as arguments a stimulus and state, and its value is the next state and software response. In essence we have replaced the stimulus history with state data[2].

For the state box function to give a response for a history, we must know the initial state, which we will write $\dot{t}$. One can think of a state box informally as a mechanism which initializes its state to $\dot{t}$ and then accepts stimuli. For each stimulus, the system issues a response (possibly the null response or illegal) and possibly changes state. We might therefore break the state box into two functions: the response function $SB_R:S \times T \rightarrow R$ which determines the response, and the state transition function $SB_T:S \times T \rightarrow T$ which determines the next state. The state box response for any sequence of stimuli is therefore given by

$$SB_R(s_n, SB_T(s_{n-1}, SB_T(s_{n-2},\ldots SB_T(s_1,\dot{t})\ldots))),$$

which should have the same value as the black box function. This demonstrates three important points. First, the state box function and black box function can, in the sense described above, be said to be the same. Thus it makes sense to discuss deriving a state box from a black box. Second, it means one can apply the notions of completeness and consistency to the state box just as they were applied in the black box. Third, it shows an unexpected sort of complexity which arises because one has introduced additional information. The state box contains more information about the implementation than the black box—it names the state data. There are many different state boxes for a given black box because we have moved toward the code, to a less abstract level.

The remainder of this section describes how to discover and document state box behavior, as well as how to verify and validate a state box specification.

State Box Creation

Once the black box has been created, verified, and validated, one can begin work on a state box specification. Alternately, one might begin specification work at the state box level and skip the black box altogether when the problem is inherently state-based, as with a database. We will cover only the former approach in this chapter.

The state box function has the same three components as any function: a domain, range, and mapping rule. The stimulus and response sets are inherited from the black box, while the state space must be invented. Since the state space is new, and the mapping rule involves the state space, we must also re-invent the mapping rule. Fortunately, the state space and mapping rule can be discovered by examination of the black box tables.

As with the black box, one may discover that it is convenient to use specification functions when defining the state box. However, the specification functions used in the state box are not defined on S^*, but on *SxT*. For black box specification functions which do not reference history, this does not change anything. The factorial function, for instance, remains the same. The max function, however, must be changed to eliminate the history references. We define a new state data item to hold the historical maximum, and re-define the max function to use the state data item.

$$\max(a,m) = a \text{ if } a>m$$
$$\max(a,m) = m \text{ if } a\leq m$$

The above is no longer sufficient, however. We must know the initial value of m in order to correctly map sequences of integers to their maximum; for this case, let $\dot{m} = -\infty$.

Before writing the state box specification, we must discover the state space required to encode the black box. Some state data items will come from specification functions (as with the max function). Others will come from examination of the black box. The entry BB:1.1, for instance, implies the necessity to remember whether there has been a Select:Main.Project.Open followed by a Select:File.Open more recently than any Select:Main.Project.Close. That is, we must be able to decide if a file is open or not. We introduce a new item of state data: ProjectOpen. This will be initially false (since the condition cannot be true when the history is empty). ProjectOpen will be set to true whenever we have a Select:Main.Project.Open followed by a Select:File.Open, and will be set to false whenever we have a Select:Main.Project.Close. This process of examination continues until all state data needed to represent the behavior encoded in the black box has been discovered.

The state box specification is also written as a series of tables, with one table for every stimulus. The content of each table is discovered by examining the corresponding black box table. The following process can be used to create a state box from a black box.

1. Beginning with the black box specification, create a table for every stimulus and trace the table to the corresponding table in the black box. Each table should have five columns: tag, response, state conditions, state transformation, and trace. The tag is used for later reference to a row of the table, and can be any unique value.
2. Consider each of the tables, and for every row copy the response from the black box to the state box and trace the row to the black box row. Examine the black box conditions, and decide what state data, if any, is required to decide the condition. Add any new state data to the state data list. Enter the appropriate initial value for every state data item.
3. For each state data item discovered, decide when its value should be modified. Add this modification information to the state box

tables in the "state transformation" column.

4. Once all state data has been discovered, encode each black box condition in terms of the state data and enter this condition into the corresponding state box "state conditions" column. Trace the state box row to the black box row.
5. Stop work when all tables are complete and review your work with your peers. Specific points to review are discussed in the next subsection.

For example, the previous black box table (Table 1) could be encoded as the following state data and state box table (Table 2 and Table 3). Again, responses are listed in a reference section prior to the tables, and can be copied from the black box. Some changes in the response descriptions may be necessary because of the replacement of history with state data.

State Migration

Definition 17. *State migration* refers to the design decision that

Name	**Description**	**Initial Value**
ProjectOpen	A Boolean value which is true if a project is open and false if no project is open.	false
ProjectEdited	A Boolean value which is true if a project has unsaved changes, and false otherwise.	false
DialogUp	A Boolean which is true if a modal dialog is up and false otherwise.	false

Table 2: State Data Items

Tag	Response	State Conditions	State Transformation	Trace
SB:1.1	R1	ProjectOpen = true and ProjectEdited = true	DialogUp = true	BB:1.1
SB:1.2	R2	ProjectOpen = true and ProjectEdited = false	DialogUp = true	BB:1.2
SB:1.3	R3	ProjectOpen = false	DialogUp = true	BB:1.3

Table 3: Stimulus Select:Project.Open (BB:Table.1)

state box components (data, responses, tests, and transformations) "will be aggregated in various ways and each aggregation [...] hidden from and unavailable to specifications regarding all other aggregations" (Mao, 1993).

State migration is, simply put, data hiding or encapsulation. Any state box component is a candidate for state migration. We may discover two types of state migration in the state box: grouping and deferment. In the first case, we may discover that state box components can be partitioned into logical groups which are largely independent. This indicates a modular implementation with procedures and data local to each module. For the second case, we may also discover as we refine the state box into a procedure in the clear box that some data items can be moved to a lower level. In this case we may defer the implementation and maintenance of those state data items to the lower level. The second case requires knowledge of the procedural implementation, and thus we cannot decide all migration details until the clear box construction phase.

State Box Properties

If any changes are discovered in the black box, these changes should be traced back to the NLS, IS, or requirements, and any changes made there. The tags for the changed information may then be followed forward to insure that all necessary changes are made. The resulting documents should be validated and, for the black box, verified. If changes are made to the NLS, IS, or requirements, domain experts must be involved in the validation.

As mentioned earlier, completeness and consistency apply to the state box as well as the black box. We must therefore verify these two important properties. Further, we must verify that the state box correctly implements the black box. This correctness verification eliminates most of the requirements traceability validation of the state box. One must still insure that every row has a trace, and that the trace justifies the row. This may be done when the row is verified for correctness, as described below.

Transaction closure must be validated for the state box since additional information has been introduced. This entails checking that the state space is sufficient to model the black box conditions, and that the state transformations are sufficient to capture the necessary state data. Verification should not be attempted until closure has been validated. For each state data item, insure that it has a definition, initial value, and that its value is modified at the appropriate points in the state box. For each black box condition, insure that every part has a corresponding state data condition. Performing this validation first will catch many problems prior to verification.

Consistency and completeness of the state box are verified in the same manner as for the black box. For example, in Table 3 we assume the condition in the first row is true. This clearly implies the conditions in the other two rows are false, indicating that row one is consistent with the other two rows.

Correctness requires that we show that histories are mapped to state data correctly. We must verify that the right choice of initial state and state transformations has been made to encode the relevant parts of the history, and that the tests are correct given the encoding. We may do this as follows.

1. Consider each row of the state box table in turn, and assume the state condition is true.
2. From the state box tables and initial state, determine what history conditions must exist for the state condition to be true.
3. Compare these history conditions with the history conditions from the black box. If they do not match, determine for which histories they do not match, and make appropriate corrections.

Correctness verification issues are similar to closure validation issues. This is no surprise. Since we have insured that the black box behavior is sufficient to model the transactions for the system, verification of the state box to the black box should insure transaction closure. The initial validation step is included as a "sanity check" on the state space.

A more detailed discussion of state box verification can be found in the chapter on development.

Conclusion

A good specification is of vital importance to the rest of the Cleanroom process. When constructing a specification, it is important to always work at the correct (most helpful) level of abstraction. This may imply that sometimes a black box is not created, and specification proceeds immediately from the NLS to the state box. However, one must balance this against insuring that enough initial work is done. It is important that the problem be understood through an IS and NLS before specification work begins on any level.

Changing the specified behavior is made manageable by breaking the black box and state box into several tables, and by requirements traceability. Whenever a change needs to be made, the change should be traced back to the highest level possible, and the requirements trace be followed down from there. This isolates the parts of the specification which must be changed for any change in requirements. The author has seen Cleanroom projects develop several hundred pages of black box specification without requirements traceability, and has seen the havoc that a single, simple requirements change creates in this situation. The result is often that changes to the specification are abandoned, and the software and specification then diverge, creating even more problems for certification, documentation, and maintenance.

The verification and validation at each step is essential to creating a good specification. If one takes care to insure that the black box and state box are complete, consistent, correct, and satisfy transaction closure, then one may proceed to develop code from them with confidence.

Endnote

[1] Correctness here refers to a domain issue; whether this is the right black box. This is different from the mathematical issue of whether one formal object is correct with respect to another. Thus correctness is validated in the black box, and verified in the state box (by comparing the state box to the black box).

[2] One could regard the black box function as such a mapping BB:$S \times S^* \rightarrow S^* \times R$ which takes a stimulus and history and returns the new history obtained by appending the current stimulus and the software response.

References

Dyer, Michael. *The Cleanroom Approach to Quality Software Development.* New York: Wiley and Sons, 1992.

IEEE Computer Society. *IEEE Guide to Software Requirements Specifications* (IEEE Std. 830-1984). New York: IEEE, July 1984.

IEEE Computer Society. *IEEE Standard Glossary of Software Engineering Terminology* (IEEE Std. 610.12-1990). Corr. ed. New York: IEEE, February 1991.

Ferguson, Paula M. *Motif Reference Manual for OSF/Motif Release 1.2* Sebastapol, California: O'Reilly & Associates, 1993.

Jacobson, Ivar, et al. *Object-Oriented Software Engineering, a Use Case Driven Approach.* Workingham, England: Addison-Wesley, 1992.

Mao, Hailong. "The Box-Structure Development Method." Dissertation, University of Tennessee, December 1993.

Mills, Harlan. D., Richard C. Linger, and Alan R. Hevner. "Box Structured Information Systems." *IBM Systems Journal.* v. 26, n. 4 (1987): 395-413.

Mills, Harlan. D. "Stepwise Refinement and Verification in Box-Structured Systems." *IEEE Computer.* June 1988: 23-36.

Mills, Harlan. D., Richard C. Linger, and Alan R. Hevner. *Principles of Information Systems Analysis and Design.* Orlando: Academic Press, 1986.

Neufelder, Ann Marie. *Ensuring Software Reliability. Quality and Reliability Series 38.* New York: Marcel Dekker, 1993.

Prowell, Stacy J. "Sequence-Based Software Specification." Dissertation, University of Tennessee, May 1996.

Stoll, Robert R. *Set Theory and Logic.* New York: Dover, 1979.

CHAPTER 3

Development Practices

Michael Deck
Cleanroom Software Engineering, Inc.

Cleanroom development combines specification and design in a management hierarchy, with significant results in both quality improvement and cost reduction. A *specification* is the abstract description or declaration of the black box behavior of software. A *design* is a stepwise refinement of a specification; a series of increasingly detailed steps toward the implementation of that behavior. Each design step reveals sub-specifications and organizes them with structures that manage their interaction. The Cleanroom development process includes several activities:

- Design, the creative act of proposing designs and implementations that meet the needs of a project;
- Review, where the project team evaluates the proposed design based on predetermined criteria;
- Abstraction, in which an unknown or poorly understood specification is derived from design materials; and
- Management, which integrates the other development activities to meet overall project goals.

This chapter will describe the Cleanroom development practices and some of their underlying theory. It assumes that the reader understands the techniques used in Cleanroom specification, in particular how black-box abstractions that meet customer requirements are created and how they are validated against requirements. This foundation understanding is critical. First, because the development process that will be described in this chapter begins when an initial software specification is defined. Second, because to write a design means knowing how to write the specifications of the next lower-level artifacts. This chapter also assumes that the reader understands the incremental nature of the Cleanroom development process. It is not necessary at this point to know how to write an increment plan, though that knowledge is required to fully implement the Cleanroom process.

The chapter begins with an overview of key concepts and foundations. This conceptual material describes the "why" of development; understanding this material will help in tailoring the practices to fit a specific project. Then, it describes specific practices that are used by Cleanroom teams. The practices describe the "how" of Cleanroom development and provide a starting point for using Cleanroom development. A final section sets the practices into the context of the Cleanroom development process.

The Cleanroom Development Process

Overview

The Cleanroom development process is guided by the *box structures* method (Mills, Linger, & Hevner, 1986, 1987; Mills, 1988). The term *black box* is used for two kinds of specification. *Process specifications* define data-transforming entities–objects that behave the same whenever they receive the same inputs. *Data specifications* define entities that abstract or encapsulate data–objects that "remember" information from one use to the next. Each type of specification begins a different design path that will ultimately lead to a single implementation. The data-abstracting black box is refined as a *state box*; the process-abstracting black box is refined as a *clear box*. At the system level, the design artifacts and their controls are called an "architecture." At the code level, they are called an "implementation." All of these are included in this chapter's use of the term, "design."

The black box, state box, and clear box are all views of the same object, offering different perspectives. The black box is a completely external view. The state box provides some details about the internal data storage but hides processing. The clear box exposes both data storage and processing.

Many of the early works on box structures, such as Mills, Linger, & Hevner (1986), can be read to suggest that every black box, whether it abstracts data or not, begins a design path whose next step is the state box. From the state box, then, the next refinement is always the clear box. This chapter will simplify the process by eliminating the state box step in cases where the black box does not describe a data abstraction. Although there are rare circumstances when one could introduce state into a process-abstracting black box (for example, a cache), generally the black box and state box of a process abstraction are identical.

The Black Box: Process and Data Specifications

The black box is a complete definition of the externally-relevant behavior of the object under all possible circumstances of use. (The word, "object," will refer to software units of any size, including systems, components, modules, and parts, as well as objects in the object-oriented sense.) In the case of a process abstraction, the black box is usually stated in terms of a function that maps inputs into outputs, hiding the details of control flow and local data. In the case of a data abstraction, the black box is most often stated in terms of transition functions that use the inputs, together with the state of the object, to produce outputs. By describing behavior in terms of an abstract model of that state, the black box hides details of data implementation. In "classic" box structures, the object's history of use acts as the abstract model of its state (Mills, Linger, & Hevner, 1986, 1987; Mills, 1988). The black box specification also defines the permitted usage of the object by identifying inputs for which the object's behavior is undefined or unpredictable.

The Clear Box: Process Designs

The clear box is the first step in implementing a process specification. The clear box defines algorithmic details of completing an intended process specification by exposing certain aspects of concrete control structures. A clear box consists of a control structure (the typical structured-programming constructs like sequence, if-then-else, and while-do), and lower-level process specifications controlled by that structure. Some of these lower-level process specifications will require no further design, like "x := y." Other process specifications may require additional design work, like "array_1 := contents of array_2 sorted by name." The clear box may also contain local data. Each local data object is an instance of a data specification that describes its abstract data model, permitted usage, and behavior.

The State Box: Data Designs

The first design step for the data-abstracting black box is to describe a state box that exposes certain aspects of concrete data structures that will be implemented: the "how" of data storage rather than the "what." A state box has two parts: the state data and the machine. The state data is a collection of data objects, each of which is an instance of a lower-level data specification. The machine is a collection of process specifications, one for each operation, each mapping inputs to outputs. The machine expresses each operation in terms of the state data. The state data objects are sometimes called the *concrete model*, in contrast to the abstract model of the black box specification. As with process specifications, some of the lower-level data specifications, like "integer" require no further effort; others, like "employee database" are likely to require substantial effort in specification and elaboration.

This idea that parts of the black box data model are apportioned out to concrete data objects that may themselves be specifications requiring further implementation is called *state migration* after Mills, Linger, & Hevner (1986).

Correctness

A design is composed of specifications linked together with organizing control or data structures. A specification is a model, or abstraction, of the design. The specification hides certain aspects and emphasizes others. Data specifications hide concrete storage mechanisms. Process specifications hide the ordering of operations as well as any short-term storage needed to accomplish those operations. Specifications exist at every level—high-level specifications are models for design languages, design languages model source code, source models object, and object models microcode. Specifications act as the contract between the user of the object, system, program, or part and its developer.

Program correctness asks whether the model reflects the objective reality of the underlying design. *Complete correctness* means the design has exactly the same behavior as its specification model. However, it is usually acceptable for the design to be different from the specification — to do more than the specification says, but not less. This is called *sufficient correctness*. In the sections on state box and clear box review, correctness will mean sufficient correctness. In this chapter, we will use the term "verification" in its narrower sense of a correctness argument.

Common Services

Depending on the environment, process specifications may be implemented as procedures or functions that can be instantiated by a variety of processes through parameter passing or other mechanisms. Likewise data specifications and instances can often be shared by many objects. The generic term for specifications that can be used in different parts of the system is *common services*.

The Development Hierarchy

A system that starts out as a data abstraction evolves as a hierarchy such as that shown in Figure 1. The initial black box, which

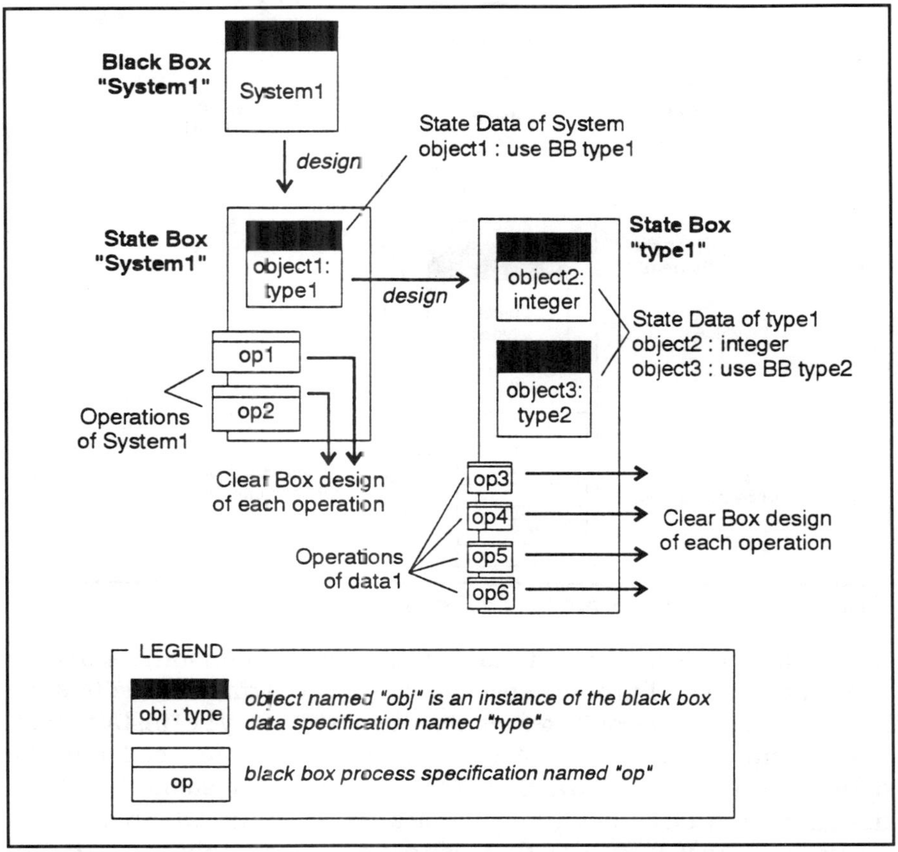

Figure 1. Development Hierarchy of a Data-Abstracting System

may be a unique object or may be an instantiable type or class, is first designed as a state box that reveals both data specifications and process specifications. Each lower-level data specification begins its own hierarchy that evolves next to a state box. Each process specification begins a hierarchy that evolves next to a clear box. Each clear box design may reveal local uses of data specifications as well as process specifications. In the figure, the data-encapsulating black box *system1* has an abstract data model and two operations (not shown). As a first step, *system1* has been designed as a state box with a single object in the state data. That object, named *object1*, is an instance of a lower-level data specification called *type1*. The state box also defines two operations, *op1* and *op2*, in terms of *object1*. The design of *type1* also requires a state box, which has been designed to have two state data objects, *object2* (an integer) and *object3* (of type *type2*). Its machine is composed of four operations defined on *object2* and *object3*. The clear boxes of all the operations, and the next design step of *type2*, remain to be done.

A system that starts out as a process specification evolves as a similar hierarchy as shown in Figure 2. The initial black box is

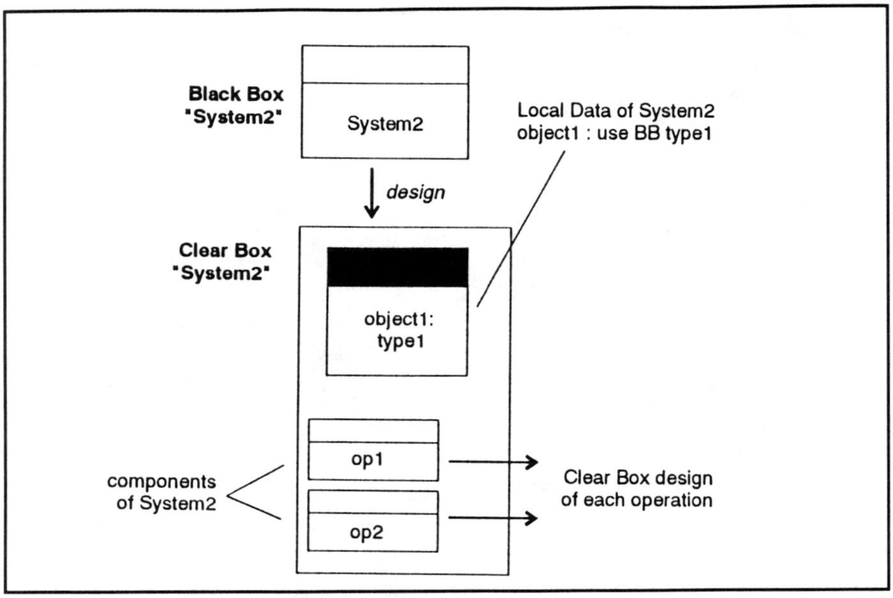

Figure 2. Development Hierarchy of a Process-Abstracting System

designed as a clear box that may reveal local data (instances of data specifications) and process specifications. The former evolve to state boxes, the latter to clear boxes. Again, this system may be "instantiable" (usually implemented via procedure calls) or not (inline code). In the figure, the process-abstracting black box called *system2* has been designed as a clear box (the graphics don't tell us whether it is a sequence or an if-then-else) that also defines a local data object, called *object1*. The specification *type1* is re-used from the previous example, in this case as local, rather than as state, data. The two components of the clear box, *op1* and *op2*, are yet to be implemented.

The leaves in both hierarchies are *primitive* data and process specifications. What is primitive depends on the project: in general, if the specification is already implemented, and the quality of the implementation is trusted by the team, that is a primitive. For example, the team that is designing an embedded system may have to actually implement the "integer" data type in more primitive terms, whereas the team that is using an upper CASE tool may be provided with database definition and access primitives in a graphical language. Likewise simple integer-to-integer assignments will be primitive process specifications for most projects. The review process links together each specification with its implementation, forming an unbroken chain of verification that integrates the entire hierarchy.

The hierarchy of specifications in Cleanroom development is an example of a "uses" or "usage" hierarchy after Parnas (1974). There are numerous other hierarchies in the software development process that are orthogonal to the usage hierarchy of specification. For example, the inheritance hierarchy of object-orientation is a way for the team to organize and re-use data specifications. Cleanroom and object-orientation are highly complementary and there are strong synergies between them (Hevner and Mills, 1993; Becker, et al., 1994; Deck, 1996). The inheritance hierarchy guides design decisions (what new objects to specify) while the usage hierarchy guides verification to ensure the correctness of the designs. These are among the many relationships that exist between development work products in a Cleanroom project. The sections that follow will focus primarily on the usage hierarchy.

Reuse in Cleanroom

There are several aspects to effective reuse of source and object code in Cleanroom. Design-quality review criteria should include reusability, by identifying parts that could be slightly changed so as to be more reusable and by noting those parts that are potentially reusable in a log or database. A second reuse aspect is to thoroughly evaluate the quality of any part that is placed in service so that those parts can be treated as primitives later on in the development process; more rigorous review is in order for those parts that are expected to be re-used. Tools for storing and retrieving reusable objects and their specifications are also an important consideration.

Cleanroom Development Strategies

Once the initial specification is drafted and at any time after that during development, the snapshot status of development is as follows:

- specifications may exist that are not primitive,
- a library of reusable parts may exist, with each item consisting of a specification and verified design that could be re-used as primitives, or can be re-worked from source,
- a body of existing design may exist whose specifications are either unknown, unreliable, or unverified,
- long-term and short-term plans are in-place and understood, and are being used to guide choices.

Each thread of the Cleanroom development process locates a specification in the current hierarchy that is not yet implemented and is not primitive, takes one or more design steps for that specification, and then conducts reviews to evaluate the progress made. During these reviews, previously approved designs may be modified, requiring re-review to ensure that the overall hierarchy is correct, meets requirements, and has appropriate design qualities. When the new leg of the hierarchy is approved through review in context, the process repeats until every specification is expressed as a primitive.

Sometimes many of these threads may be operating simultaneously and concurrency management of the shared entities is required whenever that occurs. Clearly the choice of which specification to design next, how many levels to design before convening a review, and how to manage concurrency are all important management aspects of Cleanroom development. Tactics for concurrency management and for evolving the hierarchy are discussed in more detail later.

Cleanroom Development Practices

The Design Philosophy: Proposal and Evaluation

Suppose, having completed their last specification review, a Cleanroom team is walking down a dark alley when they stumble across a thick document. Upon examining it, the team sees that it advertises itself as an implementation of that very black box specification. What should they do?

There are two criteria for evaluating that design: correctness and design quality. Correctness is judged with respect to a specification: a design is *correct* if the designed behavior sufficiently meets the specified behavior. Given an adequately-described design and specification, this is something that is possible to determine objectively, within the limits of human fallibility, without testing, through *verification*. Note that, without a specification, nothing can be said about the correctness of a design; correctness is always defined with respect to a particular specification. The "goodness" of the specification, including issues such as usability that are sometimes considered "design" issues, is determined through *validation* of the specification, discussed in Chapter 2, Specification Practices.

The other evaluation criterion, design quality, is more subjective. Assuming that the design is correct with respect to the specification, design quality asks if it is a good design. Aspects of design quality include performance, simplicity, robustness, obviousness, reusability, burden sharing among parts, narrowness of interfaces, adherence to standard practices, and many more. The relative importance of each of these aspects depends on the project, and design decisions by project members must be based on these factors.

Cleanroom teams use a variety of techniques to evaluate correctness and design quality in a *review* process. Reviews may range from informal discussions to mathematical proofs, but their goal is to convince the team members that a design is worth keeping, or if it is not, how to improve either the design or the specification to make progress toward the development goal.

In a sense, the idea of stumbling across a design in an alley is not so far off the mark. Although there are many successful Cleanroom projects, there is nothing in Cleanroom where a particular path from specification to design is dictated or recommended. Historically, Cleanroom has assumed that good designers know how to design systems and programs. Cleanroom provides guidance in two ways: It strongly focuses on the correctness argument, which encourages developers to produce simple, obvious designs (Dyer, 1988); and it encourages the use of good software engineering practices such as information hiding, modularization, and structure. But beyond this is an admission of the great difficulty inherent in teaching good design; many good designers don't really know how they do it, and two equally good designers may have radically different approaches.

The absence of a required or recommended design approach actually works in Cleanroom's favor: As new approaches are developed and improved, they can be easily incorporated into the Cleanroom framework. Thus object-orientation, which was in its infancy when Cleanroom was first used, can easily be applied to Cleanroom development (Hevner and Mills, 1993; Becker et al., 1994; Deck, 1996). Indeed, object-orientation can provide much of the guidance to designers that has been intentionally absent from Cleanroom.

A Simple Example

The example shown in Figure 3 will be used to illustrate some of the concepts and ideas of this chapter. It is small so that all of its aspects may be precisely known. The black box defines an object, called MA_12, that estimates the restocking needs of a merchant based on a 12-month moving average. It is defined using Box Description Language (Mills, Linger, & Hevner, 1986). The abstract data model consists of an array and a counter. Although these abstract data objects may seem "concrete," there is no requirement that the actual data storage be implemented using these data objects or types. The abstract model is chosen to fit the cognitive model of the reader or user.

```
define BB MA_12
model
    sales : array [1..12] of integer initial 0
    c : integer initial 0
operation AddMonthlySales(in i:integer):
    [ c < 12 → sales[c+1] := i, c := c+1
    | true → for k between 1 and 11,
        sales[k] := sales[k+1], sales[12] := i ]
operation EstimateRestocking(out e : integer):
    [ c = 0 → e := 0
    | c ≤ 12 → e := (sales[1] + ... + sales[c])/c
    | true →undefined ]
end define
```

Figure 3. BDL Black Box Example

Part of the validation of this specification against requirements will include ensuring that *c* can never exceed 12, so that the user behavior of EstimateRestocking is never undefined. The object provides two methods, each of which has its own transition function. These transition functions, AddMonthlySales and EstimateRestocking, are defined using the *conditional rule* notation of Linger, et al. (1979).

The State Box

Making progress toward completing the software product usually requires expressing both process and data designs. Box structures has traditionally suggested that data be addressed first, but with two strong caveats. First, both data and process evolve in a stepwise fashion, with verification and review at every step. So it is incorrect to assume that data implementation details are described to the last byte before process decisions are addressed. Instead, a data design step may be followed by a process design step, and so on. Second, there is considerable thinking-ahead done in every design step, so that considerations about future process-design decisions will often affect current data-design work.

Syntax

As with all syntactic conventions in Cleanroom, what is proposed here is optional and should be tailored to fit the particular team. A syntax for state box definitions is shown in Figure 4. It is motivated by Mills, Linger, and Hevner (1986). The formal syntax definition is based on the notion of a context-free grammar expressed in Backus-Naur form. For more on grammars, see Naur (1963) or any text on compiler or language theory.

The state box definition begins by giving a name to the state box, defining its state data and its operations. Each state data object is a named instance of a black box specification, though that specification may not always be written down. The usage permitted for each state data object is defined by its specification, as is the abstract model that the data object presents. Each state box operation is defined in terms of a process specification, for which a variety of notations exist.

The two forms of the operations section permit either a more OO-like viewpoint, with named methods, or a "classic" box structures viewpoint, in which a single stimulus triggers the (unnamed) operation. The arguments and responses may be named or unnamed, but they must always be "typed" using the definition of a black box data abstraction. If there are multiple arguments or responses they must be named.

Example

The example shown in Figure 5 proposes a state box design for the black box MA_12 previously defined in Figure 3. Its state data is a list-

```
<state box definition>     ::= define SB <black box name>
                               state data <state data>
                               <operations >
                               end define

<black box name>           ::= string that identifies a data-encapsulating
                               black box specification

<state data>               ::= [<object-name-list> :
                               use BB <black box name> (<initial value>)]*

<object-name-list>         ::= <object-name> [, <object-name>]*

<object-name>              ::= string that identifies the data instance

<initial value>            ::= string that defines the initial value of the
                               object's abstract model

<operations>               ::= <named operation>+
                                | <unnamed operation>

<named operation>          ::= operation <operation name>
                                (<optional-parameters>)
                                <optional-responses>
                                <process specification>

<unnamed operation>        ::= transition <parameters> <response>
                               <transition function>

<operation name>           ::= string that identifies the operation

<optional-parameters>      ::= <named parameter> [; <named parameter>]*
                                                  |<unnamed parameter>
                                                  | empty

<named parameter>          ::= [in | out | inout] <object-name-list> :
                               <black box name>

<unnamed parameter>        ::= <black box name>

<optional-responses>       ::= <named response> [, <named response>]*
                                                 |<unnamed response>
                                                 | empty

<named response>           ::= <object-name-list> : <black box name>

<unnamed response>         ::= <black box name>

<process specification>    ::= black box process abstraction (or name of)
```

Figure 4. BDL State Box Syntax

```
define SB MA_12
state data
        inventory : use BB list-of-integer (empty)
operation AddMonthlySales (in i:integer):
        [ inventory :=
           (the last up to 11 items of inventory) ⊕ i ]
operation EstimateRestocking (out e : integer):
        [ length(inventory) = 0 → e := 0
        | length(inventory) ≤ 12 →
           e := sum(inventory)/length(inventory)
        | true → undefined ]
end define
```

Figure 5. State Box for MA_12

of-integers data structure that gives access to both ends. Perhaps this choice of data implementation was made because the target language provides predefined operations on lists like sum, length, remove_first, and append. Or perhaps experience has shown that such a list provides better performance on a particular architecture. The design is incomplete because the list-of-integers data type may not yet be implemented and the operations are also not yet implemented. A shorthand notation has been used for the function of AddMonthlySales, to avoid undue formality.

It is worth noting some ways that object-orientation might influence the choice of design. In the object-oriented paradigm, one of the essential characteristics of a good design is how effectively it uses inheritance (Blair et al., 1991). So, instead of defining the object inventory to be an encapsulated member data object of the state box of MA_12, the designer could have designed MA_12 as a subclass of *list-of-integer* that adds two new member functions, AddMonthlySales and EstimateRestocking, and restricts access to the generic list functions like append and delete. If done correctly, this would be similar to the proposal of Figure 5 and might provide benefits to later designers who want to subclass further. Or, it may be a cumbersome implementation. The team that uses object-orientation and box structures will customize the BDL or other notations to allow the choice of design direction to be noted. Those teams will also want to introduce the use of "this" or "self" as a way of noting an object's use of its own or a superclass's state data.

A comparison between Figure 3 and Figure 5 shows the distinction between the abstract model of the black box, which was an abstract picture that the object's user had of the data, and the concrete model or state data of the state box, which is in this case a single data object. The state data object(s) are instances of data specifications and users of those objects are required to understand their specifications and obey their rules. Users may only access the abstract model the object presents and are forbidden from referencing an object's internal data implementation. Figure 5 assumes (for now) that the specification of the type *list-of-integers* implements the intuitive concept of a "list of integers" and that the needed operations are provided. This is something that would have to be verified later on. That unverified assumption exposes the designer to some risk, and he or she will have to exercise good engineering judgment in assessing and mitigating that risk.

It should be noted that, as a result of a single paper (Mills & Linger, 1986) some practitioners equate Cleanroom with the use of a very limited set of data abstractions, namely stacks and queues. Nothing could be further from the truth. That particular paper reported on experimental results of a single project which, taken generally, should not come as any surprise: Give preference to data abstractions that are well-understood, easy to verify, and workable in the problem domain. At the same time, hide those implementations that are complicated or cumbersome but necessary within data-abstracting black boxes. While stacks and queues are excellent tools for certain purposes, higher-level abstractions are also useful. At the same time, there are ideal applications for the judicious and careful use of arrays and pointers.

Recap: Black Box Process Specifications

The black box process specification of a process is usually defined as a mapping from inputs into outputs. Such a mapping is usually written using an assignment notation, after Linger, Mills, and Witt (1979):

```
[ output := function(input) ]
```

or as a mapping, after Mills (1975):

```
f: input → output
```

These mappings may fall into a number of types:

- a *total function*, that maps each possible domain element (input) into a single range element (output)
- a *partial function*, undefined on part of its possible domain but producing only one range element for each element in the domain of definition
- a *relation*, taking each domain element into a set of range elements

Because there are many types of mapping used in process specification, this chapter will use "specification," "mapping," "behavior," and "abstraction" in preference to the more common, but less correct, "intended function."

Partial functions are rarely used at the system level, where a system would be expected to deal gracefully with all inputs, even "unexpected" ones. However, they are commonly used for internal interfaces, where the description of the domain alerts the object's user to the necessary preconditions for its successful use. For example, a procedure that expects to be called with an argument greater than zero might be defined as:

```
[ input > 0 → output := square root of input
| true → undefined ]
```

Nondeterministic black box process specifications are defined using relations, for example

```
[ output := anything ]
```

even though the actual implementation could be deterministic. This section will start with the assumption that these are total functions, then introduce the additional machinery needed to deal with partial functions and relations.

Recap: Black Box Data Specifications

In the case of a data abstraction, the black box is defined as an abstract model of the object's state, and a collection of transitions, one for each operation. Each transition has two parts. The first, which we will call BBoutput, defines the output in terms of the input and the state of the system. From the black box point of view, this state is the value of the abstract, black box data model. The second part of the transition, which we will call BBupdate, describes how the abstract state is updated each time the system is used.

- BBoutput maps {inputs, values of the black box data model} into outputs
- BBupdate maps {inputs, values of the black box data model} into new values of the black box data model.

This definition of a data abstraction is characteristic of the model-based approach (see Hoffman & Strooper, 1995, for a recent summary of state abstraction approaches).

Before proceeding, a more careful analysis of the concept of abstract state is important to the understanding of the next sections. In "classic" box structures, the abstract state is always a sequence, called SH or S*, which consists of the history of all system use. In that view, there is only one possible BBupdate, namely the appending of the input to the history. Thus each transition had the form

```
[ output := BBoutput(input, SH)
  SH := SH ⊕• input ]
```

Because BBupdate is always the same, its documentation is usually omitted. This view has many advantages. The first benefit is pedagogical: Because it is impractical to actually implement a data structure SH, a distinction between the abstract and concrete data models is enforced. Another benefit is that this view assists in understanding a user's view of system behavior, particularly in situations where the requirements are not well defined.

However, in many practical applications, it has turned out to be difficult to write history-based transition functions that result in a sensible presentation of system behavior. Several techniques have been proposed to deal with this, including the use of functions that cast history into other abstractions, and the use of canonical histories (Mao, 1993). One particular problem with history is that every transition changes the state of the object, since every input is appended to SH for possible future use. Thus the useful notion of a constant or read-only transition is lost. In addition, for small objects like stacks and switches, the perceived need to define functions that derive *switch is on* or *top of stack* from SH may be a barrier to adoption of box structures altogether.

The examples in this chapter view the black box abstract data model as a collection of abstract objects of various types. The flavor of box structures in which stimulus history serves as the abstract data model is referred to as "classic" box structures, and is a special case of the more general view.

The example of Figure 3 defines black box functions for each operation. When the operation AddMonthlySales is requested, along with an integer *i*, BBoutput is null and BBupdate is defined as

```
[ c < 12 → sales[c+1] := i, c := c + 1
| true → for k between 1 and 11, sales[k] := sales[k+1], sales[12] := i]
```

When the operation EstimateRestocking is requested, BBupdate is the identity function (the state is unchanged) and BBoutput is defined as

```
[ c = 0 → e := 0
| c ≤ 12 → e := (sales[i] + ... + sales[c])/c
| true → undefined ]
```

State Box Semantics

The relationships between data abstractions and their concrete realizations is a well-examined subject in the literature. Guttag, et al. (1978), Liskov & Zilles (1975), Parnas (1972), and Wulf, et al. (1976) have all written on the issue. The semantics presented here, and the verification techniques, closely follow the example of Gannon, et al. (1987) and Shankar (1982).

The state box defines transition mappings that are similar in form to that of the black box. Each transition has two parts:

- SBoutput maps {inputs, values of the state data} into outputs
- SBupdate maps {inputs, values of the state data} into new values of the state data.

The goal of state box verification is to demonstrate that the state box correctly implements the black box: If identical streams of operations and input values are presented to the black box and to state box, the same total output is produced.

The black box and its state box design each define a *data space*. The data space is the set of all possible values of the data model – concrete in the case of the state box and abstract in the case of the black box.

A *representation mapping* is a function that defines a correspon-

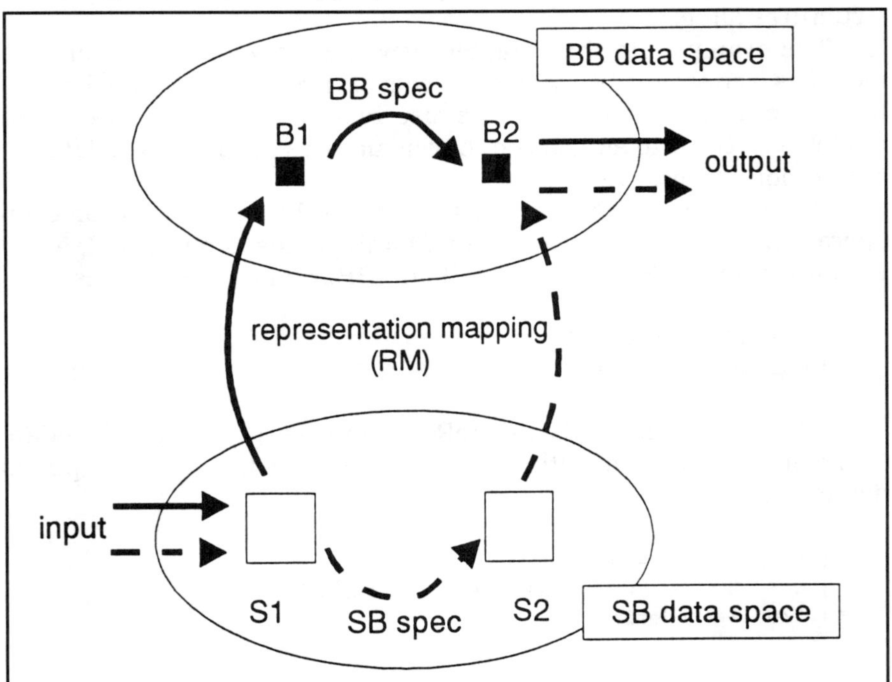

Figure 6. Commutativity Diagram

dence between elements of the black box data space and elements of the state box data space. Initially, we will assume that the representation mapping is a function that maps the state box data space to the black box data space. This mapping is usually many-to-one, but it must be onto: for every point in the black box data space, the representation mapping must map at least one point in the state box data space into it.

The essence of state box verification is to show that the diagram shown in Figure 6 commutes: following the dashed arrows and following the solid arrows must give the same B2 and same output. More precisely, if any input I is given to the state box, in any initial state S1, both of the following must be true:

- BBoutput(I,RM(S1)) = SBoutput(I,S1). The output of the state box function when applied to I and S1 is the same as the output of the black box function when applied to I and RM(S1) — the result of applying the representation mapping to S1.
- BBupdate(I,RM(S1)) = RM(SBupdate(I,S1)). The state defined by RM(SBupdate(C1)) — applying the state box mapping to C1 and then the representation mapping to the result–is the same as BBupdate(RM(C1)) —applying the representation mapping to C1 and then applying the black box to the result.

It is usually the responsibility of the state box designer to define the representation mapping at the time the concrete model is defined. This representation mapping is carried along with the state box design, either as commentary or as separate documentation. A representation mapping for MA_12 is shown in Figure 7.

The state box verification technique presented here uses a form of mathematical induction, asking three correctness questions:

1. Does the representation mapping RM carry the initial state of the state box into the initial state of the black box?
2. Given an input I, a state box data value S1, representation mapping RM, black box output function BBoutput, and state box output function SBoutput, does BBoutput(I,RM(S1)) equal SBoutput(I,S1)?

```
if length(inventory) = k > 12, c is undefined.
Otherwise, c = k.

if length(inventory) = k > 12, sales[1] through sales[k] are
undefined. Otherwise sales[1] through sales[k] are respec-
tively the head of inventory, the item after the head of
inventory, and so forth.

if length(inventory) = k < 12, sales[k+1] through sales[12]
are zero.
```

Figure 7. Representation Mapping for MA_12

	Inventory Length < 12	Inventory Length ≥ 12
Input is AddMonthlySales	case 1	case 3
Input is EstimateRestocking	case 2	case 4

Figure 8. Verification Cases of State Box MA_12

3. Given an input I, a state box data value S1, representation mapping RM, black box data function BBupdate, and state box data function SBupdate, does BBupdate(I,RM(S1)) equal RM(SBupdate(I,S1))?

The first step in verifying MA_12 asks, if the list *inventory* is empty, are *sales[1]* through *sales[12]* and c all zero? The representation mapping says they are.

For step two, the state box specification suggests four cases as shown in Figure 8.

The AddMonthlySales stimulus defines only a data update, not an output, so verification step 2 is vacuously true for cases 1 and 3. The EstimateRestocking stimulus defines only an output, so verification step 3 is vacuously true for cases 2 and 4.

For case 1, suppose S1 contains an inventory list *inventory* of length n<12. The result of applying the representation mapping of Figure 7 to S1, that is, RM(S1), is

```
c = n
sales[1] = head(L)
sales[2] = item after head(L),
sales[3] = 2nd item after head(L), and so forth up to sales[n]
sales[n+1] through sales[12] are all 0.
```

Now suppose AddMonthlySales(x) is input. SBupdate says to append x to *inventory* in this case. Applying RM to the result, or RM(SBupdate(AddMonthlySales(x),S1)) gives

```
c = new length(inventory) = old length + 1 = n+1
sales[1] = head(L)
sales[2] = item after head(L),
sales[3] = 2nd item after head(L), and so forth up to sales[n]
sales[n+1] = last item of result of appending x to inventory = x
sales[n+2] through sales[12] (if they exist) are all 0.
```

Applying BBupdate to RM(S1), namely BBupdate(AddMonthly Sales(x),RM(S1)) yields the same thing.

The other cases are similar, the only difference being the need to verify that length(inventory) never exceeds 12. This formal verification argument can be tedious, but the insights it yields, both for achieving correctness and for improving quality, are tremendous.

Extensions: Partial Functions, Relations, and Large Abstract Data Spaces

The preceding correctness questions assume BBoutput, BBupdate, SBoutput, and SBupdate are total functions with the indicated direction. In the case that any are partial functions, what is desired is that the state box be at least as powerful as the black box —that the domain of definition of the black box be a (possibly total) subset of the state box domain. More succinctly, we require that: dom(BBoutput) $\subseteq$ dom(SBoutput) (see Gannon, 1987).

However, if any of BBoutput, BBupdate, SBoutput, or SBupdate is a relation, then what we want is for the state box to be more constrained than the black box. We want the set of possible black box outputs for any input to wholly contain the set of possible state box outputs for any input. For total relations,

- BBoutput(I,RM(S1)) $\supseteq$ SBoutput(I,S1) and
- BBupdate(I,RM(S1)) $\supseteq$ RM(SBupdate(I,S1)).

Combining all of these possibilities, we add that in the case of a partial relation, the preceding two requirements must be augmented by the requirement dom(BBoutput) $\subseteq$ dom(SBoutput).

When the black box state space is very large, as it is when stimulus history is used as the abstract data model, it can be difficult or impossible to write a representation mapping function from concrete to abstract that is onto the black box state space. This is particularly true when many of the abstract states are indistinguishable from each other by the black box user. There are two possible ways to solve this. The first is to narrow the black box state space by defining a mapping from it into canonical states (Mao, 1993) that are all and only those states that the black box's user can tell apart. For example, "read-only" operations that don't change the future behavior of the box can be discarded in such a mapping. This requirement places a burden on the black box specifier, who must also declare what the canonical state space is, and some may feel this also defeats the purpose of using stimulus history.

A second solution is to reverse the direction of the representation mapping, having it carry abstract states into concrete ones. The same kind of commutativity arguments apply, with the following requirements:

- the representation mapping must be defined for every possible black box state,

- the domain of the state box functions must be at least as large as that of the black box functions, and
- the outputs and state data updates produced by the state box must form a subset of the outputs and state data updates produced by the black box.

In any of these cases, it should be noted that Cleanroom teams using classic box structures have concentrated their verification efforts on the clear box, and have given a somewhat less prominent role to the state box. Many of the examples shown in literature such as Mills, Linger, & Hevner (1986) suggest that a system might only have one state box, namely the design of the highest-level data-abstracting black box, and that all further refinement be through clear boxes. In such a world, proficiency in state box verification is of secondary importance. We suggest, however, that the important tool of state migration, and the rising popularity of object-orientation, will give new significance to the state box and to the techniques for its verification.

Abstraction: Obtaining a Black Box from a State Box

There are many occasions when one may want to use abstraction to recover the black box behavior of an existing state box. One of these is when dealing with legacy systems or "old code." There, a complex concrete state may present difficulties for maintenance and understanding, and a more focused and understandable abstract state is desired. A second occasion is during development, when a team may have moved ahead into state box design without having fully completed the black box specification. In either case, the black box behavior of the existing state box can be abstracted and compared to a desired or expected behavior.

Recovering an abstract model of state from a concrete one is difficult because there are no clear guidelines as to what constitutes a good abstract model. The simplest approach and the one used most often is to expose the concrete model— the state data —as the abstract model. In the MA_12 example, to follow this approach would mean

```
specification function GetEstimate
      (sh : history of MA_12 stimuli) returns integer
   ( there are no AddMonthlySales stimuli in sh → 0
   | true →
      sum of i's in up to 12 last AddMonthlySales
      stimuli in sh)/ max(number AddMonthlySales stimuli
      in SH, 12)
   )
 end specification function
```

Figure 9. Specification Function GetEstimate

using a list of integers as the abstract black box model. This approach certainly has the advantage of simplicity, both in abstraction and in later verification, but the abstraction it presents may not be ideal for the object's user, and it may expose too many internals whose change might require informing that user. There are two other approaches to deriving black box behavior from a given state box: via stimulus history; and via proposal-and-verification.

State Box Abstraction via Stimulus History

In this approach to state box abstraction, the first step is to identify the history of stimuli, SH, as the abstract data model. Writing the part of the black box behavior that updates the abstract model is easy: every operation appends argument and operation information to the permanent, infinite, sequence of stimuli. The second part is more difficult, because it requires the writing of functions that use that stimulus history to produce the desired system responses. More often than not, the way this is done is to write *specification functions*—initially termed "single-valued functional abstractions" in Pleszkoch, et al. (1990). Specification functions would be used to cast stimulus history into more manageable abstractions, or directly into values. Figure 9 shows one way of doing this.

Figure 10 shows how a function could be used to return a sublist, similar to a canonical history. It also shows a black box defined using that function.

```
specification function InventoryList
      (sh : history of MA_12 stimuli) returns list of integer
   ( there are no AddMonthlySales stimuli in sh
        → empty list
   | true →
        up to 12 most recent i's of AddMonthlySales
        stimuli, in order, most recent last
   )
end specification function

define BB MA_12
model
   sh : list of MA_12 stimuli initially empty
operation AddMonthlySales(in i:integer):
   [sh := sh ⊕ ("AddMonthlySales",(i))]
operation EstimateRestocking(out e : integer):
   [ length(InventoryList(sh)) = 0 → e := 0
   | true → sum(InventoryList(sh))/length(InventoryList(sh)),
        sh := sh ⊕ ("EstimateRestocking",())]
end define
```

Figure 10. Stimulus-History Black Box MA_12

State Box Abstraction via Proposal and Verification

The final technique for state box abstraction is to propose an abstract model, write down a black box definition in terms of this abstract model, write down a representation mapping, and then attempt to verify the state box against the new black box. This is similar to a technique called "specification interposition" in Deck (1995). This technique is most useful if a particularly appealing abstraction is known to exist, or has been suggested by a domain expert.

The Clear Box

The black box view of a process hides algorithmic details. The clear box is the first step in implementing a process specification. It exposes certain aspects of concrete control structures and defines algorithmic details of the process. A clear box consists of a control structure (such as a sequence, if-then-else, and while-do) and lower-level process specifications controlled by that structure. This partial exposure of details at every level permits intellectual control over development. The clear box may also contain local data and it may be defined as a procedure, with a name and parameters.

Syntax

Early Cleanroom teams used design languages such as PDL (Process Design Language) to express clear boxes. Design languages have some advantages over programming languages. They have simple syntax, clear semantics, and are generic enough to be understood by all programmers. Unfortunately, the use of design language necessitates an implementation step to translate the PDL into a compilable programming language. This step is non-trivial, and can be dangerous if the programming language is not equally well-understood. The use of a design language also can require a team to either eschew powerful features of the implementation language, or to augment the design language so that it ends up looking like the implementation language. Recent trends in Cleanroom usage have moved away from design language toward using implementation language. However, most teams will still use a subset of the implementation language such as the Design/C described by Rosen (1992) for better understandability.

The syntax in Figures 11 follows the guidance of Linger, et al. (1979). This syntax is usually augmented with structures such as CASE, for-next, and do-until.

Example

The state box MA_12 shown in Figure 5 leaves two process specifications to be designed: one for each of the operations AddMonthlySales and EstimateRestocking. Figure 12 shows a clear

```
<clear box definition>     ::= <named clearbox>
                                | <proc-body>
                                | use BB <black box name> (<optional-parameters>)
                                | <assignment-statement>
                                | <process specification>

<named clearbox>           ::= proc <black box name> (<optional-parameters>)
                                <optional-responses>
                                <proc-body>end proc

<black box name>           ::= string that refers to a black box definition

<optional-parameters>      ::= <named parameter> [; <named parameter>]*
                                | <unnamed parameter>
                                | empty

<optional-responses>       ::= <named response>  [, <named response>]*
                                | <unnamed response>
                                | empty

<named parameter>          ::= [in | out | inout] <object-name-list> :
                                <black box name>

<unnamed parameter>        ::= <black box name>
<named response>           ::= <object-name-list> : <black box name>

<unnamed response>         ::= <black box name>

<proc-body>                ::= <optional-local-data>
                                (<sequence> | <ifthenelse> | <whiledo>)

<assignment-statement>     ::= object-name := value

<optional-local-data>      ::= data
                                [<object-name-list> : use BB <black box name>
                                  (<initial value>)]*
                                end data

<process specification>    ::= black box process abstraction

<sequence>                 ::= do
                                <clear box definition>;
                                <clear box definition>
                                end do

<ifthenelse>               ::= if
                                  <predicate>
                                then
                                  <clear box definition>
                                else
                                  <clear box definition>
                                end if

<whiledo>                  ::= while
                                  <predicate>
                                do
                                  <clear box definition>
                                end while
```

Figure 11. BDL Clear Box Syntax

```
[ inventory := (the last up to 11 elements of inventory) ≈ i]
proc AddMonthlySales (in i:integer)
      do
       [length(inventory) < 12 → identity
      | true → inventory := remove_first(inventory)];

      [ inventory := inventory ≈ i ]
     end do
end proc
```

Figure 12. Clear Box for MA_12 Operation AddMonthlySales

box design for AddMonthlySales. It expresses the design using a sequence of two parts, each of which is a process specification. A typical element of Cleanroom style is to copy the intended specification on top of its design, for ease of verification.

The clear box for EstimateRestocking, shown in Figure 12, demonstrates the idea of combining unnamed and named clear boxes. In it, a sequence clear box (do...end do) nests a call to a process-abstracting common service black box, SumList, and an if-then clear box.

Each of these clear boxes has access to the state data *inventory* which is an unstated *inout* parameter. The design also mixes specifications that are known to be non-primitive (in square brackets) with

```
[ length(inventory) = 0 → e := 0
| length(inventory) ≤ 12 →e := sum(inventory) / length(inventory)
| true → undefined ]
proc EstimateRestocking(out e : integer):

   data
      len : use BB bounded_int (0)
      tot : use BB bounded_int (0)
   end data

   do
      [ len := len + length(inventory),
        tot := len + sum(inventory) ]
      use BB SumList(inventory)

      [ len = 0 → e := 0
      | true → e := tot / len ]
      if len = 0
      then e := 0
      else e := tot / len
      end if
     end do
end proc
```

Figure 13. Clear Box for MA_12 Operation EstimateRestocking

specifications (such as e := 0) that are thought to be primitive. A further element of Cleanroom style is to leave intermediate specifications on top of the unnamed, inline clear boxes such as the inner if-then-else. This permits the stepwise verification of the design: this design can be verified in two steps, first verifying the outer sequence and then verifying the inner if-then-else *independently* of the outer sequence.

The other important point of this example is to show that a clear box can contain instantiations of data specifications (in this case bounded_int) as local data objects that survive only for the duration of the clear box. Depending on the underlying semantics of the design or implementation, the instantiation may have effects that should be considered if not documented. Instantiation may initialize values of a local object's abstract model (remember, as users we can't see the implementation) or it may have other side effects that must be documented in order to verify correctness. In many languages, allocation of a local data object has a side effect of reducing the amount of stack space available to the rest of the program. Allocation may even fail if the necessary stack space is not available. Rigorous, mathematical proof of correctness would require the understanding and documentation of all such side effects. Cleanroom teams must constantly judge whether each program or part is sufficiently critical to warrant such rigor, or whether to accept the risk of leaving conditions like stack overflow to less-rigorous inspections or walkthroughs.

Semantics

There are several approaches to assigning meaning to programs. The axiomatic approach of Hoare (1969) is most often taught in university courses. The functional, or denotational, approach of Mills (1975) and Linger, et al. (1979) is almost universally used in Cleanroom, though there is no particular requirement that it be used. Basili and Noonan (1982) compare the two approaches. The functional approach models programs and program-parts as state-to-state mappings. Expressions, predicates, and assignments are the primitive notions of this semantics, and each is modeled as a function or relation on program states. This chapter omits some of the mathematical niceties; the purist should consult other sources.

Clear Box Correctness

As described previously, this section will deal with sufficient correctness: If the specification says to accept inputs A and B but is undefined when C is input, it is acceptable for the actual design to accept input C and return an error message. Likewise, if the specification says on a particular input either X or Y might be output, the actual design can decide to always output X. We say a design is correct with respect to its specification whenever all of the following are true:

- if the specification defines a unique response for input A, then the design produces that same response on input A
- if the specification defines a set of possible responses for input A, then the design can produce a subset of those responses on input A
- whenever the specification is undefined for an input A, the design may take any action on input A

Sometimes the specification will be considerably looser than the design, because it wishes to hide details from the higher levels in the hierarchy. For example,

```
[ i, j, t := j, i, j ]
```

is sufficiently correct with respect to

```
[ i, j, t := j, i, either i or j ]
```

which is sufficiently correct with respect to

```
[ i, j, t := j, i, anything ]
```

which in turn is sufficiently correct with respect to

```
[ i = 0→ undefined | i, j, t := j, i, anything ].
```

A chain of progressively weaker specifications forms this correctness hierarchy.

Figure 14 illustrates the general theory of clear box verification. Beginning with an intended specification, an initial clear box design is

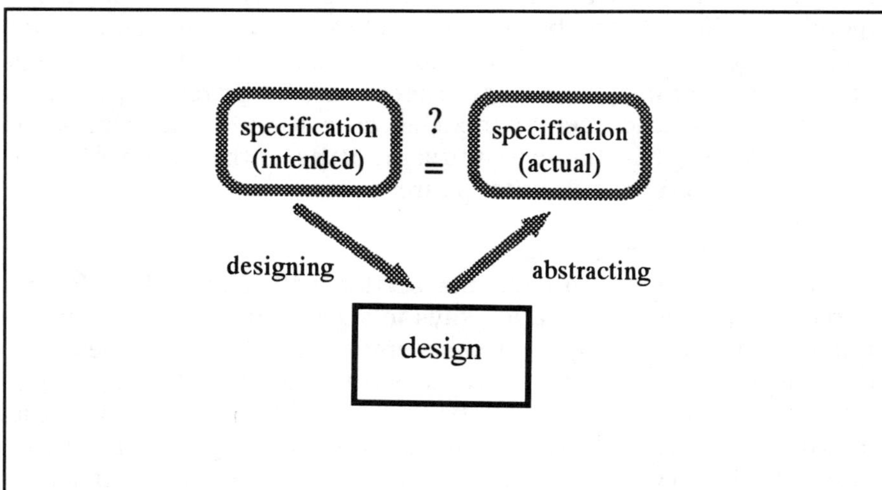

Figure 14. Schematic of Clear Box Verification

proposed. Then, abstraction takes place to yield the actual behavior specification of the design. The two specifications are compared, and if the actual specification sufficiently meets the intent, the design is correct. In the next few sections we will look at the techniques of clear box correctness verification based on Linger et al. (1979).

The State Space of a Process

Every process—whether it be a large procedure or a single program part—is specified by a mapping that is defined on the program's state space. The *state* of the system is the set of all variables, together with their values at a particular point in time. The *state space* is the collection of all possible states. A process transforms the system from a before state to an after state. Typically, these state transformations are defined using the conditional-rule syntax of Linger et al. (1979) or precise natural language, or a combination of the two.

Function Composition

The meaning of a sequence of program parts is the *composition* of their mappings. If program part P is specified by mapping f, and program part Q is specified by mapping g, then the meaning of **do** P; Q **end do** is the composition mapping f o g. For example, suppose:

- f = [inventory := remove_first(inventory)]
- g = [inventory := inventory ⊕ i]

The composition of these two functions is the specification of program part **do** P; Q **end do**:

- f o g = [inventory := remove_first(inventory) ⊕ i]

step	specification	new "len"	new "tot"	new "e"
0	before 1st step	unknown	unknown	unknown
1	len := 0	0	unknown	unknown
2	tot := 0	0	0	unknown
3	len := len + length (inventory)			
	tot := tot + sum (inventory)	length (inventory)	sum (inventory)	unknown
4	len = 0→ e := 0 | true → e:= tot / len	length (inventory)	sum (inventory)	0, if len = 0 else tot/len

Figure 15. Trace Table for EstimateRestocking

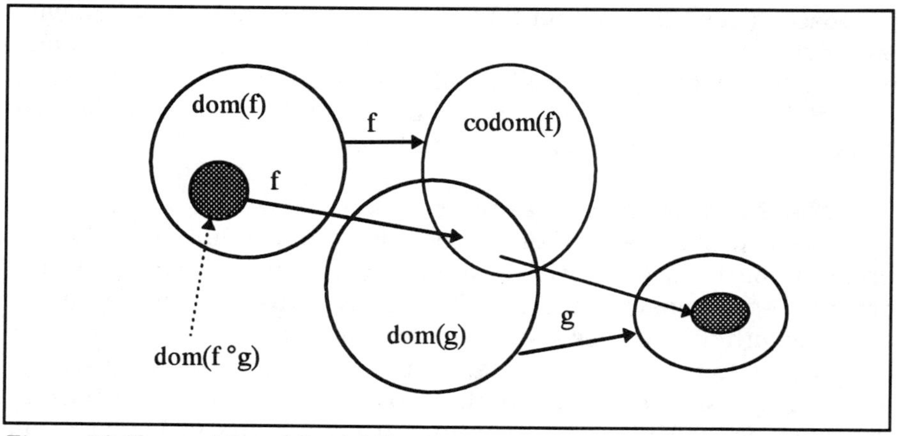

Figure 16. Composition of Partial Functions

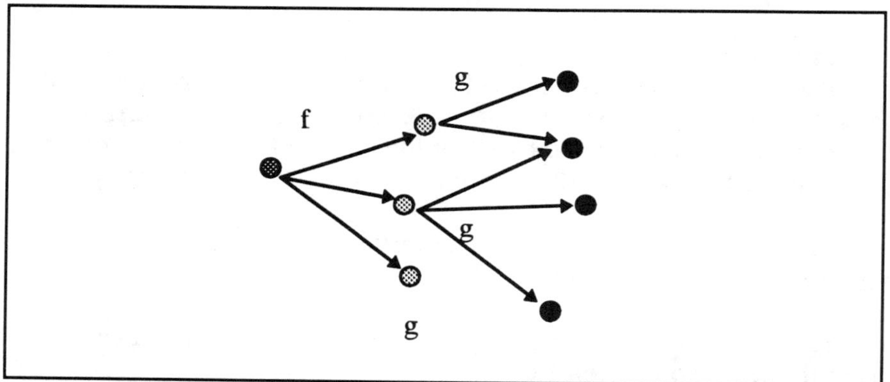

Figure 17. Composition of Relations

Notice that the resulting function is still a *specification* because it hides the sequentiality of processing.

A typical technique for composing sequences of conditional rules is to substitute the results of earlier assignments for the before values of later assignments. In the preceding example, we substituted *remove_first(inventory)* everywhere *inventory* appears on the right-hand side of function g. A more thorough substitution technique uses the trace table, identifying the values of each variable after each step, and substituting those values appropriately in the next step. An example of this technique, applied to the EstimateRestocking clear box, is shown in Figure 15. Note that the data initializations have the effect of assigning a value and must be included.

Composition of Partial Functions and Relations

Some care must be taken when composing partial functions and relations. The composition of partial functions f o g is defined only on the intersection of the codomain(f) and the domain(g) as shown in Figure 16.

specification: F

design: do P; Q **end do**

Correctness Question: does [P] followed by [Q] do F?

Figure 18. Sequence Correctness Questions

In the case of a relation where *f* maps a single value into a set of values, and *g* maps a single value into a set of values, the composition results in all of the values *g* produces from each f-result, as shown in Figure 17. Bear in mind that some of the g result sets could have duplicate elements, and *g* may be undefined on some of the *f* results.

The Correctness of Sequences

We have already touched on the fundamental issues of correctness:

- Is the domain of the actual specification at least the domain of the intended specification?
- For every element of the domain of the intended specification, does the actual specification produce the same result?

Many Cleanroom teams follow Linger et al. (1979) in stating correctness questions for each clear box verification. Figure 18 states the correctness questions for the simple two-part sequence. The notation [P] is read "the function computed by program part P."

Abstracting a sequence is therefore as simple as composing the mappings that make up the sequence. The only difficulty may come in comparing the composition [P] o [Q] with F.

The Correctness of Alternations

Alternation (if-then, if-then-else, and CASE) is verified in a similar manner: abstract the actual behavior specification of the part, and compare with the intent. If we abstract the program part

```
if (length(inventory) < 12
then
   [inventory := inventory ⊕ i]
else
   [inventory := remove_first(inventory)⊕i]
end if
```

we derive the overall function of the if-then-else:

```
[length(inventory) < 12 → inventory := inventory ⊕ i
| true → inventory := remove_first(inventory) ⊕ i]
```

specification: F
design: if condition then P else Q **end if**
Correctness Question 1: if condition is true does [P] do F?
Correctness Question 2: if condition is false does [Q] do F?

Figure 19. Alternation Correctness Questions

Verification is completed by arguing that this is the same function as

[inventory := (the last up to 11 items of inventory) ⊕ i]

Some discussion may be required during the verification review, in which cases are described, or the meaning of the intended function is further explored. The team may agree that this verification is complete, or it may decide at this point to improve the wording of the intended function so as to prevent misunderstandings, not to mention having the same discussion every time this part is re-reviewed.

A simple technique for verifying nested alternations and sequences is to take each case of the intended behavior and, using that as an assumption, walk through the actual behaviors to see if the result is as specified. This technique would yield a three-step verification of the outer sequence in Figure 13. In the first step, suppose length(inventory) = 0. The desired behavior is e := 0. We can walk through the sequence or use a trace table, picking only those cases that fall within that assumption, and arrive at that same behavior. In the second step, assume length(inventory) ≤ 12. We really don't have to verify the third, because any design will satisfy "undefined."

The correctness questions for alternations are summarized in Figure 19.

Correctness of Loops

Establishing the correctness of looping constructs like while-do and do-until is somewhat more complicated. The basic technique used most often in Cleanroom requires first introducing the interchangeability of iteration and recursion. Suppose we have the following loop that forms the body of the SumList common service:

```
proc SumList (inout len, tot: integer;
              inout inv : list-of-integer)

    data
        curr : list pointer (inv.head)
    end data

    while (curr not at end of inv)
    do
      [ len := len + 1,
        tot := tot + inv.curr
        curr := next of inv ]
    end while
end proc
```

First, let us suppose there are no remaining elements of the list (i.e., the current pointer is at the end of the list). Then the overall function of the loop is to do nothing at all–the identity mapping. If there are elements after the current pointer, then the overall function begins by updating some variables and moving to the next inv element. What happens next? There are again two cases. If there are now no remaining elements, nothing more is done. Otherwise, do the assignment, move to the next item, and continue. This looks like an infinite sequence:

```
do
    [empty(inv) → identity
    | true →
     len := len + 1,
     tot := tot + inv.curr,
     curr := next of inv ] ;

   [empty(inv) →identity
   | true →
      len := len + 1,
      tot := tot + inv.curr,
      curr := next of inv ] ;
   ...
end do
```

If we look at just the value of len, we can see the trace table unfolding to have an infinite number of cases:

```
no more elements → identity
| no more elements after next → add 1 to len
| no more elements after next 2 → add 2 to len
```

and so forth. To compress this into a simpler form, we write the function of the while loop as a summary of the net effect of this infinite sequence. The most important aspect of this summary is that the while loop is a process of *completing* an action rather than *doing* an action.

In the preceding loop, we would say that the function of the loop is to remove all the *next remaining* elements of the list, add that number to len and add the sum of those elements to the total. This point of view has several benefits in addition to making verification possible. First, it highlights any missing initialization (such as setting len and tot to zero). Second, it makes the loop function independent of the initialization, so that it could be used in a different place with a different initialization.

If we take advantage of this kind of loop-summarization, then the overall function of the while loop has two parts. In the first part, the while test is initially true, in which case the loop does no (more) work. In the second part, the while test is initially false, in which case the loop does its body exactly once and then does the loop all the rest of the times. In order to take advantage of this substitution of recursion for iteration, however, the loop must be guaranteed to terminate.

The creative part of while-loop verification is to suggest a function for the loop that is amenable to this composition. Let's suggest an overall function for our while-loop:

```
[ curr := position at end of inv
  len := len + number of next remaining elements in inv
  tot := tot + sum of next remaining elements in inv]
```

There are three parts to the correctness verification of loops. First, we have to establish that the loop will always terminate on the domain of the function. We could argue this formally, but informally it would appear that the end of the list will eventually be reached.

The second part to the correctness verification asks whether, if the predicate is initially true, the identity function is a correct realization of the overall intent. So, if we are at the end of the list, does doing nothing set *curr* to point to the end of *inv*, add the number of remaining elements to *len*, and so forth? Since there are no remaining elements, the implementation is vacuously true.

The third part of the verification asks us to compose two functions: if there are remaining elements, does

```
[ len := len + 1,
  tot := tot + inv.curr
  curr := next of inv]
```

composed with

```
[ curr := end of inventory
  len := len + number of next remaining elements in inv
  tot := tot + sum of next remaining elements in inventory ]
```

correctly implement the overall intent? For *len*, we can argue that adding one, followed by adding all the rest of them, is the same as

specification: F

design: while condition **do** P **end do**

Correctness Question 1: does the loop terminate on the domain of F?

Correctness Question 2: if condition is false does identity do F?

Correctness Question 3: if condition is true does [P] o F do F?

Figure 20. While-do Correctness Questions

adding all of them. The same kind of argument is used for *tot* and *curr*.

The preceding rules are summarized in the three correctness questions for the while-do, shown in Figure 20.

While-loop verification is not really that much more complicated than sequences and alternations, since it is essentially a sequence verification itself. What is difficult in practice is writing an overall while function that assists verification.

When the overall intended while-loop function is a partial function or relation, things get considerably more complex. With partial functions, one must establish that no execution of the loop can carry the state out of the domain of the subsequent execution. With relations, the complexity lies in composing the relations. For more detail in this area, see Stotts and Ruiz (1991).

Clear Box Abstraction

Clear box abstraction provides benefits similar to those of state box abstraction. It allows the recovery of the specification of an undocumented or poorly-documented piece of code or design. It also supports the notion of developers "thinking ahead" by trying out some design ideas, then abstracting them to a black box and comparing that black box with the original intent.

The composition of functions using trace tables is sufficient to recover the specification of any program composed solely of sequences and alternations. For programs containing iterations, the usual approach is to guess the while-loop function and then verify it. In abstraction, just as in design, the number of intermediate specifications that are actually documented and maintained depends on the skill of the team, the complexity of the project, and the reliability that the product demands. Basili and Mills (1982) and Hausler, et al. (1990) describe some of the techniques and benefits of clear box abstraction in more detail.

Concurrency and Real-Time Considerations in Cleanroom Development

The general category of real-time systems includes systems where there is either actual (e.g., multiprocessing) or apparent (e.g., multitasking and multithreading) concurrency, systems where concurrent processes share resources, and systems where there may be nondeterminism caused, e.g., by interrupts. In the real-time environment, timing of processes may be critical.

In Cleanroom projects where real-time issues have been important, the division between informal evaluation of correctness and more formal verification techniques has typically been at the real-time interface (e.g., Brewer, 1995). Sequential units of code are verified against their mathematical specifications, but real-time issues such as timing, locking, resource contention, and serialization are enforced using traditional techniques (e.g., semaphores). The adequacy of those techniques is confirmed using discussion, experience with similar problems, and, in some cases, simulation. The success of these projects in meeting their goals and in improving their quality and productivity is well-established. Thus, it is quite likely that this mixture of approaches will be adequate for most Cleanroom projects.

Specification is the central issue in the verification of real-time systems. Additional specification rigor is needed in three areas where the functional model is deficient: nondeterminism, timing, and termination. The approach of Stotts and Ruiz (1991) maps input states into sets of valid output states. Becker & Hevner (March, 1991) have suggested a white box to complement the black, state, and clear boxes. Deck, et al. (1992) proposed a conceptual framework in which stimulus histories are expressed in terms of formal languages. Mills (1988) proposes the concept of a *Resolve* function at strategic points in the concurrent operation. All of these notions reflect the influence of denotational semantics (see, e.g., Tennant, 1976) and functional semantics. No specific method has predominated in Cleanroom practice–each has shown its applicability to one specific problem domain or another.

In the area of timing, Becker and Hevner (July, 1991) propose combining Petri nets (and associated analytical tools) with box structures. A simpler but less powerful approach is to augment the functional semantics with attributes such as time. For example, an intended function could read "swap X and Y returning a value to register R1 no sooner than x and no later than y microseconds after invocation." Of the suggested approaches, Petri nets are the most promising technique for confirming that a design would meet this expectation. Some of these confirmations take the form of verification (proof) while others take the form of certification (acceptably high probability). The third area, termination, has been the subject of extensive research. The notations proposed include Communicating Sequential Processes (Hoare, 1978) and Communicating Modules (Witt, 1985). These formalisms are exacting and tools for verification assistance are largely absent.

```
black box of data type MA_12
state box design of MA_12
   state data object inventory, instance of list-of-integers
      • black box of data type list-of-integers
   process specification, named AddMonthlySales
      clear box of AddMonthlySales
         sequence of two unnamed parts
            • part1 expected to use list-of-integers operations
            • part2 expected to use list-of-integers operations
   process specification, named EstimateRestocking
      clear box of EstimateRestocking
         local data len and tot, instance of bounded_int
            • black box of data type bounded_int
         sequence of two unnamed parts
            • part 1 named SumList, uses list-of-integers
              operations
            part 2 if-then-else with two unnamed parts
               • part 1 expected to use bounded_int
                 operations
               • part 2 expected to use bounded_int
                 operations
```

Figure 21. Box Hierarchy for MA_12

Final Thoughts on the Example

It is difficult, in a presentation such as this, to show the false starts and rewriting that take place in the Cleanroom development process. What looks like a clean, error-free initial implementation is in fact the result of several failed passes of verification followed by rewriting and more review. That said, there are a couple of remaining aspects to the MA_12 example (of course not yet complete and ready for testing) that bear mention.

At some point the careful reviewer would have asked how it is that len, of type bounded_int, is used in integer arithmetic, since it apparently does not provide an operation for retrieving an integer value. This would come out in a verification review when the reviewers examine whether those arithmetic statements are, in fact, primitive. This might be resolved in a variety of ways, including retyping of len as integer, or writing an operation for bounded_int that permits this kind of operation, or determining that the necessary operations already exist.

Figure 21 shows the box hierarchy so far for object MA_12. The outline levels show the parent-child relationships. The bullet (•) indicates a node that has not yet been designed.

Cleanroom Quality

The Cleanroom practices have been shown in many studies such as those summarized in Linger (1993) to reduce development costs and improve software quality. There are a number of reasons for this. First, the development of a coordinated hierarchy of specifications, all linked together by verification, improves the manageability of projects, especially large ones. Second, team reviews have a variety of benefits in addition to eliminating defects, including cross-pollination, development of backup resources, and solicitation of improvements. Finally, the iterative cycle of review gives some qualitative techniques for measuring progress within an increment while the incremental process enables quantitative measures for the entire development. Each of these benefits will be described in the sections that follow.

One of the key success factors of any methodology adoption is to tailor the methodology to the specific needs of the project and its environment. Hausler, et. al (1994) describe a phased approach; Deck (1994) describes a framework for tailoring and provides several additional examples.

Architecture-Driven Development

The Cleanroom-developed system evolves as a hierarchy of specifications managed by data and control structures. In this way the system itself mimics the structure of an effectively-managed organization. Higher-level contracts (specifications) are negotiated with the customer. Then, the task is subdivided into subcontracts (subspecifications). The overall contract manager ensures that the subcontracts, together with the controls over their interaction, produce the desired result. A subcontractor may further delegate parts of the work. Dependencies among the various parties are limited, so that one party is not affected by the internal decisions of another party. Although equal effort is not devoted to documenting all of these contracts—some are written, some verbal—they exist at every level. In addition, one does not simply hand out the contracts, send the developers into their offices, and await successful results. Instead, project management standards define how interactions among subcontracts will take place, certain control functions are retained for management, and protocols for renegotiation are established for addressing changing circumstances. In a software project, design is the activity of allocating work to such subcontracts, and deciding how to control them.

One of the critical parameters in defining a management hierarchy is the notion of span-of-control: how many subordinates does each manager control? Cleanroom has traditionally applied the "rule of five" when recommending the number of lower-level objects in each design step. Generally the span of control is between 3 and 7. Formal studies in other domains have suggested that short-term memory operates best in a similar range (Miller, 1956). While many have disputed the applicability of this knowledge to software development, one can argue that the act of reviewing ends up being dominated by short-term memory, and hence lends itself to narrower, rather than larger, spans of control.

Organization and Management

Unfortunately, the Cleanroom development hierarchy is not strict; common services will necessarily have multiple "parents" or users. For this reason the usual practices of configuration and shared-object management will apply. One example of this is when the developer of a shared common service wishes to change its specification (if only the design changes, users need not be informed). The developer of the changing object must inform all of its users, since their objects may require re-verification, and they should therefore concur in the change. Depending on the size and complexity of the project, the mechanics of this notification may have to be decided up-front. Usually, a message can be broadcast to all team members announcing the possible change. Those who use the object are expected to know that, or to check, and reply. This can be problematic if key team members have left the team temporarily or permanently, or if they overlook their use of the object. Text-searching facilities (such as "grep") may be necessary, or the team's tools may provide appropriate search engines. Some teams have proposed maintaining a "used-by" list with the documentation of each object, but this has the disadvantage that a potentially reusable object should not have to know who uses it, and should not inform others of that usage. It also places a burden on the maintainer of that object, since every time it is re-used in another place the object must be updated. No matter what mechanism is used, the central principle remains that the verification links in the hierarchy must be examined and possibly refreshed whenever anything changes.

Although programming teams frequently focus on getting the code out at all costs (and management frequently abets this by measuring lines of code "complete"), the real intellectual effort comes higher in the hierarchy. The step from precise, complete module specifications to code is relatively straightforward and is constantly being further automated. This automation has the effect of making higher-level specifications primitives but has nevertheless not seemed to solve the "software crisis." That is because, without great attention to documenting and reviewing the high level specifications, the lower-level artifacts must constantly be re-written, fixed, and changed. The careful documentation of specifications at every level, and the maintenance of these specifications whenever circumstances change, are the foundations of a highly productive development environment.

The development hierarchy also guides the decomposition of a larger project into a team of teams (Hausler, et al., 1994). A small project of two to five developers would probably have a single team review all of the work products. A medium-sized project of up to fifteen developers might apportion the first-level design artifacts out to three teams of five developers each. Most reviews of the highest-level specification, and the verification of the first design level, would involve one or two representatives from each sub-team. Design reviews of the lower level artifacts would be limited to individual teams of five. A large project of, say, 75 developers would be organized into several layers. A lead team would own the highest-level specification and the first level of design. The lead team would be composed of representatives from each of four component-group areas, plus (for example) three system-level staff and architects. Each component group would own the designs of their assigned components, and would be composed of representatives from four module-group teams, plus component staff if necessary. Each module-group team would own a collection of module designs, and would have three to five members. The glue that keeps this structure together is the intermediate specifications. The component specifications, for example, are negotiated contracts between the system designers (who are the users of the components) and the component designers. The module specifications are negotiated contracts between component designers and module designers. Shared common services are typically owned at the highest level common ancestor, but some teams will move these into global pools.

Naturally the structure of specification documents is very important, and highly specific to a project. In each project, the documentation will reflect the balance of two competing needs. First, there is a desire to have a specification document be self-contained without a lot of external references. This promotes re-use and assists the review of the specification. Second, there is a desire not to duplicate effort, and especially to not have multiple copies of the same object or definition that must all be located and updated for every change. Thus, a definition that is found in multiple specifications might be placed in a shared document library. But, without a mechanism for displaying library objects at the time the using document is read, the goal of self-contained specifications is less well attained. Teams usually find their most comfortable balance point on the side of less duplication, even if this makes specifications and designs less self-contained. Tools for on-the-fly replication, and hypertext tools, offer promise in bridging these competing goals.

It is important to use the preceding as guidelines for tailoring an organization to meet specific project goals. The overriding principles are to maintain intellectual control over the development by enforcing consistent review practices and by keeping the hierarchy fairly narrow through small spans of control.

Team Design Review

A specific goal of the development process is to arrive at a hierarchy of specification objects that is not only correct, but obviously so. This characteristic of obviousness is one of the components of the design quality part of the team design and specification reviews. Simple, obvious designs result in systems that are easier to maintain and improve, and easier for new team members to learn.

The team review practices described in this section are representative, and perhaps even typical, but are always tailored to meet specific project needs. We will focus exclusively on the kinds of reviews that are applied to designs, specification reviews having been covered in an earlier chapter.

Each design work product follows a path through a series of reviews by the team that owns it (often drawing in others as needed). The goal of these reviews is consensus. Although voting, management or team-leader tie-breaking, and the like may be necessary, these should be seen as a last resort. Instead, it should be the role of managers and other leaders to propose consensus points of agreement and to assist the team toward consensus. Consensus also requires the entire team to participate, whereas voting potentially permits minority viewpoints to lead to disaffection and faction. Each of these reviews essentially has the same wide range of possible outcomes. The team could completely reject the design and send it back for fundamental rethinking, accept the design with no changes, or anywhere in between. There are several reasons for having a progression of short design reviews:

- reduce the potential re-work involved if the design requires substantial changes;
- limit the amount of new work to be reviewed each time;
- permit the team to see and comment on the evolution; and
- expose design decisions to other team members whose concurrent work is potentially affected.

Prototype Reviews

We will call the first phase of review "prototype" review. In this phase, preliminary solution strategies are discussed, unworkable alternatives rejected, and the team becomes generally informed about work directions. Informal methods such as chalk-talk are used to brief the team, and prototype reviews may be conducted without significant advance preparation by the reviewers. Traditionally, Cleanroom reviews have used low-tech tools such as printed document review, note-taking, and post-review modification. However, some teams have experimented with the use of specialized rooms where materials are viewed and updated on-line (Kaplan, 1995). The cost-effectiveness of these approaches depends on the ease-of-use of the facility. One unsuspected barrier to effective Cleanroom reviews may be the physical unavailability of review rooms on short notice. The more successful Cleanroom projects have acquired one or more special rooms, sometimes even a vacant cubicle, dedicated to their reviews. Such a room also permits team-owned documents to be stored in a central place.

The prototype-review phase for a particular object ends when the team feels that the proposed strategy forms a workable basis for continuing work. It is often omitted at the lowest levels of design, where the range of strategic options may be more constrained and the penalty for skipping the phase (namely rewriting code) is less severe.

Development Reviews

The second stage of review is the development review. The early development reviews of a design primarily focus on design-quality aspects such as structure, simplicity, understandability, obviousness, potential for reusable parts, performance, robustness, and maintainability. Development reviews also begin to look at correctness. Although a later review will do a specific correctness check, development reviews have to make sure that the foundations for easy correctness verification are laid, including sufficient intermediate specifications.

The individual preparation period for development reviews will vary depending on the level of scrutiny required, the amount of material, and its technical complexity. Some teams, believing that the goal of obviousness makes advance preparation unnecessary, have done much less advance preparation. Others, faced with inherently complex systems and algorithms, have mandated it.

Verification Reviews

Verification reviews focus on verifying the correctness of a design through the application of the verification practices described in earlier sections. However, there is still opportunity to re-open design-quality issues or even to question the overall design strategy (though this is hoped to be rare). A typical verification review outcome is to agree that the design is correct, or will be correct if a few small changes are made.

It is not unusual for a review to start out as a verification review, find significant correctness or design-quality problems, and to proceed in the form of a development review. This is especially frequent when a team tries to rush the process, skipping earlier review phases in order to "save time."

Individual preparation for verification review is important, and it significantly reduces the amount of time spent in review. On occasion a re-review will be done on short notice, but only small changes should be reviewed in that manner.

Tailoring the Review Process

The Cleanroom review practices leave many opportunities for tailoring the review process to a particular team. For example, suppose a verification review ends with only a few small changes to be made. Should another review be convened to examine the changes? Should a mini-review, such as a buddy system, be employed? Or should it be left to the discretion of the developer? The choice of strategy should be determined by the team, taking into account the balance between a need for more rapid progress and the risk of faults being introduced through an unreviewed change.

In an effort to formalize the review process, some teams (Hausler et al., 1994) have agreed to adopt elements of the inspection protocol recommended by Fagan (1976). These elements include a separation between reader and designer, the use of a trained facilitator or moderator, and the appointment of an individual to record decisions. Dyer (1992) uses the phrase "verification-based inspections." On the other end of the scale, teams have adopted the practice of having each team member record design decisions, and using the review-preparation period to compare the actual changes with the record. Again, the decision on specific review techniques must be made by the individual project.

Discussion of all possible review-process tailoring opportunities is outside of the scope of this chapter. Votta (1993) suggests that many inspections may not require a formal meeting. Porter et al. (1995) make additional observations about inspections. New tools, such as electronic mail and shared electronic documents, can reduce the amount of face-to-face review time. When using these tools, care should be taken to ensure that the primary goals of review are not compromised.

Comparing Inspections with Verification Reviews

Cleanroom verification reviews are organized around the evaluation of correctness which, using the functional approach, is a closed-ended process: once all the program parts are verified, the review is complete. Verification review is a constructive argument of correctness that applies to design as well as to code. Inspection usually emphasizes looking for bugs (or "issues"), guided by checklists that reflect the prior experience of the organization. This suggests a form of the "pesticide paradox" of Beizer (1995)–the developers are trained over time to not make those particular mistakes, so checklist-based inspection is in some sense "fighting the last war." Design-quality questions are not off-limits in verification, as they may be in code inspection.

With that said, it is the opinion of this author that the ideal approach is to merge verification with inspections; to add "correctness shown" as a checklist item for every design and code artifact. In this way, the organization still learns from past mistakes and can apply specific design-quality guidelines. Further, in an organization that is not yet ready for correctness verification, checklist-based inspections are still better than the alternative of unrestrained, ad-hoc unit debugging. A process that employs the kind of hierarchical designs described in the preceding section, but which uses traditional inspections as the Cleanroom "review" techniques, would be a Cleanroom process though not necessarily an optimal one.

Measuring Progress

The best, most quantitative measurement of progress for a Cleanroom team is its meeting of incremental goals with acceptable quality and reliability. It is for this reason that the number of increments is usually rather large, and the duration of each rather small. But it is also important for a team to be able to measure and assess progress toward delivering an increment. This can be especially important during the first increment being developed by a new Cleanroom team. Although it is highly subjective, the best way to measure this progress is to track the evolution of each subtree of the development hierarchy through its phases of review, using the best engineering judgment of the designers to assess how far they are from primitives, and how close each design step is to its final verification review. Some experience is required to make these judgments, which is why it is important for the first-time Cleanroom team to choose a relatively small piece of functionality for its first increment. A good manager can see that a team which is reviewing major rewrites of a large component specification is further from completion than a team which is reviewing small changes to a module design, provided the latter team has completed the reviews for the work products above it in the hierarchy. Insisting that the major directional emphasis be top-down makes it possible to map levels in the hierarchy into approximate completeness.

Risk-Driven Goal Setting

Every step of the development process necessitates the selection of a specification to take forward into design. It is important that there be a general strategy for this selection, lest individuals pursue a kind of random walk through the tree. A depth-first policy is perhaps the least desirable. There, each specification is taken all the way to primitives before the next high-level specification is worked. Breadth-first is better, since high-level designs will be completed first, and any problems with those designs found. Other approaches apply some intelligence to the selection of a next development thrust. It is true that some engineers will select the specification that seems most interesting or challenging, while others will select the easiest one. The best approach, though, is to assign a risk of failure to each specification – a measure that represents the possibility that a successful or optimal design cannot be found using the resources allotted. Then, at each iteration select the specification that presents the highest risk. Each design step should produce sub-specifications that have lower risk than their parent, so that the team will mix depth-first and breadth-first strategies.

The selection of development targets may be influenced by resource availability–if only one person is qualified to design a particular part, it must wait until that person is available. It will also be influenced by dependencies among parts, and by the increment plan. Making hard choices and setting clear priorities is a difficult management task. Weinberg and Schulman (1974) showed how giving conflicting directions, or suggesting that many factors have equal weight, has a significant negative impact on the performance of software professionals.

Summary

The division of Cleanroom development into the general categories of specification and design, where the latter reveals simpler specifications, provides a management framework for the application of all Cleanroom development practices. Team organization is guided by this hierarchy, as is the iterative review process. It is that review process, in which designs are evaluated both for correctness and design quality, that ensures the overall quality of the delivered software.

The development process begins when an initial specification is sufficiently complete for the first design step to take place. The appropriate level of completeness will depend on the project and environment. Each increment of development ends when each specification that belongs in that increment represents a primitive needing no further design, and when the entire design hierarchy for that increment has passed its last verification review. It is at this point that the increment is handed off to the test team for certification.

Cleanroom development practices are guided by strong principles but are also highly flexible. This chapter has described some of the alternatives available to Cleanroom developers, but it is by no means an exhaustive list. Judgment and experience are required to make full use of the Cleanroom development practices, and a phased and tailored approach to their introduction is strongly recommended.

ACKNOWLEDGMENTS
The author would like to thank the editors and the anonymous reviewers for their helpful comments. Special thanks go to Mark Pleszkoch, for his help with the semantics of state box verification under partial functions and relations, and to Alan Spangler, for carefully reviewing and correcting many of the examples.

References

Basili, V.R., & Noonan, R.E. (1980). A Comparison of the Axiomatic and Functional Models of Structured Programming. *IEEE Transactions on Software Engineering*, SE-6(5), 454-465.

Basili, V.I., & Mills, H.D. (1982). Understanding and Documenting Programs. *IEEE Transactions on Software Engineering*, SE-8(3), 270-283.

Becker, S.A., & Hevner, A.R. (1991). A White Box Analysis of Concurrent

System Designs. *Proceedings of the Tenth Annual IEEE International Phoenix Conference on Computers and Communications,* (Phoenix, March).

Becker, S.A., & Hevner, A.R. (1991). A Dynamic System Modelling Tool using Box Structures and Petri-Nets. *Proceedings of the Second International Working Conference on Dynamic Modeling of Information Systems,* (Washington, July).

Becker, S., Beiler, P., & Hevner, A. (1994). Object-oriented Box Structures for Developing Complex Systems. *Proceedings of the 27th Hawaii International Conference on Systems Sciences,* IEEE Computer Society Press, Los Alamitos, CA.

Beizer, B. (1995). *Black Box Testing,* Wiley, New York, 9.

Blair, G., Gallagher, J., Hutchison, D., & Shepherd,.D. (1991). *Object-Oriented Languages, Systems, and Applications,* Halsted Press, New York, NY.

Brewer, M., Fisher, P., Fuhrer, D.A., Nielsen, K. & Poore, J.H. (1995) The Application of Cleanroom Software Engineering to the Development of Embedded Control Systems Software. *Proceedings of the Second Annual European Industrial Symposium on Cleanroom Software Engineering,* (Berlin, March).

Deck, M.D. (1994). Cleanroom Software Engineering: Quality Improvement and Cost Reduction *Proceedings of the Twelfth Pacific Northwest Software Quality Conference,* (Portland, October), 243-258.

Deck, M.D. (1995). Cleanroom Software Engineering and "Old Code": Overcoming Process-Improvement Barriers. *Proceedings of the Thirteenth Pacific Northwest Software Quality Conference,* (Portland, September), 126-147.

Deck, M.D. (1996). Cleanroom and Object-Oriented Software Engineering: A Unique Synergy. *Proceedings 1996 Software Technology Conference* (Salt Lake City, April).

Deck, M.D., Pleszkoch, M.G., Linger, R.C., & Mills, H.D. (1992). Extended Semantics for Box Structures. *Proceedings of the Twenty-Fifth Hawaii International Conference on System Sciences,* vol. 2 (software track), IEEE Computer Society Press, Los Alamitos, CA, 382-393.

Dyer, M. (1988). Designing Software for Provable Correctness: the direction for quality software. *Information and Software Technology,* 30(6), 331-340.

Dyer, M. (1992). *The Cleanroom Approach to Quality Software Development,* Wiley, New York.

Fagan, M. (1976). Design and Code Inspections to Reduce Errors in Program Development. *IBM Systems Journal,* 15(3), 219-249.

Gannon, J.D., Hamlet, R.G., & Mills, H.D. (1987). Theory of Modules. *IEEE Transactions on Software Engineering,* SE-13(7), 820-829.

Guttag, J.V., Horowitz, E., & Musser, D.R. (1978). Abstract Data Types and Software Validation. *Communications of the ACM,* 21(12), 1048-1063.

Hausler, P.A., Pleszkoch, M.G., Linger, R.C., & Hevner, A.R. (1990). Using Function Abstraction to Understand Program Behavior. *IEEE Software,* (January), 55-63.

Hausler, P.A. (1992). A Recent Cleanroom Success Story: The Redwing Project. *Proceedings of the Seventeenth Annual Software Engineering Workshop, NASA Goddard Space Flight Center,* (Greenbelt, Md., December) 256-285.

Hausler, P.A., Linger, R.C., & Trammell, C.J. (1994). Adopting Cleanroom Software Engineering with a Phased Approach. *IBM Systems Journal,* 33(1),

89-109.

Hevner, A.R., & Mills, H.D. (1993). Box-Structured Methods for Systems Development With Objects. *IBM Systems Journal,* 32(2), 232-251.

Hoare, C.A.R. (1969). An Axiomatic Basis for Computer Programming. *Communications of the ACM,* 12(10), 576-583.

Hoare, C.A.R. (1978). Communicating Sequential Processes. *Communications of the ACM,* 21(8), 666-677.

Hoffman, D., & Strooper, P. (1995). Abstraction and Modular Software Development. *ACM SIGSOFT 95,* (Washington, October).

Kaplan, C. (1995). *Secrets of Software Quality: 40 Innovations From IBM* McGraw-Hill.

Linger, R.C. (1993). Cleanroom Software Engineering for Zero-Defect Software. *Proceedings of the Fifteenth International Conference on Software Engineering,* (Baltimore, May).

Linger, R.C., Mills, H.D., & Witt, B.I. (1979). *Structured Programming: Theory and Practice.* Addison-Wesley, Reading, MA.

Liskov, B., & Zilles, S. (1975). Specification Techniques for Data Abstractions. *IEEE Transactions on Software Engineering,* SE-1(3), 7-19.

Mao, H. (1993). *The Box-structure Development Method.* Ph.D. Dissertation, (December), University of Tennessee, Knoxville.

Miller, G.A. (1956). The Magical Number Seven Plus or Minus Two. *Psychological Review,* 63, March, 81-97.

Mills, H.D. (1975). The New Math of Computer Programming. *Communications of the ACM,* 18(1), 43-48.

Mills, H.D., Linger, R.C., & Hevner, A.R. (1986). *Principles of Information Systems Analysis and Design,* New York: Addison-Wesley.

Mills, H.D., & Linger, R.C. (1986). Data Structured Programming: Program Design without Arrays and Pointers. *IEEE Transactions on Software Engineering,* SE-12(2), 192-197.

Mills, H.D., Linger, R.C., & Hevner, A.R. (1987). Box Structured Information Systems. *IBM Systems Journal,* 26(4), 395-413.

Mills, H.D. (1988). Stepwise Refinement and Verification in Box-Structured Systems. *IEEE Computer,* (June), 23-36.

Naur, P. (1963) Revised Report on the Algorithmic Language ALGOL 60. *Communications of the ACM,* 6(1), 1-17.

Parnas, D.L. (1972). A Technique for Software Module Specification with Examples. *Communications of the ACM,* 15(5), 330-336.

Parnas, D.L. (1974). On a 'Buzzword': Hierarchical Structure. *IFIP Congress 74,* North Holland Publishing Company, Amsterdam, 336-339.

Pleszkoch, M.G., Hausler, P.A., Hevner, A.R., & Linger, R.C. (1990). Function-Theoretic Principles of Program Understanding. *Proceedings of the Twenty-Fifth Hawaii International Conference on System Sciences,* vol. 2 (software track), IEEE Computer Society Press, Los Alamitos, CA, (January), 74-81.

Porter, A., Siy, H., Toman, C.A., Votta, L.G. (1995). An Experiment to Assess the Cost-Benefits of Code Inspections in Large-Scale Software Development. *ACM SIGSOFT 95,* (Washington, October).

Rosen, S. (1992). Design Languages for Cleanroom Software Engineering *Proceedings of the Twenty-Fifth Hawaii International Conference on System Sciences,* vol. 2 (software track), IEEE Computer Society Press, Los Alamitos, CA, (January), 406-417.

Shankar, K.S. (1982). A Functional Approach to Module Verification. *IEEE Transactions on Software Engineering,* SE-8(2), 147-160.

Stotts, P.D., & Ruiz, J.C. (1991). *Nondeterminism and Nontermination in Mills' Functional Verification Method. CS-TR-2460* (revised), University of Maryland, College Park, Department of Computer Science.

Tennent, R.D. (1976). The Denotational Semantics of Programming Languages. *Communications of the ACM,* 19(8), 437-453.

Votta, L.G., Jr. (1993). Does Every Inspection Need a Meeting? *Software Engineering Notes,* D. Notkin, ed., 18(5), 107-114.

Weinberg, G.M., & Schulman, E.I. (1974). Goals and Performance in Computer Programming. *Human Factors,* 16(1), 70-77.

Witt, B.I. (1985). Communicating Modules: A Software Design Method for Concurrent Distributed Systems. *IEEE Computer,* (January), 67-77.

Wulf, W.A., London, R.L., & Shaw, M. (1976). An Introduction to the Construction and Verification of Alphard Programs. *IEEE Transactions on Software Engineering,* SE-2(4), 253-265.

CHAPTER 4

Certification Practices

James A. Whittaker
Florida Institute of Technology

The Motivation for Statistical Testing

As previous chapters have demonstrated, Cleanroom allows software to be developed under intellectual control. While it cannot guarantee zero defect software, Cleanroom can reduce the number of defects found in testing dramatically. Thus, the primary focus of testing in Cleanroom is not finding failures. Instead, testers are able to focus on measuring aspects of the product and the process that enable effective decision making and continuous process improvement. Finding failures also occurs but only as a side-effect (albeit an important one) of the primary goal of measurement. The important attitude for Cleanroom practitioners to develop is that defect prevention in design allows testing to be conducted more systematically and scientifically.

The goal for measuring software quality is to establish the probability that a software system will not fail while it is in use (Poore et al, 1993). However, finite testing resources prevent the possibility of applying each and every input sequence that a user could apply during the lifetime of a software system. Thus, we are limited to *estimating* quality based on the application of only a relatively small sample of test cases.

The process of estimating particular quantities of interest from only a small sample is the state-of-the-practice in many business and engineering fields. For example, in the manufacture of automobiles it is impossible to check every feature of every vehicle that comes off the assembly line. Thus, it is standard practice to check only a sample of vehicles for their quality and to estimate, based on the sample results, the quality of all the vehicles manufactured. Political polls are another common example of sampling. In order to gather information about voter disposition, candidates often take opinion polls of a small sample of voters and draw conclusions about their position among the opposing candidates.

The information that sampling provides is useful in many ways. Automobile manufacturers use their samples to determine which plants are building the best vehicles, which car lines are the most reliable and so forth. This information allows them to make business decisions based on real data. For example, they may choose to reorganize the management structure of a poorly performing manufacturing site or decide to replace an unreliable car line with a new design. Politicians use their polls to plan campaign strategy or to form a position on a certain issue. In other words, uses for the information that sampling provides are varied. Creativity is required of engineers who want to put the information to work for them.

In light of the important decisions made based on sample information, it is critical that the sample be obtained in a manner consistent with scientific practices. No manager wants to make decisions based on unreliable data. However, there is never a guarantee that a particular sample is a "good" sample. Thus, one must take extreme care in forming a sample correctly to minimize the risk of obtaining misinformation. There are two important properties that a sample should possess. These are (1) that the sample be free of human bias and (2) that the sample be a reliable representation of the real population of possibilities.

The first criterion, unbiased sampling, is very important for the validity of the decisions based on the sample. As an analogy, consider the automobile company that samples only those vehicles which it knows are high quality and advertises that their vehicles never break down. Imagine the public protest when the true quality is discovered by customers. Politicians would be equally dissatisfied if their polls predicted they would win by a landslide when, in reality, the race is very close. The loser in each of these cases is everyone. The automobile manufacturer would lose business to more honest companies and their customers would be stuck with lousy vehicles, likewise, the politician may make poor strategy decisions because he or she feels that the election outcome is already determined. This is why samples are drawn randomly. Random samples erase human bias and maximize the probability that the information obtained from the sample is valid.

The second criterion, reliability of the sample, determines how well the results taken from the sample apply to the real population. Even though a sample may be unbiased, it still may not yield estimates

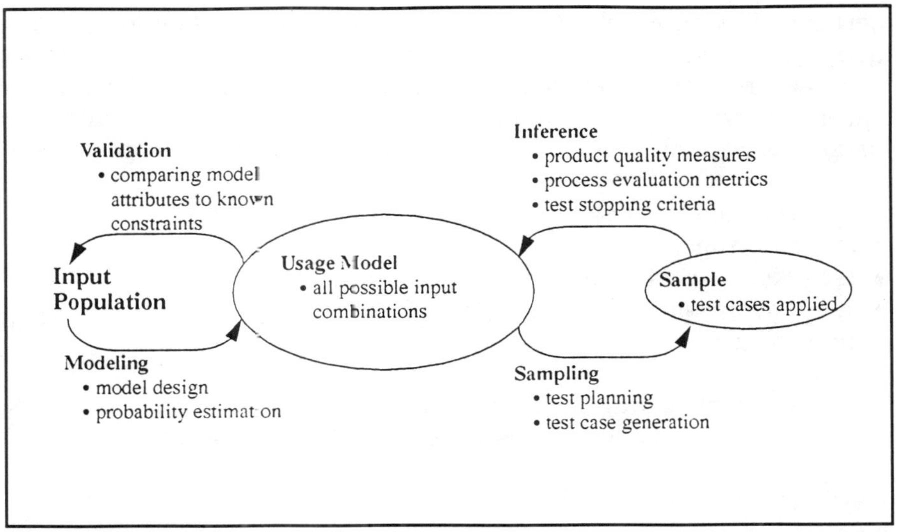

Figure 1: Software Testing as Sampling

that truly match the population of interest. This may be because the sample is too small or that certain key events did not occur in the sample. Thus, the credentials of the sample itself must be considered when using it to make business decisions.

In order to satisfy these two criteria, the Cleanroom approach to software testing is to view testing as a sampling problem (see Figure 1). First, testers construct a model of the input population. This *usage model* is a representation or interpretation of the real input population and must be validated against known real world constraints. The validated model is then used to choose the sample in such a way as to make it unbiased and reliable. This sample becomes the set of test cases that are applied to the increment under test and is the basis for inferring the quality of the software product and also to assess the process that created the software. The method is called *statistical testing* and is described in detail in this chapter.

Overview of Statistical Testing

Statistical testing can be performed in many different ways for many different purposes. In general, it can be used in any testing phase and at any specific level of operation (i.e., unit-level, system level and so forth). However, the incremental nature of Cleanroom affects the way in which statistical testing is applied when it is used in Cleanroom.

Scope

Statistical testing requires exercising the functionality of a system to determine its correctness. In Cleanroom, the statistical test is performed by assembling sequences of external inputs and applying them to an increment of the product. Statistics enter the picture because the sequences are constructed randomly based on some specific distribution. Common choices for the distribution, called the *usage distribution*, reflect some or all of the following perspectives:

- typical or normal usage,
- adverse usage,
- usage for a specific user type,
- safety or mission critical usage and
- uniform usage.

Statistical testing in Cleanroom is concerned with testing the correctness of the following aspects of product operation:

- system correctness and
- system usability.

It does not address:

- function or unit correctness (except in the context of the whole system) or
- system performance.

In Cleanroom, statistical testing is performed on the current accumulation of increments. Each increment is compiled as a single unit and tested at the system level. Although certain functional parts may be isolated in testing, testing is always performed on the entire increment with minimal use of non-product scaffolding code. In other words, only a single executable is created for testing each increment.

Process

Statistical testing can be accomplished with or without a model of the input population. Generally, it is preferable to build a model and use it to control sampling. Sampling without a model, also called *random testing*, was performed on some early Cleanroom projects but has not been used in Cleanroom practice for many years.

Sampling with a model requires that the input population for a system be modeled and then specific input sequences, or test cases, be generated from the model. Although any model of a formal language could work, the most popular model used in practice is the finite-state, discrete-parameter *Markov chain* (Whittaker and Poore, 1993). This model is described in detail later in this chapter.

The certification process tasks and the artifacts created during process execution are listed in Table 1.

The first step in the process is to create the test plan. Sources for this task include all available system documentation, i.e., specifications, prototypes, prior software versions, user and reference guides, and usage information. Usage information is available in the form of customer interviews, data captured from fielded systems and developer intuition. The test plan itself contains information relating to the models that are to be constructed to test the system, the abstraction levels for these models, the system boundaries that the models will operate under and real world constraints on testing such as schedule, budget and available personnel. Further, metrics collected from prior projects also play a role in test planning as they provide feedback that may alter how the models are defined. For example, if we have determined that a high degree of abstraction in a usage model has caused failures to be masked in a prior project, then we may plan for more detailed models to be constructed.

The models defined by the test plan are developed from the black box and any available usage information. These models describe how

Process Task	Sources (Inputs)	Artifacts (Outputs)
Test planning	• increment plan • top-level black box • usage information • metrics from prior projects	• test plan (model definitions, abstraction levels, test resources/constraints)
Model development	• top-level black box • usage information • test plan	• usage models (Markov chains)
Model analysis	• usage information • test plan • usage models	• validated usage models • validation arguments • model analysis reports • updated test plan
Test generation	• validated usage models	• test scripts • coverage reports
Test processing	• test scripts	• executable test cases • expected results
Test execution	• system under test • executable test cases • expected results • failure information	• failure log • testing models
Test measurement	• failure log • testing models	• product certification measures • process assessment metrics • test stopping criteria

Table 1: Certification Process Tasks and Artifacts

the system can be used when it is fielded.

The models are then analyzed to determine their consistency with known usage information and the testing constraints defined in the test plan. Often, it is necessary to adjust certain parameters of the models to obtain consistency. The updated models are called *validated usage models*. This step also creates data useful for helping test executors prepare for the upcoming statistical test. An important point is that this analysis is only possible when the usage model is a Markov chain.

The validated models are used to automatically generate test scripts which serve as a sequence of commands and actions to use to test the software. These scripts can be processed into executable test cases and amended with expected results to make them suitable for automated execution. The test cases are then executed against the system and the results are logged in a failure log.

Finally, measurements are made on the quality of the product (as indicated by the statistical test) and on the effectiveness of the development and testing processes. These measures serve as the exit criteria for the test and as objective data to allow managers to make informed decisions about the software's fitness for release to customers.

Test Planning

During the test planning phase, the scope of the statistical experiment is determined. Specifically, the system under test is scrutinized to determine system decomposition, or *stratification*, possibilities that will allow testing resources to be focused on different system components.

System stratification lends significant insight into testing. It helps testers form a complete testing strategy by exposing all the areas that could be tested (although all might not be tested); and, it eases the modeling burden by separating the testing concerns of multiple software components. Thus, multiple models can be constructed, each representing a different aspect of usage of the system under test. For example, stratification could allow a critical function to be isolated and thoroughly examined in a separate model.

There are two levels of stratification. A *user-level stratification* is performed in order to identify how the system is stimulated by different users, groups of users or viewpoints on use. For example, it is often the case that multiple tests are desirable when there are distinct classes of users, such as general users and administrative users of a network. Also, one might choose to stratify based on how the system boundary is defined. This is the case in device certification where there are application-level users and protocol-level users. In any specific application, each user type should be enumerated so it can be considered

User Type	Classes
Human	network user, novice user, professional user, publisher, graphic artist, classroom user
OS	standard format, text format, interchange format, all supported import formats, illegal or unsupported formats, corrupted files, error messages and resource allocation

Table 2: User Level Stratification for User Type and Class

for stratification.

To illustrate user-level stratification, consider a typical word processor. Stratification begins by enumerating the types of users that we expect the system to interact with, and documenting the reasons for stratifying the system for these users. Another viewpoint is that we are enumerating the possible sources of input for the system under test. In this word processor example, inputs come from two distinct sources: keystrokes (and input from a mouse or other device) from human users and files from the operating system. Obviously, the top-level black box is an excellent source of information about the user types that are necessary to consider.

Associated with each user type are user classes which further decompose the user types into meaningful subsets. Table 2 lists the user types and classes for the word processor example.

The second level of system decomposition is usage-level stratification. This consists of enumerating system objects, functional units and modes of use that could potentially be tested in isolation. Whereas in the prior user-level category we are interested in who is using the system, in this step we are interested in what the system does. For example, for the word processor we could begin simply by listing the features of the specific system we are testing: document creation and retrieval, figure drawing, printing and so forth. These would allow us to identify the list of possible features that make candidate usage strata.

Also included in *usage-level stratification* are modes of use of the software that represent possible performance or availability problems. Items such as large data files, critical use scenarios and so forth, fit into this category. For a word processor, large documents and documents with excessive graphics and formatting codes could be considered. Also, potential error situations such as full storage areas and missing document files should also be listed.

To illustrate usage-level stratification, we proceed as above,

Usage Type	Classes
Document editing and retrieval	new files, existing files, imported files, text-based editing features, document formatting features
Table editing	data entry, changes to table structure
Graphics editing	equations, figures, special fonts and characters
Macro definition	macro creation/modification, macro execution
Printing	network printers, local printers, files
Large documents	files with text and formatting characters, files with tables and graphics, large imported files
Adverse operating conditions	full storage area, files deleted while open, read only files, locked files

Table 3: Usage Level Stratification for Usage Type and Class

enumerating the usage types and classes in Table 3.

Using the stratification classes identified in the tables above, a decision must be made to choose which classes form valid strata for testing. This requires test management to use all available information about customer requirements, expected sales volume and the expected distribution of user classes in the field. Some of the user classes might subsume others, making the list of possible strata shorter. However, it is often the case that many user classes are conflicting and a test of one would not indicate anything about the other; testing them both is necessary.

After each stratum is selected, a percentage of test resources, called the *sampling percentage*, is allocated to each. Assigning sampling percentages requires intimate knowledge of the specification for the system under test and is also aided by knowledge about how the

	Sampling Percentage	
Stratum	Typical Use (80%)	Adverse Use (20%)
Professional user	55%	
Novice user	10%	
Standard format	20%	
Text format	5%	
Interchange format	3%	
All supported import formats	2%	
Unsupported formats		5%
Corrupted files		5%
Macro definition (all classes)	5%	
Large documents (all classes)		50%
Adverse operating conditions (all classes)		40%
total:	100%	100%

Table 4. Assigning Sampling Percentages

system will be used in its intended environment. Multiple sampling percentages can be assigned for cases in which different perspectives on quality are desirable, e.g., a typical user perspective could be one goal and an adverse usage perspective could be another. Table 4 shows sampling percentages for a subset of the strata identified in the word processor example.

The specific strata that are chosen for the test, i.e., given nonzero sampling percentages, are based on the business goals and user/ sponsor requirements for the software. Managers are faced with the task of spreading the available budget over the possible strata that satisfy the requirements of the system and address the quality concerns of the user to the highest degree.

Usage Models

Constructing usage models is the primary certification task in Cleanroom. The most common model used in practice is the finite-state, discrete-parameter Markov chain. Markov chains fit into a class of models called *stochastic processes*. A stochastic process is a process which unfolds randomly and takes place in stages. In the case of modeling software, the stages are, of course, specific stages of software execution. For example, a stage of a user interface application might be "the main window has the focus;" while a real-time application might have the stage "error condition being processed." The stages of the software are being encoded as states and arcs of a Markov chain and the inputs that are possible from each stage are assigned probabilities based on the specific criteria described in a later section.

Markov chains have three components: states, arcs, and transition probabilities.

Type	Component Definitions	Usage
Stimulus Model	States: system inputs Arcs: unlabeled Probabilities: represent likely sequencing of inputs	To generate data files, initialization files, protocol streams or batch input
Usage Variable Model	States: combination of usage variable values Arcs: system inputs, input abstractions Probabilities: represent the probability of making transitions among states-of-use	Basic modeling technique, applicable in a wide variety of applications
Response Model	States: system responses Arcs: system inputs, usage variable abstractions Probabilities: represent likelihood of applying inputs from specific response states of the software	A starting point for building large models

Table 5: Types of Markov Chains for Cleanroom Certification

The states must obey the *Markov property*, i.e., the information necessary to determine the next state in the process must be wholly contained in the current state. This is traditionally stated as: *the future is independent of the past given the present.* Markov chains can be represented by either a matrix with the states as indices and the transition probabilities as entries, a directed graph with the states as nodes and the arcs (labeled with the transition probabilities) as edges or a table of from-state/to-state/probability entries. We will depict Markov chains as directed graphs in this chapter.

Current practice of Cleanroom certification has identified three useful forms of Markov chains for different types of software systems and their usage. The models are enumerated and described in Table 5. Construction of each of these models is illustrated in the next section.

An Example of Markov Modeling

In order to illustrate the three modeling options, we will construct a certification scenario for a hypothetical clock program for a graphical user interface. Most windowing systems allow a clock to be displayed which indicates current system time and date in either an analog or digital format. We will model clock software called "Timepiece," which is described in Figure 2.

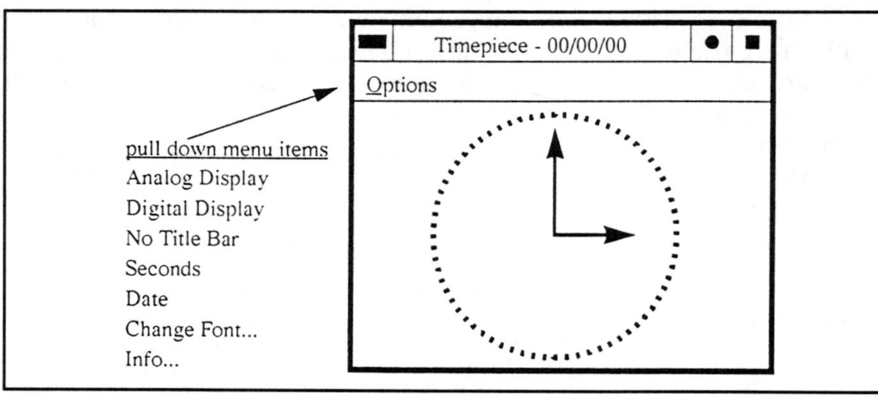

Figure 2: Description of Timepiece

```
******
.timerc
******
[Timepiece]
Maximized=0
Options=1,0,0,0
Position=639,0,800,190
Font=Times
```

Figure 3: An Example Timepiece Startup File

User Type	Classes for this Type
Human	typical user, novice user
File	missing .timerc, legal .timerc, illegal text .timerc, binary (illegal) .timerc
OS	clock pulses, time/date

Table 6: User Level Strata for Timepiece

Usage Type	Classes for this Type
all functions	n/a
special fonts	standard fonts, extended font set, fonts from other suppliers

Table 7: Usage Level Strata for Timepiece

Timepiece works as one would expect a clock to work and can be initialized with a startup file called ".timerc." Each item in the *Options* menu can be set from this startup file. An example file appears in Figure 3.

The first step in the certification process is to determine the system boundaries so that usage models can be selected and constructed. The following user and usage level strata are extracted from the Timepiece problem description.

From these lists of strata, testers and their management must decide which models to construct and how strata might be combined into a single model, or which strata might be tested nonstatistically. In most Cleanroom projects, multiple models are the rule and not the

Stratum	Model to be Constructed?	% of Total
all users	Model necessary to test the input sequences from the user. No distinction between typical or novice user.	~80%
missing .timerc	Model not necessary, this can be tested in a single crafted test case.	<1%
legal .timerc	Model necessary to test the variation in the startup file.	~20%
illegal .timerc	Can be modeled in the same model as legal cases.	
binary .timerc	Model not necessary, this can be tested in a small number of crafted test cases.	<1%
clock pulses	Model not necessary, these stimuli will be present during all testing because they occur automatically. Might want to consider testing a small number of cases with a faulty internal clock.	n/a
time/date	Separate model not necessary, this stimulus can be incorporated into the typical user model. We might consider leap year and the year 2000 as special cases for this input.	n/a
all functions	Covered in the "all users" strata above.	n/a
all fonts	Model not necessary but the testers should vary the fonts available to Timepiece during testing to see if it behaves appropriately. Different fonts can be installed off-line at specific points in testing.	<1%

Table 8: Model Selection Scenario for Timepiece

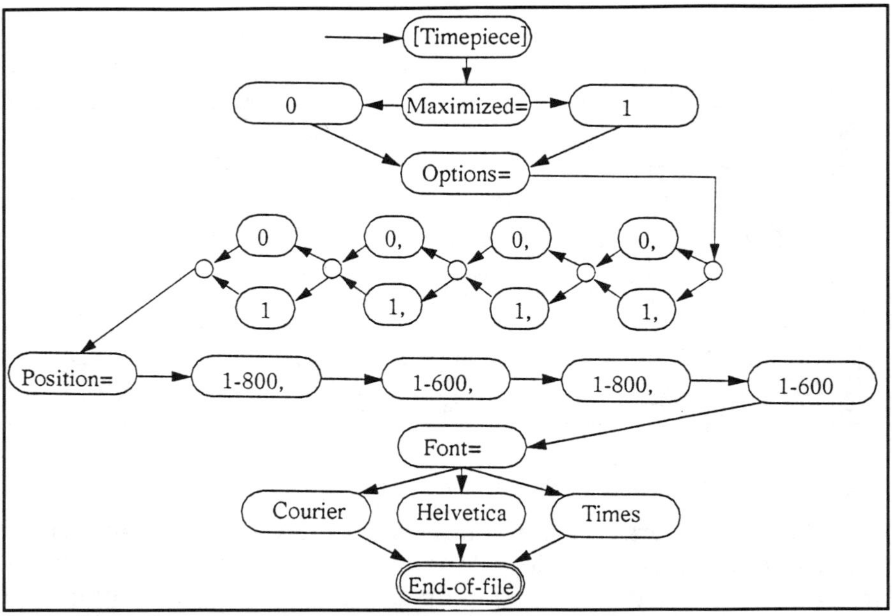

Figure 4: Stimulus Model for Legal Timepiece Startup Files

exception. In fact, even this simple example requires multiple usage models. Table 8 contains the models that require construction and the justification for them.

Thus, two models are required for our testing scenario, one for the startup file and the second for usage of the Timepiece application itself. Stratification is a very crucial step in testing. Generally, a major review is held of these strata with managers, specifiers and end users to get agreement about which models are necessary for testing. If the review exposes a scenario that is not covered by the test strata then the stratification must be updated. The goal is to have all scenarios covered by the union of the strata defined.

The next step is to build the models identified in Table 8. The model for legal startup files appears in Figure 4. The start state is denoted by an incoming arc without an attached state and the terminate state is marked with a double circle.

Illegal cases can be added to this model by installing arcs to form illegal sequences and by adding some new states to model unexpected input. Note that this model falls into the "stimulus model" category.

The Timepiece usage model is the next model to construct. For the purposes of this illustration, both the usage variable model and the response model will be constructed.

The usage variable model requires a two step development process. First, testers must discover the usage variables and then develop the model from them. Usage variables are "externally visible" modes of the system under test. A *mode* is characterized by the changes in usage possibilities that it enforces when it is active. To discover usage

1. {analog, on, none}	2. {analog, off, none}	3. {digital, on, none}
4. {digital, off, none}	5. {digital, on, change font}	6. {analog, on, info}
7. {digital, on, info}	~~8. {analog, on, change font}~~	~~9. {analog, off, change font}~~
~~10. {analog, off, info}~~	~~11. {digital, off, change font}~~	~~12. {digital, off, info}~~

Table 9: State Enumeration for Timepiece Usage Variable Model

variables, one considers each input from the user (i.e., the user represented by the stratum in question) and determines which modes of the software affect the application of that input. For the Timepiece example, the following usage variables exist:

- Setting = {analog, digital}
- Title bar = {on, off}
- Modal windows = {none displayed, change font, info}

which define the states shown in Table 9.

Notice that the full cross product of the usage variables is not used because many of these states are not possible to reach. For example, all states associated with the title bar being turned off cannot reach any modal window, making the states {*, off, change font or info} impossible to reach. The impossible states are crossed out, leaving only seven states in the usage model, plus states for invocation and termination.

Figure 5 shows the usage variable model for Timepiece. Note that it includes usage after Timepiece has been invoked with a legal startup file since invocation with an illegal file would cause the program not to be executed (this behavior is being tested in a different stratum).

Most of the inputs in Figure 5 are simple inputs in that no additional information is required for the tester to execute them. The exception is "select a font" which requires choosing a predefined font from a pick list. In practice, there are several possible ways in which this input might be handled; the most common are:

- The arc labeled "select a font" might be expanded into a submodel that randomly chooses the specific font to use. The Markov chain submodel for this situation appears in Figure 6. This entire chain replaces the arc labeled "select a font."

- The input "select a font" can be treated as "tester's choice" so that at execution time, the tester is responsible for choosing the specific font to enter. Tester's choice items are normally documented in advance

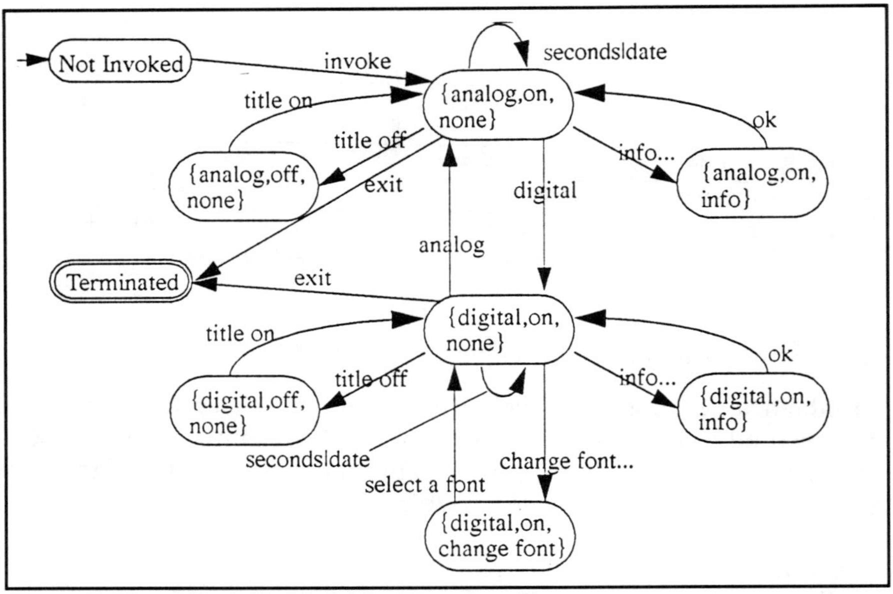

Figure 5: Usage Variable Model for Timepiece Usage

of testing and whenever a choice is required, the tester will select from the possible values according to a predefined rule, e.g., choosing the fonts in alphabetical order. Tester's choice is often used when there are multiple alternatives, e.g., hot keys or keyboard equivalents, for the same user action.

Replacing single arcs with submodels is called *hierarchical modeling* and is common practice among Cleanroom practitioners. In general, models are constructed in small, abstract pieces and then detail is added by expanding the arcs into more detailed submodels. When Markov chains are used it is important that each submodel is a valid Markov chain and that the composition of the submodels into the overall model is also a valid Markov chain.

The next step is to augment the usage model with inputs from the operating system. Specifically, we need to be able to change the system

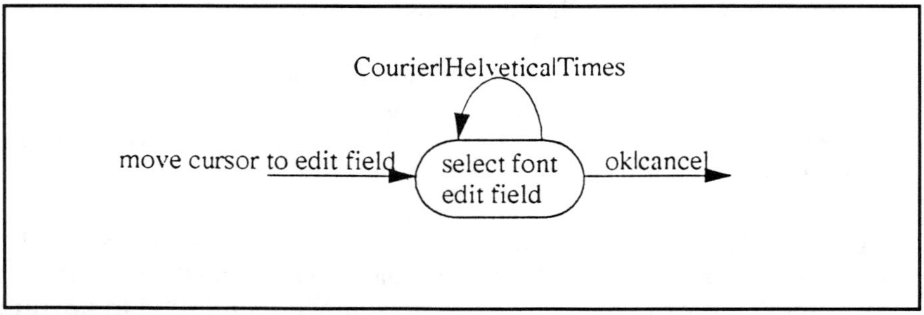

Figure 6. Change Font Submodel for Timepiece

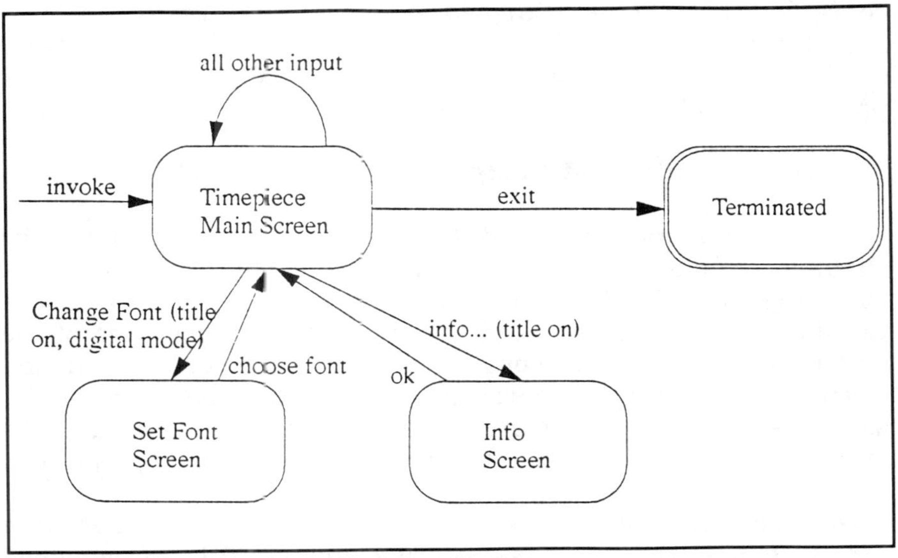

Figure 7: Response Model for Timepiece Usage

time and date from outside the program and make sure that the program reacts appropriately. These operating system stimuli are modeled like any other stimulus to the system; they become arcs in the usage model. In this case, they are "loopback" arcs from each of the states: {analog, on, none}; {analog, off, none}; {digital, on, none} and {digital, off, none}. They could also be added to the remaining states except that the response of Timepiece cannot be seen until one of the above states is reached. However, it would be interesting to test that this behavior is indeed correctly implemented.

The time/date arcs could be further decomposed to select specific dates or times of interest like February 29 of a leap year or the end of the century. As with font selection, this could be achieved through submodels or tester's choice.

As an alternative usage model, Figure 7 depicts the response model for Timepiece usage. Clearly, this model is not as rich as the usage variable model, however, on very complex systems it can be much easier to build.

Hierarchical modeling is particularly useful for the response model. For example, the main screen state can be listed in an abstract form as in Figure 7, then expanded into multiple states and arcs that define usage variables. Most large systems are defined in exactly this way: a "top level" response model is first drawn and then the usage variable models are constructed to replace each state in the top level model.

It should be noted that since the response model is constructed based on externally visible inputs, the state space can often be constructed automatically from the black box specification. It is conceivable too that the code could be used for this purpose, however, specifications are much better since they define what the software should do. The code defines only what it actually does, which will provide a test of limited effectiveness.

Defining and Manipulating Usage Variables

As the example illustrated, the process to construct a Markov chain usage model begins by analyzing the physical inputs of a software system and determining the usage variables. Creating usage variables is a design step and requires detailed knowledge of the system being modeled. Although the variables may be encoded (i.e., given a name with enumerated values) in different ways, they should, as an ensemble, capture all the *usage states* that the software can be in. Usage states are differentiated by one of the following properties:

- **User choices:** There are different choices available to the user when the system is in one state as opposed to another. This is exemplified by the *Setting* usage variable, different choices are available depending on whether the setting is digital or analog.

- **External behavior:** The system behaves differently in each of the states given the same user input. This is exemplified by the *seconds* stimulus which shows a second hand for an analog clock and a second counter for a digital clock, i.e., two different responses for the same stimulus.

- **Input likelihood:** An input is more likely in some states than in others. For example, we may decide that the *date* stimulus is more likely from the digital display than from the analog display.

Thus, if one can identify two modes of software operation that are different with respect to user choices, external behavior or input likelihood, then those modes are different usage states of the system under test.

For systems of any size or complexity, the usage variables may define a set of states that is too large to be practically constructed, even using hierarchies of models. In such cases, it is important to determine whether the size of the model is a side effect of an inefficient design or simply due to the nature of the application. In the case of the former, re-design of the product, driven by the usage model, should produce a more testable system. In the case of the latter, there are several techniques to deal with complexity. Each technique has the effect of removing states from consideration during testing. Thus, it is important to reach team consensus that the techniques do not significantly reduce the effectiveness of testing or the applicability of the quality measures taken during the actual test. The techniques for reducing model size are outlined below.

1. Limit the values of some of the usage variables. Let's say that we are modeling the operation of embedded automobile software and that we have identified the usage variable: *Gear Status* which can assume the values: {1, 2, D, N, R, P}. We may decide the operation of the vehicle in neutral and park is not useful, therefore, we would remove the values N and P from the variable.

2. Define equivalence classes for the values of some of the variables. Using the same automobile example as above, imagine a usage variable Speed = {0, 1, 2, 3, 4...}; which may be rewritten as four *equivalence classes* {0, 1-29, 30-55, 55 and above}. It is important to define the classes so that each value in a class is essentially the same in terms of user choices, external behavior and input likelihood.

3. Create abstract inputs by pushing usage variable detail onto the physical inputs. Abstraction has always been an important part of successful system modeling and usage modeling is no exception. Abstract inputs are created by combining physical inputs with the information stored in one or more usage variables. Using the automobile example one last time, suppose that we have the inputs *press accelerator pedal* and *press brake pedal.* We can push the Speed usage variable onto these physical inputs and create the abstract inputs: *accelerate to 1-29 mph, slow to 0 mph,* accelerate to 30-55 mph and so forth. Now when we take the cross product of the remaining usage variables, we can leave out the *Speed* variable because the abstract inputs have the information we need embedded into them.

No matter which method of model simplification is used, practitioners have found it useful to determine the complete set of physical usage variables, even though some equivalences and abstractions may be immediately obvious. Determining the variables in advance has never proven overly difficult or costly, and it can guide abstraction and partitioning so that testers always know exactly what is given up with each decision to move away from the completely physical point of view. Decisions can be more informed and the implications of the abstraction more completely understood.

The Role of Partitions and Boundary Values

Whenever a software system is being modeled that accepts variable input like character strings or integer data, the possible set of values must be partitioned. Usage models can support this partition-

Goal	Information	Sources
Typical usage certification	Frequency of feature usage	User questionnaires, monitoring usage of prior versions/prototypes
Critical function certification	Ordering of features/functions based on their criticality	Requirements specification/domain expertise
Stress test	Ordering of features/functions based on their expected quality	Development/design documentation

Table 10: Establishing Initial Probability Estimates

ing by creating separate arcs for each possible partition created. For example, in the case of an integer input, we might create the partitions: *negative, zero, positive* and *illegal.* Thus the state that models the input field will have four exit arcs labeled with each of the four partitions, respectively. It follows that boundary values, e.g., *illegal negative, smallest negative, other negative,* -1, *zero,* 1, *other positive, largest positive* and *illegal positive* follow the same rules.

Analyzing Markov Chains

Once the states and arcs of the Markov chain are defined, the next step is to estimate the transition probabilities. The following procedure can be used to form the estimates:

1. Determine the goal of the model:

- to certify typical usage,
- to certify critical functionality or
- to stress the system.

2. Identify all known information pertaining to the goal. Table 10 summarizes the type of information to gather for each of the goals named above.

3. Establish initial estimates of the probabilities based on the information gathered.

4. Perform analysis of the estimates and adjust the probabilities as needed.

5. Repeat the analysis until the probabilities are acceptable.

Once the goals for a model are determined and documented in the test plan, data is gathered from the sources listed in Table 10. When data is available and used to form the initial probability estimates then the model is called an *informed model*. When little or no real data is available then two choices remain. First, an *intended model* can be developed by estimating probabilities based on how the product is intended to be used in the field. Second, an *uninformed model* can be obtained by assigning uniform probability distributions over the exit arcs for each state. Slight modifications to a strictly uniform distributions are generally still classified as uninformed; unless the probabilities reflect real or intended behavior. Uninformed models are often used for stress tests.

Analyzing the probability assignments occurs in two phases. First, the *model validation* phase determines the ability of the model to achieve its objectives. For example, if the objective is to model typical usage then a valid model is one that behaves like a typical user (or, at least, what we know about typical usage). During validation the probability assignments can change to reflect new information and to make the model match usage more closely. Next, the *model analysis* phase determines what test procedures can be put into place in order to optimize testing. For example, automation planning takes place during model analysis. In general, the probabilities do not change during the model analysis phase. However, if they do, then the model

Result	Definition/Usage
Long Run Probability for state *i*	DEFINITION: the relative frequency of appearance of state *i* in a very long sequence of states generated from the usage model USAGE: • feedback to design for increment planning, i.e., ordering the increments based on frequency of use • to compare model behavior with known usage information • to install arcs for interrupts and error conditions, i.e., these stimuli are more likely to occur in high frequency states
Mean First Passage Time for state *i*	DEFINITION: the expected number of transitions (from the start state) until state *i* occurs in the test cases USAGE: • to compare model behavior with known usage information • to determine expected test case length and model coverage
Probability of Occurrence for state *i* in a test case	DEFINITION: the probability that state *i* occurs in a single test case USAGE: • to compare model behavior with known usage information • to plan test automation, i.e., to determine test automation priority based on the most frequently occurring states
Mean Number of Occurrences of state *i* in a test case	DEFINITION: the expected number of occurrences of state *i* in a single test case USAGE: • to compare model behavior with known usage information • to plan test automation
Source Entropy	DEFINITION: the complexity of the usage model as a stochastic process USAGE: to determine the complexity of testing with a model

Table 11: Some of the Analytical Results from the Markov Chain

validation phase must be performed again to make sure the model is still in sync with its objectives.

The fact that the usage model is a Markov chain greatly enhances the validation and analysis tasks by providing high level usage information that is otherwise difficult or impossible to determine. Table 11 lists several analytical values that are readily computable from the Markov chain and help testers perform the validation and analysis.

The mathematics underlying the calculations is standard Markov chain theory and is described in further detail in Whittaker (1992) and Whittaker and Thomason (1994).

These measures are computed for the usage variable model of Timepiece in Table 12. All transition probabilities leading up to this analysis are uninformed and were obtained by giving each exit arc equal probability, with the exception of the "exit" input which received half the probability of the other inputs.

Some of the measures of general interest are shaded in Table 12:

- The states {analog, on, none} and {digital, on, none} have the highest long run probabilities. Together they possess nearly sixty percent of the total probability mass of this distribution. Thus, if we desired, we might install the arcs representing operating system stimuli on these states only since they are the most probable states.
- The mean first passage for "Terminated" is the expected test case length which is 15.6 inputs for this model.

State Label	Long Run Prob.	Mean First Passage	Prob. of Occurrence	Mean No. of Occurrences
Not Invoked	0.06		1	1
{analog,on,none}	0.33	1	1	5.4
{analog,off,none}	0.07	13.4	0.55	1.2
{analog,on,info}	0.07	13.4	0.55	1.2
{digitial,on,none}	0.26	8.5	0.67	4.4
{digital,off,none}	0.05	28.25	0.36	0.8
{digital,on,info}	0.05	28.25	0.36	0.8
{digital,on,change font}	0.05	28.25	0.36	0.8
Terminated	0.06	15.6	1	1

Table 12: Analytical Results for the Timepiece Usage Variable Model

- The time to occurrence for the least likely state is nearly 29 transitions. Thus, 2 test cases are expected to be necessary to cover this state in the test suite.
- The state {analog, on, none} occurs in every test case and is also expected to occur most often. Thus, any test automation budget (for test case execution and evaluation) should be first spent on this part of the system as opposed to the other states which occur less often.
- Overall, this table shows significant user activity for a clock—which we assume is not the focus of user input when it is executing. This model may be a good one to test the system to find bugs, but may not provide accurate reliability statistics.

When these results are computed, the report generated is reviewed by a team of project stakeholders which generally includes managers, testers, developers and users. The overall behavior of the model is scrutinized to determine how well it fulfills its purpose (e.g., how similar it is to typical usage) and how well it supports testing. If it is deemed inadequate in either respect, then the probabilities are adjusted and the analysis process repeated until a successful model is obtained.

Statistical Testing

Once the analysis results have been accepted, changes to the model's structure or probabilities are not allowed. At this point, test scripts are generated by starting in the initial state, generating a random number and choosing the next state based on the transition probabilities. This process is continued until the final state is reached.

Input to Apply	State Reached
1. invoke	{analog,on,none}
2. digital	{digital,on,none}
3. change font...	{digital,on,change font}
4. select a font	{digital,on,none}
5. title off	{digital,off,none}
6. title on	{digital,on,none}
7. exit	Terminated

Table 13: An Example Test Script

The state and arc labels of the specific path traversed become the test script. It follows that since the scripts are selected at random, some could be quite short while others can be longer. Properties of both individual test scripts and large numbers of scripts can be described in advance of generation by the analytical measures of Table 12. An example test script for the Markov chain of Figure 5 is pictured in Table 13.

The general method used in practice is that a large number of test scripts are generated (usually by a tool) in advance of testing and then applied, in the order generated, to the system under test. In the case that automated tools are used to execute the scripts, an additional step to parse the scripts into usable format is taken. Execution and evaluation (determining success or failure) methods are inherently domain specific and very few general solutions apply, thus we will not discuss the details of these practices in this chapter. Further discussion of the execution and evaluation problem for a specific domain can be found in Agrawal and Whittaker (1993).

When the software is first delivered to the certification team from development, it is labeled as "version 1." Testing is initiated on version 1 and data about success and failure is logged. Data collection during statistical testing is important in order that the measures about the product and process be as accurate as possible. The following data needs to be collected for each test case applied to the system under test:

- sequential test case number,
- the result of applying the test case (pass or fail),
- sequential transition number that the failure was observed on and
- whether testing was continued after the failure or halted.

This data is input to measurement engines to compute stopping criteria and quality measures. Testing continues until one of the following criteria are met:

- The measures indicate that the increment is ready to be released. In the case that it is an intermediate increment, testing is halted until the next increment is ready. If the increment is the last one, the software is released. The increment itself is labeled as "certified."

- The measures indicate that the increment is of unacceptable quality and the team determines that additional testing will not sufficiently increase quality. Whenever this occurs, the code is put back into development (or possibly into specification depending on the nature of the failures) and testing is halted until the code is changed and verified by the development team.

- The measures indicate that the increment is of unacceptable quality but the nature of the changes to the code are such that, once made, testing can continue. When the changes are made and the code is verified and re-compiled, it is labeled "version 2" and testing continues on this new version. In most Cleanroom projects, multiple versions are required to eventually certify an increment.

The measures are intended to augment expert opinion by providing quantitative evidence of quality. Obviously, the longer the measures have been in use by a particular Cleanroom team, the larger their role in making important decisions becomes. We turn now to the topic of computing the measures and interpreting the results.

Certifying Software Quality

The usage models represent the input possibilities of the system under test. In Cleanroom certification the goal is to estimate the quality of the software for any given input sequence from the population of possibilities. Obviously, it is not practical to execute every test case from a model or any reasonable budget for testing would be quickly exhausted. Thus, the best that can be achieved is to generate a sample of test cases from the model and certify the entire population based on the sample. The technology that enables this is called *statistical inference* and is common practice in most other engineering disciplines.

Statistical inference requires the definition of the population of interest and the assignment of a probability distribution to the population elements, a sampling procedure to randomly draw sample data from the population and an inference engine to compute properties of the sample that apply to the population. Table 14 defines each of the necessary items for statistical inference when applied to software testing. The rest of this section focuses on the last two items: sample measures and inference engines.

Population	Usage Model
Population Distribution	Transition probabilities in the usage model
Sampling Procedure	Random walks through the usage model based on the transition probabilities
Sample	Test cases generated from the usage model
Sample Measures	Quality measures, stopping criteria
Inference Engine	Testing Markov chain reliability model

Table 14: Test Artifacts for Statistical Inference

The most common quality measure is *software reliability*, which is defined as:

> *Definition:* Software reliability is the probability that a software system performs according to its specification for any randomly chosen use of the software system under a specific usage profile.

This conditional probability can be computed with a number of mathematical models. These models generally fall into one of two categories:

- *reliability models*, in which reliability is measured from the current software version only and
- *reliability growth models*, in which reliability is computed using data from successive software versions.

Reliability is a dual-conditioned probability. It depends on both the definition of a use and also the usage profile that governed the sampling process. A reliability estimate reflects the definition of a use that was established in the usage model (as defined by the start and terminate states in the Markov chain) and the probabilities assigned to the transitions. Thus, the estimate is accurate for users whose usage patterns are represented by the usage model.

The Testing Markov Chain Reliability Model

The *testing Markov chain reliability model* exploits the fact that the population is represented by a Markov chain to estimate reliability. This insight gives us significant information about the sample and its relationship to the population. This allows the estimates to account for more information from the statistical test than many other published reliability models.

The following definitions are necessary to begin the discussion about testing chains.

- The Markov chain usage model is denoted *U* and is called the *usage chain.* It is the model of the input population.
- A second Markov chain is introduced to model the testing sample. It is called the *testing chain* and is denoted *T.*

Since well defined stochastic models exist for both the population and the sample, analysis takes one of two forms. First, we can use statistical measures to compare the two models, giving insight about how representative the sample is of the population. These class of measures are called *stopping criteria* and measure test completeness. Second, we can derive quality measures directly from the testing chain. Measuring in this manner allows us to avoid the assumptions that many published software reliability models make about unknown failure rates and distributions. Specifically, these distributions can be observed directly from the testing chain without any assumptions.

Constructing the Testing Chain

Usage chain *U* has stationary transition probabilities (i.e., they do not change throughout the test); however, we allow the testing chain *T* to be updated as each test case is applied. Thus, the testing chain will actually be a sequence of Markov chains $T_0, T_1, \ldots, T_N$ where T_0 represents no testing yet performed, T_1 represents the testing experience of the first test case, T_2 represents the first two test cases, and so forth.

Specifically, the initial chain T_0 is a copy of usage chain *U* with all arc probabilities set to 0. If no software failures occur in the first test case, T_1 is obtained from T_0 by incrementing arc frequencies along the path of states from the start state to the terminate state in the first test case. Similarly, T_2 is obtained from T_1 by the second test case; and, in general, T_i is obtained from T_{i-1} by test case *i*. In this way, frequency counts on arcs in *T* are always obtained from specific test cases executed against the system under test.

The testing chain can be used as an inference engine for both reliability modeling and reliability growth modeling. In either case, the arc frequencies for the most recent testing chain are normalized to relative frequency probabilities when computation is required.

For the reliability model, the testing chain's arc counts are reset when new system versions are created. Thus, as the software changes, a new testing chain is created to model only the test cases applied on that version. In this manner, the testing chain remains an accurate model of the testing experience of the current software version.

For the reliability growth model, a testing chain is maintained that is not reset between system builds and incorporates testing experience across different software versions. This latter testing chain is a model of the process of failure discovery and fault removal. Both types of models provide valuable feedback about software development activity.

Regardless of which testing chain is being maintained, the series $T_0, T_1, \ldots, T_N$ provides important analysis capability. If no failures are detected, the evolution of *T* is dictated solely by test cases from *U*. The fact that the model is a Markov chain guarantees that the test cases generated will become "statistically typical" of *U* when enough are generated. This means that the relative frequencies on *T*s arcs will converge to the probabilities on *U*s arcs.

Incorporating Failure Data

Suppose now that failures occur and that the jth failure f_j is detected during execution of test case *i*. To incorporate this failure event into *T*, a new state labeled f_j is placed in T_i exactly as it was ordered in *i*. The arcs to/from the new state f_j have frequency count 1. If f_j is a halting failure (i.e., the remaining states in the test cases were not executed), then the test case is aborted and the arc from f_j goes to the terminate state; otherwise, the test case can continue and the arc from f_j goes to the next state in *i*. In this way, T_i is maintained as a Markov chain that incorporates both the underlying structure of the source of test cases, *U*, and the frequency count history of test cases-plus-failures as testing evolves.

Convergence of *T* to *U* is adversely affected by failures during testing. To achieve convergence when failures have been observed, the relative-frequency probabilities on arcs to failure states in T_i must approach 0. In this way, the probabilities on the non-failure arcs are still forced to converge to the corresponding probability in *U*. If even one failure occurs, this can only be accomplished if the system under test responds to more test cases without exhibiting failures. Thus, failures automatically impose additional testing to overcome their adverse impact on the convergence of *T* to *U*.

When no failures occur in testing an increment, convergence will ultimately be achieved. Intuitively, comparison of the actual evolution of *T* (including failures) with its expected evolution (without failures) supports statistical estimation of the software's characteristics based on the software's actual performance. At any point in the testing process, the most recent test history T_i is available for analysis. Because T_i itself is a well-defined Markov chain, computations are based on the theory of Markov chains.

The testing chain incorporates each event of each test case, recognizing the probabilistic relationship between states and arcs established in the usage chain. Any computation based on *T* incorporates this information as well.

To illustrate testing chain construction, consider the example usage chain in Figure 5. The initial testing chain, before any test cases are executed, is a copy of this chain with each arc frequency initialized at zero. A randomly generated test case is then obtained and executed against the software. The testing chain is updated to reflect the states and arcs traversed in that test case. For example, the following test case causes the corresponding transition arcs in the testing chain to be updated (states are included in the test case for reference, individual inputs are indented).

Suppose now that a failure appears in the next test case during the display of the "Info" window. This test case, would achieve the following updates in the testing chain.

Thus, the testing chain is updated with frequency counts that reflect the actual events that occurred when the test case was executed. If the failure had caused the system to halt, then the testing chain would be updated with the failure state followed by an immediate

Test Case	Modifications to the Testing Chain
Not Invoked	
invoke	
{analog,on,none}	update transition: (Not Invoked, {analog,on,none}) from 0 to 1
digital	
{digital,on,none}	update transition: ({analog,on,none}, {digital,on,none}) from 0 to 1
change font...	
{digital,on,change font}	update transition: ({digital,on,none}, {digital,on,change font}) from 0 to 1
select a font	
{digital,on,none}	update transition: ({digital,on,change font}, {digital,on,none}) from 0 to 1
title off	
{digital,off,none}	update transition: ({digital,on,none}, {digital,off,none}) from 0 to 1
title on	
{digital,on,none}	update transition: ({digital,off,none}, {digital,on,none}) from 0 to 1
exit	
Terminated	update transition: ({digital,on,none}, Terminated) from 0 to 1 update transition: (Terminated, Not Invoked) from 0 to 1

Table 15: Building a Testing Chain without Failures

Test Case	Modifications to the Testing Chain
Not Invoked	
invoke	
{analog,on,none}	update transition: (Not Invoked, {analog,on,none}) from 1 to 2
info...	
{analog,on,info}	create failure state *j* update transition: ({analog,on,none}, failure *j*) from 0 to 1
ok	
{analog,on,none}	update transition: (failure *j*, {analog,on,none}) from 0 to 1
title off	
{analog,off,none}	update transition: ({analog,on,none}, {analog,off,none}) from 0 to 1
title on	
{analog,on,none}	update transition: ({analog,off,none}, {analog,on,none}) from 0 to 1
exit	
Terminated	update transition: ({analog,on,none}, Terminated) from 0 to 1 update transition: (Terminated, Not Invoked) from 1 to 2

Table 16: Integrating Failures into a Testing Chain

transition to the terminate state. The remainder of the test case would be unexecuted and no credit is given for it.

Analytical Results from the Testing Chain

The testing chain is the inference engine for computing product quality measures and stopping criteria for testing. Whenever computation is desired, the frequency counts in the testing chain are normalized to probabilities.

Quality Measures

The testing chain represents the test history of the system under test during correct functioning and during software failure. Thus, it is possible to define random variables that characterize the relationship of failure states to non-failure states in order to describe the impact of failures on the testing process.

Reliability can be computed directly from the testing chain T at any time during testing. There are two measures of reliability available from the testing chain:

- The single-use reliability, R_S, is the probability that an arbitrarily selected use of the software will not cause a failure. Technically, it is the probability that a sequence of states from T beginning with the start state and ending with the first occurrence of the terminate state will not contain a failure state.
- The long-run reliability*, R_L, is the proportion of total time, over the lifetime of the product, that the software does not fail. Technically, it is the sum of the long run probabilities for all the nonfailure states in T.

Both the above probabilities assume that additional use beyond what occurs in testing (i.e, in the field) matches the statistical profile described by the usage chain. Thus, the validation of the usage model is crucial in order to have high confidence in the reliability calculations.

The reason that these measures for reliability represent an improvement over many published reliability models is that they avoid any assumptions about the distribution governing the appearance rates of failures. First, they are based on actual failure occurrences and, second, no explicit assumption about the interfail times is necessary since the failures occur within a well defined stochastic process.

Table 17 enumerates some values for a testing chain where 20 test

* This definition of Reliability is still under study at SET, and may or may not be included in subsequent versions of toolSET_*Certify*®.

Test Case	Result	R_S	R_L
1	Fail	0.4817	n/a
2	Pass	0.7172	n/a
3	Pass	0.8174	n/a
4	Pass	0.8647	n/a
5	Fail	0.7333	n/a
6	Fail	0.6767	0.7465
7	Pass	0.6875	0.8456
8	Pass	0.7222	0.8921
9	Pass	0.7481	0.9104
10	Pass	0.7641	0.9278
11	Pass	0.7835	0.9425
12	Pass	0.7972	0.9597
13	Pass	0.8110	0.9628
14	Pass	0.8212	0.9711
15	Pass	0.8323	0.9789
16	Pass	0.8421	0.9854
17	Pass	0.8497	0.9898
18	Pass	0.8575	0.9911
19	Pass	0.8636	0.9954
20	Pass	0.8698	0.9967

Table 17: Some Sample Values for RS and RL

cases were generated and applied to a software system. Measurements are reported for every test case. Notice that R_L is generally much higher than R_S. This is due to the nature of the computation and, in practice, generally holds. R_S is based on a single arbitrarily selected use whereas R_L is computed using the long run characteristics of *T*. Thus, if the failure states truly represent rare events, their effect diminishes (or "washes out") over time. R_L is only computed when the testing chain has begun to "converge," i.e., *T*'s statistics begin to resemble *U*'s statistics despite the failure states. That is why the early values for this metric are labeled "not applicable."

Stopping Criteria

The Testing Markov Chain model enables a number of analytic stopping criteria based directly on the statistical properties of the usage and testing chains. Among those computed in practice are goodness of fit criteria, discrimination and distance. Each involves the comparison of properties of the testing chain *T* with the usage chain *U* (i.e., comparing the sample to the population).

Measure	Definition
Discrimination	The stochastic dissimilarity between the usage and testing chains. Achieved through the comparison of transition probabilities of *U* and *T*.
Distance	The Euclidean distance between the usage and testing chains when interpreted as vectors in multidimensional space. Each dimension is represented by a transition probability.
Chi Square Test	The square root of sum of the squares of the difference between the long run distributions of *U* and *T* (not including failure states).
State Coverage	The percentage of usage chain states that have been incorporated into *T*.
Arc Coverge	The percentage of usage chain arcs that have been incorporated into *T*.

Table 18: Stopping Criteria from the Testing Markov Chain

The usage chain is a model of ideal testing of the software, i.e., each arc probability is established with the best estimate of actual usage and no failure states are present. The testing chain, on the other hand, is a model of a specific test sample, including failure data. Thus, the usage chain represents what would occur in the statistical test in the absence of failures and the testing chain represents what has occurred. Dissimilarity between the two models is therefore a useful measure of the progress of testing. When the dissimilarity is small, the sample is an accurate representation of the population.

The measures to determine this similarity are summarized in Table 18. The *discrimination*, denoted *D(U,T)*, measures the stochastic dissimilarity of *U* and *T* as stochastic sources and the distance, denoted *d(U,T)*, measures the distance between the two models by comparing the respective transition probabilities. The Chi square test* can be performed on the long run distributions of the two chains as an additional measure of convergence.

The last two values in Table 18 are simple structural coverage criteria. We call these *structural stopping criteria* and the former are *analytical stopping criteria.* In practice, it is the analytical stopping criteria that more accurately predict stopping times.

The two sources *U* and *T* are likely to generate a similar set of typical sequences only if the values for the analytical stopping criteria are very small. A value of one or more of these measures approaching zero has several implications for software testing. First, it ensures that each state in *U* appears in the test history in the correct proportion as computed in the long run distribution of *U* and that the sequencing properties of the test history closely match those of *U*. Second, it forces the probability of occurrence of the failure states in *T* to be pushed towards zero. This means that confidence must be gained in every path through the testing chain before the stopping criterion is acceptably small. Third, it recognizes the limitations of the usage chain for testing the software. When the statistics of the testing chain and usage chain match, the usage chain is unlikely to generate a test case that adds any

* This and other stopping criteria are under study at SET, and may or may not be included in future versions of toolSET_*Certify*®.

additional information to the statistical testing experiment.

To monitor the testing process, the stopping criteria can be computed with each test case applied to the software. A downward trend in the analytical values signifies growing similarity of the two models. Usage chain *U* never changes; however, the measures reflect the impact of each additional test case on the stochastic characteristics of the testing chain. *D(U,T)* can, for example, rise when no failures are observed if a test case reinforces some low probability event. Of course, a rise is expected when a failure occurs. When the discrimination drops below some predefined threshold and experiences little change for an extended period, it is implied that additional test cases will not significantly impact the statistics of the testing model and testing can stop.

Table 19 shows some example data for the stopping criteria from the same 20 test cases as shown above. Each measure is computed after every test case (except the discrimination which is only computable after all arcs have occurred in *T*, beginning at test case number 7). This table illustrates typical behavior of the stopping criteria during both failure and non-failure test cases. For example, when no failure occurs, the stopping criteria either fall or rise depending on whether the current test case causes the testing chain to become more or less similar to the usage chain. Note that the general trend is downward under this circumstance. When a failure is observed, a rise in the measures occurs which is sustained over several subsequent failure-

Test Case	Result	*% States*	*% Arcs*	*D(U,T)*	*d(U,T)*
1	Fail	44.4	17.6	n/a	0.9421
2	Pass	55.6	35.3	n/a	0.7085
3	Pass	77.7	68.4	n/a	0.7096
4	Pass	77.7	68.4	n/a	0.7101
5	Fail	88.8	73.6	n/a	0.8715
6	Fail	100	89.4	n/a	0.9276
7	Pass	100	100	0.0209	0.7954
8	Pass	100	100	0.0201	0.7431
9	Pass	100	100	0.0144	0.6949
10	Pass	100	100	0.0149	0.5385
11	Pass	100	100	0.0087	0.5306
12	Pass	100	100	0.0086	0.5301
13	Pass	100	100	0.0087	0.5286
14	Pass	100	100	0.0072	0.5265
15	Pass	100	100	0.0071	0.5266
16	Pass	100	100	0.0070	0.5250
17	Pass	100	100	0.0069	0.5248
18	Pass	100	100	0.0065	0.5250
19	Pass	100	100	0.0058	0.5224
20	Pass	100	100	0.0056	0.5201

Table 19: Some Example Values for the Stopping Criteria

free test cases. The effect of the failure starts to diminish only after multiple failure-free test cases are incorporated that reinforce the paths that avoid the failure state.

The analytical results computed for the testing chain can account for the entire test history of the software or for a specific subset representing a single software version. These measures have several beneficial features. First, they are based on actual occurrences of failures. No assumptions about the distributions of failures are required in order to measure these quantities. Second, each state generated is accounted for in the computations. Each sequence of states contributes to the model in proportion to its length and probability of occurrence. The computations on the model take into account the fact that the test cases are not equally likely and that some have more impact than others. Third, each failure is probability weighted according to its location in the testing chain. Failures attached to relatively high probability paths will impact the testing stochastic process more than failures attached to lower probability paths. Thus, the testing chain delivers results which are explicitly based on the usage patterns described in the usage model.

Non-Statistical Tests

Cleanroom dogma maintains that only statistical testing be performed on each increment. In practice, this restriction is not yet practical. Although most teams have indeed forsaken developer testing and other unit test activities, non-statistical system (i.e., the increment in test) testing has occurred in two main areas:

1. "Pre-certification" system testing. These tests are performed before the statistical test using a small number of test cases. In general, the test cases are hand selected from the usage models. The purpose of this test is to give a "sanity check" of the software, to ensure that it is of sufficient quality to perform well during full statistical testing. This test is often called *biased sampling* for obvious reasons. Although it is conducted using the usage models, no statistics are possible since the tests are not randomly sampled.

2. Single purpose tests. These tests are performed to test aspects of the system that are not included in the model. For example, when we stratified Timepiece, we decided not to include missing initialization files in the model because this needed to be tested only once and there was no useful way to randomly vary the input. Thus, a single test case is handcrafted and executed. Like the biased sample, these tests are performed before statistical testing.

In all cases of testing in Cleanroom known to this author, all program execution occurs with the same executable, including tests performed on specific strata and nonstatistical tests. Testing at the unit level is replaced by developer verification of the code which was covered in an earlier chapter.

ACKNOWLEDGMENTS

Publication of this work was made possible by permission of Software Engineering Technology, Inc. (SET). This material draws heavily on the proprietary training products, documentation, and prototypes associated with toolSET_*Certify*®, a CASE tool which supports the methods and calculations described in this chapter. I thank SET for investing in the theoretical development, tool development and commercialization of these certification practices, and the many individuals at SET who have applied their talents to all aspects of this work. I am pleased to have been a part of the team for four years, and appreciate the autonomy and trust that SET accords its employees.

Special thanks go to Professor Michael G. Thomason of the University of Tennessee for his contributions to the research. I also recognize with thanks the valuable contributions of SET's customers, the practitioners of the methods, especially Mike Houghtaling and Bill Bostic of IBM, and Johan Sjoblom and Mika Rautakorpi of Ericsson. Finally, I thank Jason Selvidge of SET who is a master model builder.

References

Agrawal, K. and J. A. Whittaker (1993), "Experiences in Applying Statistical Testing to a Real-Time, Embedded Software System," *Proceedings of the Pacific Northwest Software Quality Conference,* (Portland, October) pp. 154-170.

Cobb, R.H. and Harlan D. Mills (1990), "Engineering Software Under Statistical Quality Control," *IEEE Software,* (November) pp. 44-54.

Poore, J.H., H. D. Mills & D. M. Mutchler (1993), "Planning and Certifying Software System Reliability," *IEEE Software,* (January) pp. 88-99.

Rautakorpi, M. (1995), Application of Markov Chain Techniques in Certification of Software, Master's Thesis, Dep. of Mathematics and Systems Analysis, Helsinki Univ.

Sjoblom, J. (1995), *Statistical Usage Testing of Telecommunications Software,* Dep. of Mathematics and Systems Analysis, Helsinki Univ.

Whittaker , J.A. (1992), Markov Chain Techniques for Software Testing and Reliability Analysis, Ph.D. Dissertation, Dep. of Comp. Sci., Univ. of Tenn.

Whittaker, J. A. and K. Agrawal (1994), "A Case Study in Software Reliability Measurement," *Proceedings of Quality Week* 94, (San Francisco, May) paper 2-A-2.

Whittaker, J.A. & M. G. Thomason (1994), "A Markov Chain Model for Statistical Software Testing," *IEEE Transactions on Software Engineering,* Vol. 20, No. 10, pp. 812-824.

Whittaker, J.A. & J.H. Poore (1993) Markov Analysis of Software Specifications, *ACM Transaction on Soft. Eng. Methodology,* 2(1), 92-106.

CHAPTER 5

Using Cleanroom to Raise Software Process Maturity Levels

Rick Gibson
American University

Software engineering practitioners have been inundated with methodologies, models, techniques, paradigm shifts, tools, and assorted other proposed solutions to software's chronic illnesses. The stimulus for the past decade's overwhelming array of answers is best understood by recalling, as Jones (1995) does, the state-of-the-art of large software projects in 1984:

- over 50% of systems were late by over twelve months
- on average, cost overruns were 200% of budget
- the cancellation rate was 15%.

Linger (1994) observed that our increasing dependence, as a society, on software has led to a new focus on the associated development processes. Two manifestations of this new focus are explored in this chapter: A model from the Software Engineering Institute (SEI) and Cleanroom Software Engineering, both of which had their origins along with the software crisis in the mid–1980s, but are only now coming into widespread acceptance.

In November 1986, the SEI with assistance from the Mitre Corporation began developing a process maturity framework that would assist organizations in improving their software process. After four years of experience with the software process maturity framework and the preliminary version of the maturity questionnaire, the SEI[1] has evolved the software process maturity framework into a fully defined model. Using knowledge acquired from software process assessments and extensive feedback from both industry and government, an improved version of the process maturity framework has been produced called the Capability Maturity Model (CMM) for Software, Version 1.1 (CMU/SEI–93–TR–24).

The Cleanroom philosophy, with its origins in 1980, represents one of the first practical attempts at continuous improvement of the software development process. However, Cleanroom itself is variously described as a "process" (Linger, 1994), a "method" (Dyer, 1992), a "technique" (Sorensen, 1995), and an "approach" (Burch, 1992). Presently, there appears to be some consensus for adopting a designation for Cleanroom as either a method or a technique due to the observation that organizations start by using only selected component techniques of Cleanroom and adopt additional facets later. This usage implies something less than a complete process, which can be defined as a sequence of steps performed for a given purpose (IEEE–STD–610). In the conceptual discussion that follows Cleanroom will be referred to as a subprocess.

In contrast, the CMM is a true process that defines five levels of maturity and provides step–by–step guidelines to progressively improve capability. The CMM has had a profound impact on the global software industry, but has been criticized by many experts (Bollinger and McGowan, 1991, Jones, 1995), largely due to a lack of emphasis on technology or automation.

Semantics aside, a careful study of the strengths of the Cleanroom technique and the unresolved weaknesses of the CMM suggests a synergistic blending of the two for the purpose of achieving higher maturity levels. A useful starting point for this discussion is provided by Fuggetta (1993), who decomposed software development[2] into two subprocesses: production and metaprocess, as shown in Figure 1.

The Production Process includes activities used to design, develop, deliver and maintain a software product. Cleanroom, described by Linger (1994) as satisfying the need for higher quality and produc-

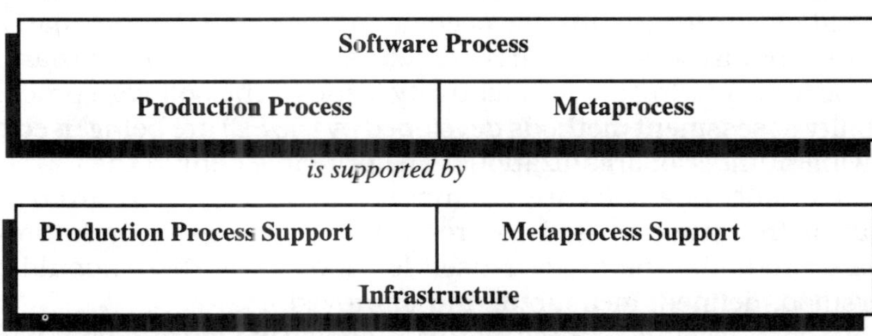

Figure 1: Reference Framework of Process Concepts

tivity in software development, unquestionably satisfies this definition. The purpose of a Metaprocess is the acquisition and exploitation of new software production activities, and more generally, the improvement and innovation of the procedures, rules and technologies used to deliver artifacts. The production subprocess is defined, assessed, and evolved through a systematic continuing Metaprocess. Fuggetta (1993) observes that, in the last decade, efforts aimed at understanding the metaprocess include those of the SEI, with its CMM.

The next layer in Figure 1 explores support for the software process. The common infrastructure shared by both the Production Process and the Metaprocess support activities provides services and functionalities for integration and a homogeneous environment. An example of an ongoing effort in this domain is the Reference Model for Frameworks of Software Engineering Environments[3], which includes a set of interrelated services for object management, process management, user interfaces, communication, policy enforcement, and configuration.

With Figure 1 providing the conceptual framework, the remainder of this chapter will examine Cleanroom as a Production Process and the CMM as a Metaprocess, with the goal of demonstrating that a synergistic blend of these two approaches is possible and desirable. The next section points out some of the important issues raised by critics of the CMM in order to set the stage for a demonstration that solutions to CMM weaknesses fall nicely within the domain of Cleanroom component techniques.

Capability Maturity Model: Metaprocess Concept and Weaknesses

Though now associated with Humphrey, the CMM foundation is with W.A. Shewhart's plan/do/check/act cycle from the Bell Telephone Labs in the 1930s, and further expounded by Deming (1986) and Crosby (1986). In September 1987, the SEI released a brief description of the process maturity framework and a maturity questionnaire (CMU/SEI–87–TR–23). The SEI intended the maturity questionnaire to provide a simple tool for identifying areas where an organization's software process needed improvement. Unfortunately, the questionnaire was too often regarded as "the model" rather than as a vehicle for exploring process maturity issues. The software process capability assessment methods developed by the SEI are being used by a growing number of organizations. The principle behind the CMM is that the quality of a software product stems, in large part, from the quality of the process used to create it. To consistently improve software products, the process used for developing them should be understood, defined, measured, and improved.

Five basic levels of process maturity, shown in Figure 2, have been

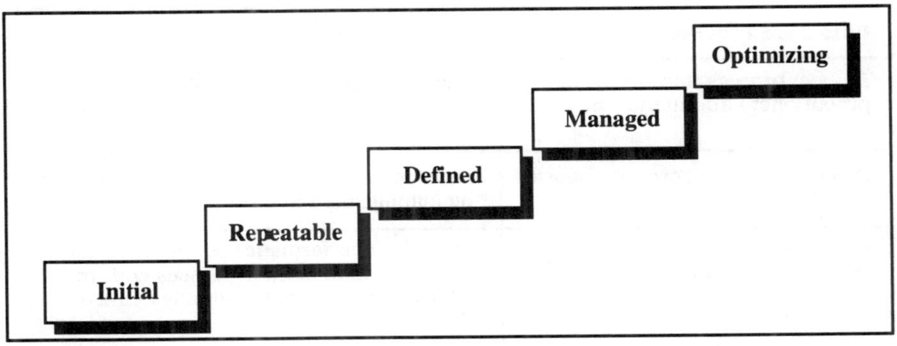

Figure 2: Capability Maturity Model

defined to describe this progression from an ad hoc software process to one that is under statistical control. Increases in maturity are associated with increasing productivity and decreased risk of failure.

The typical level 1 (initial), crisis–driven, organization has serious cost and schedule problems and uses ad hoc development. At level 2 (repeatable), the organization, although still intuitive and too dependent on key individuals, has installed project management controls and learned to manage costs and schedules. As such, it is able to repeat previously attempted tasks. In level 3 (defined), the process is well understood because the organization has introduced a structured framework for software development and dedicated resources to process improvement (e.g., an SEPG). At level 4 (managed), the process is measured and controlled by established relationships that are understood quantitatively. Data are available to establish improvement priorities and to support technology and tool investment. Variations in early life cycle activities can be analyzed rigorously to determine their effect on later activities. Finally, at level 5 (optimizing), process data are collected automatically and used for continuous measured improvement in response to new and evolving issues.

Curtis and Paulk (1993) comment on the maturity concept by contrasting mature and immature process impacts on organizations, as summarized in Figure 3.

Card (1991) built his criticism of the CMM with the contention that there are two basic approaches to process improvement: analysis and benchmarking. The analytic approach relies on quantitative evidence to determine where improvements are needed. Few software organizations have the measurements needed. Benchmarking depends on identifying an excellent organization and documenting its practices. This introduces special problems. First, in 1987, there were no excellent firms—80% were Level 1. Second, any maturity model is self–fulfilling. Improvement means doing what the model requires for the next level.

Jones (1995) faults the CMM model for asserting that both productivity or quality will improve at higher levels without providing

Immature Process	Mature Process
Ad hoc; process improvised by practitioners and management	Work gets done in a consistent, define, documented and continuously improving way.
Procedures not rigorously followed or enforced	Development efforts are supported visibly by management and others
Highly dependent on current practitioners, key individuals	Individual performance is still important, but institutionalized processes endure after the people who originally defined them are gone
Product functionality and quality may be compromised in order to meet schedule.	Product and process measurement is used.
Use of new technology is risky	Disciplined use of technology
Quality is difficult to predict	Process fidelity is controlled, audited and enforced

Figure 3: Maturity Concept

quantitative benchmarks of either. Similarly, Dyer (1992) faults conventional design methods with exclusively focusing on functional requirements and their detailing not software logic, without regard for data. In this the CMM mirrors the mistakes in practice. (Cleanroom can help).

Bollinger and McGowan (1991) use the analogy of the factory paradigm to explain the idea of replication risks inherent in CMM, especially at Level 4 (which Cleanroom will solve) They also fault the CMM for lack of an obvious reason for defect prevention not to be used

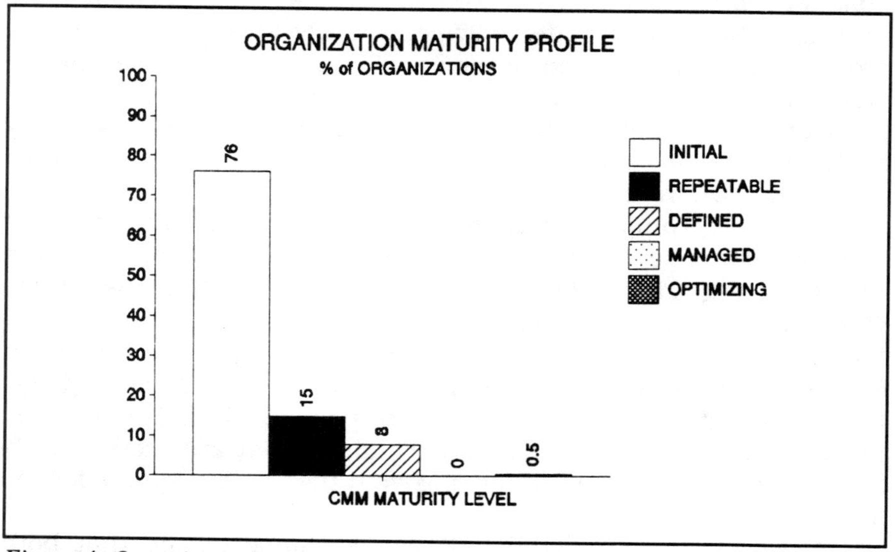

Figure 4: Organization Maturity Profile

effectively at earlier levels rather than level 5.

As more firms move past the understood levels (2&3) to higher, a frantic search for an experience base will ensue. Dyer (1992) asserts that the Cleanroom method may suggest one practical approach to achieving Level 5.

Saiedian and Kuzara (1995) point out that there are other maturity models besides the CMM, such as Capers Jones's Software Productivity Research (SPR) model and the ISO 9000 standard, prompting companies to extend the CMM and make it applicable. Paulk (1995) argues for a strong correlation between ISO 9001 (the standard in the 9000 series that pertains to software development and maintenance) and the CMM. The most relevant comparison deals with statistical techniques. ISO 9001 (clause 4.20) states that organizations must identify adequate statistical techniques and use them to verify the acceptability of process capability and product characteristics. In the CMM, Level 3 describes the establishment of organization-wide process database for collecting process and product data. If an auditor infers statistical process control from this clause, Level 4 is needed for satisfaction

Tate et al. (1992) responded to the criticisms of the CMM as due to its significant impact on the software industry. Stating further that the effects have been mainly beneficial, they then explored the overlap of CASE and software improvement paradigms as initiatives for improving software processes and products. Tate et al. (1992) argue for increased use of CASE tools by insisting that progress up the maturity ladder steps requires metrics. Pfleeger (1991) also views process maturity in accordance with the measurements required to understand the process. Table 1 portrays a combination of these two studies.

In spite of the benefits enjoyed by some firms shown in Table 2,

Level	**Metric**
1	etimates of software size, resources, schedules, code and test errors
2	function points, actual effort, requirements changes, tracking quality and process.
3	process measurement, requirements design and code complexity.
4	process activities and product properties are measured.
5	automatic data collection, metrics for technology improvement plan.

Table 1: Metrics Associated with Maturity Levels

Company	Improvement Focus	Results
Bull HN Information Systems	Customer Reported Defects	10% reduction per year
Hughes Aircraft	Coding Defects per Stage	80% of defects found in coding stage prior to unit or integration testing
Schlumberger	Average difference between estimate and actual completion times	Reduction from 35 weeks to 1 week
Texas Instruments	Comparison of two projects: A at Level 1 B at Level 2	Cost per line of source code: A = $ 10.20 B = $ 3.60 Number of defects per thousand lines of source code A = 6.9 B = 2.0

Table 2: Benefits of CMM-Based Improvements (Source: Herbsleb et al., 1994)

Goldenson & Herbsleb (1995) report on the survey of SEI results that suggest that what is still needed is more guidance on how, not just what to improve.

A continuing subject of debate is whether process capability can improve until the higher levels are achieved. Perhaps, maturity is necessary but not sufficient for true process improvement. Of the organizations SEI has collected data on, 19% reassessed still at Level 1.

Figure 5, from Card (1991) illustrates the increase in control and corresponding decrease in risk anticipated at higher CMM levels.

CMM is a common–sense application of process management and

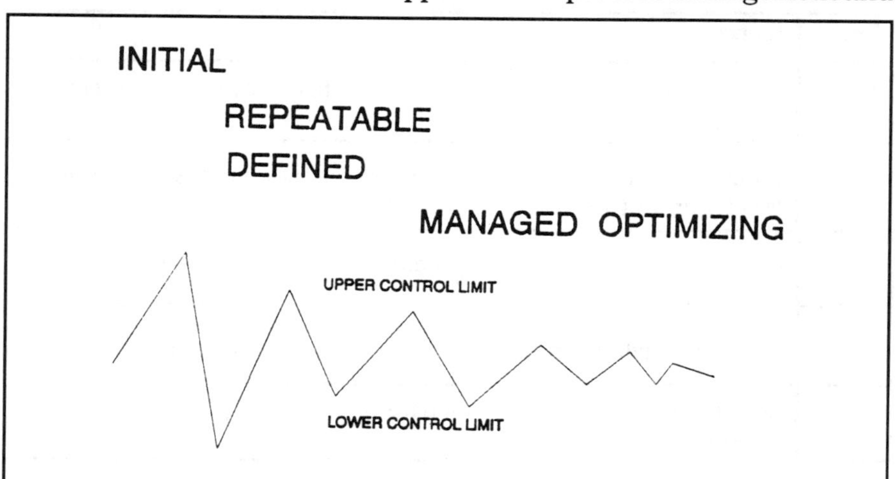

Figure 5

quality improvement concepts to software development; a community owned guide; a model for organizational improvement; the underlying structure for appraisal. CMM does not cover directly: specific tools, methods, technologies, concurrent engineering or teamwork; human resources, organizational behavior.

Bottom line, what we have here is a distinction between process capability and process performance. Process capability — the range of expected results that can be achieved by following a process, initially established at the organization level—serves as a predictor of future outcomes. The CMM process improvement premise is that the quality of a software system is largely governed by the quality of the process used to develop and maintain it. Process performance — a measure of the actual results achieved from following a process— is a strength of Cleanroom, as discussed in the next section.

Cleanroom Strength—Quality Performance

Linger (1994) complied a collection of success stories associated with the remarkable quality improvements made possible with Cleanroom that included those listed in Table 3.

Of fundamental importance is the distinction that, with Cleanroom, correctness is built in by the development team through formal specification, design and verification. Dyer (1992) offers a threefold explanation for using Cleanroom: First, Cleanroom provides the capability of producing software of higher quality and demonstrated reliability in terms of mean time to failure (MTTF). Second, Cleanroom has the potential of delivering software that approaches zero defects. Third, productivity improvements accrue from development efficiencies and reduced maintenance as a result of the first two points.

Linger (1994) explains that unlike hardware, where the statistics

Company/Project	Quality Results	Productivity Results
NASA / Satellite Control	4.5 error per 1000 lines of code	80% improvement
Martin Marietta / Automated Documentation System	0.0 errors per 1000 lines of code	
IBM/ 3090E Tape Drive	1.2 errors per 1000 lines of code	
Ericsson Telecom / OS32 Operating System	1.0 errors per 1000 lines of code	Increased by 70% in development, increased by 100% for testing

Table 3: Cleanroom Quality/Productivity Results

used to establish quality control limits are based on slight variations in physical properties; software copies are constructed from identical bits. So instead, execution behavior is the statistical property of interest. Basically, how long will it execute before failure (mean time to failure), derived from a usage probability distribution of program stimuli (e.g., update or print)

Cleanroom development teams perform no unit testing. Instead, every line of design undergoes proof of correctness.

Hausler at al., (1994) provide data, shown in Figure 6, that demonstrate the defect prevention potential of Cleanroom.

Sorensen (1995) explains it this way. The strengths of Cleanroom include: reliability (weakness of CMM) and ability to gradually introduce into an organization (common to CMM). The major weaknesses of Cleanroom is that it needs a complete set of requirements (a strength of CMM). As will be shown in the next section, these weaknesses and strengths are ideally suited to integration with offsetting weaknesses and strengths of the CMM.

While crediting cleanroom with a 90% success in defect detection Pressman (1994) also commented on its lack of widespread industry application. He contends (as does Poore, 1990) that Cleanroom demands considerable changes in technical and managerial approaches to software development in order to be effective. Thus, the next section offers a synergistic combination of Cleanroom and the CMM to enable such changes to occur.

Combining Cleanroom and the CMM in Practice

Practical advice on the use of Cleanroom can be found in several published sources (for one example see Trammell et al., 1995). Com-

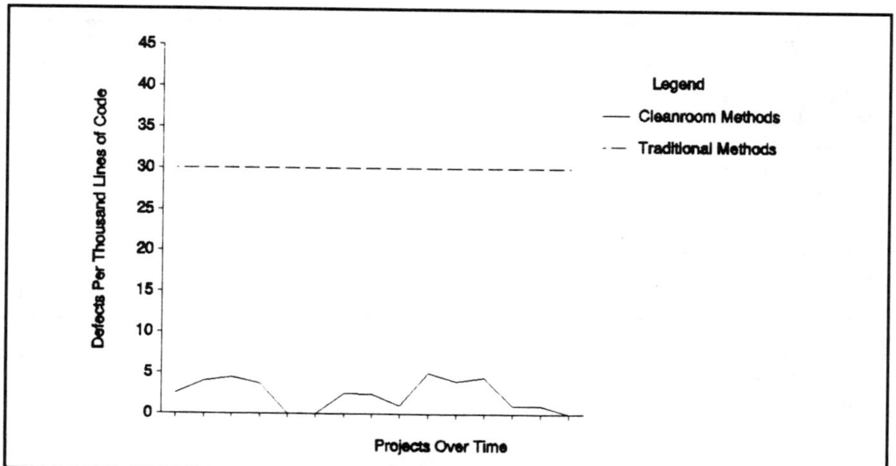

Figure 6: Cleanroom Defect Prevention Potential

parable guidelines abound for the CMM (for one example see Daskalantonakis, 1994). In contrast, Ahlgren and Sixtensson (1995) provide a single fabricated scenario, which serves as the solitary appeal for defining a relationship between Cleanroom and the CMM.

It can be shown that a synergistic blend of these two approaches is possible and desirable. In fact, several major areas of overlap and commonalities exist. Both Cleanroom and the CMM rely on analogous problem solving—from hardware manufacture and population ecology respectively. Recently, software improvement using a "maturity" analogy[4] has increasingly been emphasized and praised for conceptual and empirical basis. Like CMM, cleanroom is rich enough that it does not have to used in total, but allows choices.

Both Cleanroom and the CMM have an amazing consistency in content of reported literature due to the collaborative nature of the work. The CMM assessment process results in a profile of Key Process Areas and a Cleanroom Process Profile (described by Sixtensson, 1993) is used for assessment of Cleanroom practices.

Example of Synergistic Approach

Use Cleanroom to:
- Prevent defects
- Certify reliability
- Increase productivity

Use the CMM to:
- Evaluate deviations identified by measurements
- Select process improvement targets
- Assess process improvement progress

Using BOTH provides:
- As maturity increases, Cleanroom techniques become even more valuable

Paulk et al. (1993) explain that the five–level CMM partitions the software process into management, organizational and engineering subprocesses, each with associated Key Process Areas (KPA) as shown in Figure 7. KPAs most directly associated with Cleanroom are in bold.

The most obvious categorization of Cleanroom is in the engineering subprocess category, which exists only at and above Level 3. This is especially noteworthy due to the fact that there is a paucity of information about higher maturity levels. Recall that virtually all firms in the SEI database are Level 3 and below. Pressman (1995) pointedly observes that if all that was needed for solid software engineering was a well defined process, then the methodologies adopted by the majority of firms during the 70s and 80s should place most firms at Level 3.

Nevertheless, the lower level Key Process Areas are relevant to this discussion for several reasons. For instance, Dyer's (1992) "Roadmap

	Management	Organizational	Engineering
Level 5: Optimizing		Technology Change Management KPA Process Change Management KPA	**Defect Prevention** KPA
Level 4: Managed	Quantitative Process Management KPA		**Software Quality Management** KPA
Level 3: Defined	Integrated Software Management KPA Intergroup Coordination KPA	Organization Process Focus KPA Organization Process Definition KPA Training Program KPA	**Software Product Engineering** KPA **Peer Reviews** KPA
Level 2: Repeatable	Requirements Management KPA Software Project Planning KPA Software Project Tracking KPA Software Subcontract Management KPA Software Quality Assurance KPA Software Configuration Management KPA		
Level 1: Initial	No KPAs ad hoc process		

Figure 7

for Introducing Cleanroom Component Techniques," shown as Figure 8, assumes a baseline practice, which is the essence of CMM level 3.

Therefore, it seems worthwhile to explore interdependencies with management and organizational categories at lower levels. For example, the defect and reliability efforts of cleanroom affect schedule, cost and other tracking.

Although it is claimed that the CMM provides guidance as to how to gain control and to evolve to a culture of excellence, it appears that the real benefit of the CMM is to narrow the scope of improvement activities to those that provide the next foundation layer for growth.

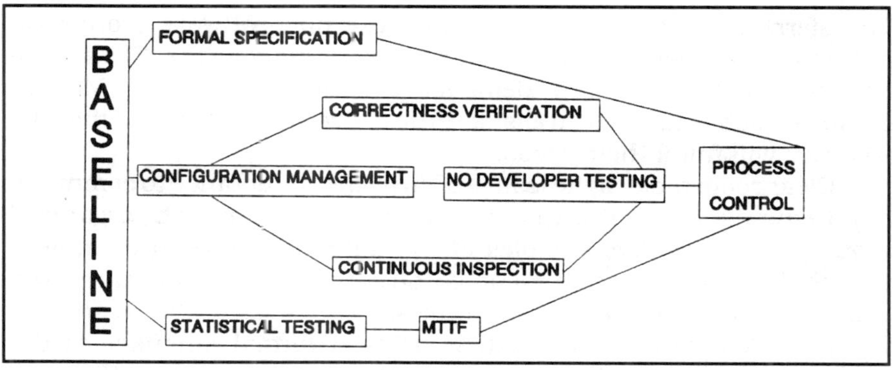

Figure 8

Thus, it is left to Cleanroom to provide the how. The next subsections explore, in a practical way, opportunities for the integration of Cleanroom as a Production Process at each CMM Metaprocess maturity level.

Level 2 — Repeatable

As was shown in Figure 7, no engineering subprocess categories are present at Level 2. Nevertheless, activities performed at this level provide the foundation for higher level capabilities. Two KPAs are relevant regarding integration of Cleanroom (Requirements Management and Configuration Management) and two more because of possible adverse consequences (Project Planning). Further, Sorensen (1995) argues that in order to use Cleanroom the organizations needs only the following abilities: systematic design methods, formal inspection procedures, documented requirements in a natural language, developer performed unit testing, configuration management of software after release into the independent test organization, and ad hoc functional testing. From a CMM perspective, these abilities are assessed at Level 2.

Requirements management activities establish and maintain agreement with the customer on the requirements of the software project. Software plans, products and activities are kept consistent with requirements.

The six Cleanroom specification volumes combine to form a complete description of the software product under development. The mission volume—which includes purpose, requirements, context, and a validation argument—is the least rigorous specification component. Cleanroom projects typically start with a focus on development–related features, e.g., verification–based inspections. As the benefits are realized, attention is turned to the formality of the software requirements specification, which becomes recognizable as the key to correctness verification. The difficulty in this step is organizational––the specifiers are not in the software engineering organization.

Transferring software methods into these non–software groups requires commitment and diplomacy. For instance, the Cleanroom Specification Volume V provides a usage profile in the form of a Markov chain—which is unlikely to assuage the concerns of end users that the software will fulfill their needs.

Cleanroom tackles the issues of customer reluctance to commit to requirements by insisting that the entire testing program be organized around representative samples of the intended usage environment and that software development be structured to permit early and continuous exposure to these samples.

Requirements documentation using a formal language is described by Dyer (1992) as "accepted but unresolved" (p. 67). Until recently most cleanroom experience has relied on natural language specifications, supported by formal grammars and tabular notations to add conciseness and precision. He suggests that three methods are emerging as viable: Vienna Design Method (see Jones, 1986), Z Specification Notation (see Spivey, 1987), and Box Structure Methodology (see Mills et al., 1986)

Software project planning activities develop documented estimates for the work to be performed, establish the necessary commitments, and define the plan to perform the work.

The Cleanroom constraint of incremental planning hinders satisfaction of Project Planning KPAs. Cleanroom increments must operate end–to–end, as testable, even if only part of the functionality.

Software configuration management activities identify the software work products and their descriptions, at given points in time, and systematically control changes to the configurations, and maintain the integrity and traceability of the configuration (CMU/SEI–93–TR–25).

Cleanroom approach forces a shift on configuration management responsibilities. Generally, the CMM suggests maintenance of controlled libraries of sources code for a product on the host machine on which the product executes. Using Cleanroom, separate controlled libraries are needed for the developers, which are typically not housed on the host machine. While this new role requires minimal extra work, it does demand procedures to ensure consistency between the two libraries.

Level 3: Defined

Software Product Engineering tasks are defined, integrated, and consistently performed so that software work products are kept consistent.

Kitson and Masters (1993) examined the SEI database and discovered that only 7% of firms had an institutionalized process for software engineering.

Subprocesses of both engineering and management are integrated into an organization–wide process. Baumert and McWhinney (1992) describe the role of the SEPG in determining state of the practice software engineering tools and techniques to be used.

Paulk et al. (1993) explain that the idea of Integrated Software Management is centered on the organization's taking a defined process and tailoring it to the specific technical and business needs of the project. The guidelines for this tailoring are described in Software Product Engineering. This returns to the earlier notion of a common infrastructure for both production process and metaprocess.

Peer reviews activities are planned so that defects in software work products are identified and removed (CMU/SEI–93–TR–25).

Paulk et al. (1993) explain that the KPAs are organized by a set of common features, which are considered as indicators of implementation and institutionalization. One common feature, ability to perform, describes preconditions such as resources, structure and training. Examples of training related to peer reviews include: methods, roles, and reporting. The use of cleanroom does not occur without some investment in terms of training people and expert consultation during start–up.

Level 4: Managed

Software Quality Management activities are planned to provide measurable goals for software work products and their priorities. Actual progress toward achieving the quality goals is quantified and managed.

Baumert and McWhinney (1992) describe Level 4 as use of statistical methods to establish quantitative boundaries and control limits. Paulk et al. (1993) explain that the Quantitative Process Measurement KPA is concerned with the institutionalization of the use of control charts and other statistical analytical tools for better decisions. Cleanroom's use of MTTF provides answers to the who and why questions of metric data collection. Flexibility also, if you want to measure the project, use current version test data. To measure the process, use all test data since the last incremental build. An improvement ratio can be calculated as a delta MTTF.

The Cleanroom Software Technology Center suggests the following key activities for adopting Cleanroom:

1. Quality Improvement Team (QIT) for development process recommendation.
2. Management overview
3. Team education
4. Process Working Group (PWG) for process definition and documentation and continuous process improvement

Compare this with CMM key activities:

1. Software Quality Assurance (SQA) Group –
2. Software Process Engineering Group (SEPG) — specialists who facilitate the definition, maintenance and improvement of the software process used by the organization.

Level 5: Optimizing

Defect prevention activities are planned so that common causes of defects are sought out, identified, prioritized and systematically eliminated.

Hausler et al. (1994) demonstrate that in comparison with traditional development methods, cleanroom reduced defects found during first test execution by an order of magnitude. Cleanroom is non–traditional in the sense that teams rely on formal (CMM uses the word differently), mathematical–based methods to prevent defects. Perhaps more importantly, they contend that traditional coverage type testing can provide no more than anecdotal evidence of reliability—if the number of defects is high is that good testing or bad code? Regarding the CMM, counting defects offers little insight into process maturity (but interfail times does).

Cleanroom component techniques piloted in an attempt to reduce defects fall within the intent of Defect Prevention KPA, and also provides evidence of behavior characteristic of the Organization Process Focus KPA. Management sponsorship of cleanroom projects as new technological process is characteristic of more mature organizations.

Bollinger and McGowan (1991) fault the CMM for lack of an obvious reason for defect prevention not to be used effectively at earlier levels rather than level 5.

Deming (1986) addresses both continuous improvement and statistical control. He asserts that without statistical control, a process has undefined capability (N.B. level 3 is labelled Defined). Further, Deming cautions that efforts to improve process in the absence of statistical methods usually make matters worse.

Whittaker & Poore (1993) contend that the present emphasis on information systems quality has focused attention on development methods based on cleanroom methods that rely on the availability of usage probabilities.

The certification team executes the test cases and checks results against system specifications. The team records execution time up to the point of any failure. The interfail times represent quality and are passed into a quality certification model that computes the systems quality (MTTF). These measures provide a scientific basis for management decisions as opposed to number of errors found (good news or bad testing?). Although statistical control is directed at process improvement, it can play a risk analysis role.

Importantly, statistical usage testing (vs. random) finds high–rate errors first, leaving only infrequent to be encountered by users—thus, increasing MTTF and user perception of quality. A corollary benefit of a well–engineered development is good documentation, providing the data needed by managers to replan schedules, reallocate resources, and accommodate functional changes. Error correction after release "hostages" are freed to start new development.

Evidence is unavailable to support that cleanroom development teams have made continuous process improvements based on statistical analysis of trends in defect data gathered over time, without which cannot determine if satisfied Level 5 defect prevention KPA (SEI database could help). With the CMM, measurement deviation is reduced systematically at each higher level until a statistically stable environment is attained at Level 5.

Conclusion

Solutions to the software crisis exist, but we have a gap between the state of the art and the state of the practice. This chapter has proposed the suitability of (state of the art) Cleanroom techniques as a practical execution of the requirements of the higher maturity levels suggested by the (state of the practice) Software Engineering Institute. The purposes for doing so are twofold:

- First to provide Cleanroom practitioners with yet another starting point for their techniques. The notion that Cleanroom method is a viable method has been hampered by concerns that it was too theoretical for practical application. A joint venture with the CMM as industry practice can help overcome that notion.

- Second, to strengthen the CMM. For the few organizations that have achieved Level 3 maturity, Cleanroom offers a practical approach to Level 4 KPA Software Quality Assurance, and Level 5 KPA Defect Prevention.

A combination of Cleanroom and CMM enables solutions to the following barriers commonly reported by firms attempting to reaching higher maturity levels:

- Lack of guidance on how (not just what) to improve;
- Organizational politics;
- Cynicism from previous experiences;
- Too many options with no method of assigning priorities;
- Successful pilot efforts that cannot be sustained;

- Vague concept of a baseline from which to start;
- Internal capability for either effectiveness or efficiency, but not both;
- Desire for an incremental approach to organization–wide improvement.

In conclusion, the CMM focus was not developed to establish which method, process, or tool was most effective. Instead, it recognizes that each organization must determine the relative effectiveness of these components for itself. Firms that select Cleanroom, have assessed their environment and decided that the essential characteristic of effective software development is reliability. Having made this choice, these firms can turn to the CMM for establishing an incremental approach to improving the development environment.

Endnotes

[1] SEI activities encompass far more than CMM alone. Krasner et al. (1992) describe the SEI PAL project using three process models: Cleanroom Software Engineering Process, IEEE P1074 Process for Configuration Management, and the AT&T Quality Function Deployment Process.

[2] In an analogous manner, but at a higher level of abstraction, Sorensen (1995) defines a methodology as a combination of a software development model (e.g., waterfall, incremental, or spiral) and techniques (e.g., prototyping, cleanroom or object-oriented). Also, Tate et al. (1992) proposed a comparable integration of CASE tools with a suitable process model.

[3] Jointly published as ECMA Technical Report TR/55, European Computer Manufacturers Association, Geneva and NIST Special Publication 500-201, National Institute of Standards and Technology, Gaithersburg, Maryland, 1991.

[4] According to Carbonell (1985) problem solving by use of analogies consists of transferring knowledge from past problem solving efforts to new problems with corresponding past experience to construct solutions to new problems.

References

Ahlgren, M. & Sixtensson, A. (1995). "Cleanroom and the capability maturity model," In *Proceedings of the 2nd Annual European Industrial Symposium on Cleanroom Software Engineering* (EISCE'2), Berlin.

Baumert, J.H. & McWhinney, M.S. (1992). *Software Measures and the Capability Maturity Model.* Technical Report CMU/SEI–92–TR–92. Software Engineering Institute, Carnegie Mellon University, Pittsburgh, PA.

Bollinger, T.B. & McGowan, C. (1991). *A Critical Look at Software Capability Evaluations.* IEEE Software (July), 25–45.

Burch, J.G., (1992). *Systems Analysis, Design, and Implementation.* Boyd & Fraser, Boston.

Carbonell, J.G. (1985). *Derivational analogy: A theory of reconstructive problem solving and expertise acquisition.* Technical Report CMU–CS–85–115, Computer Science Department, Carnegie Mellon University, Pittsburgh, PA. (March).

Card, D. (1991). Understanding Process Improvement. *IEEE Software,*

(July), 102–103.

Crosby, P.B. (1979). *Quality is Free: The Art of Making Quality Certain.* McGraw–Hill, New York.

Curtis, B. & Paulk, M. (1993). Creating a Software Process Improvement Program. *Information and Software Technology,* 35, (July), 381–386.

Daskalantonakis, M.K. (1994) "Achieving higher SEI levels," *Crosstalk,* Summer, pp. 12–19

Deming, W.E. (1986). *Out of the Crisis.* MIT Center for Advanced Engineering Study, Cambridge, MA.

Dyer, M. (1992). *The Cleanroom Approach to Quality Software Development.* John Wiley & Sons, New York.

Fuggetta, A. (1993). A Classification of CASE Technology, *IEEE Computer,* (December) 25–37.

Goldenson, D. R. & Herbsleb, J.D. (1995). "What Happens After the Appraisal? A survey of Process Improvement Efforts." Technical Report CMU/SEI. May.

Hausler, P.A., Linger, R.C., and Trammell, C.J. (1994). Adopting Cleanroom Engineering with a Phased Approach. *IBM Systems Journal,* 33(1), 89–109.

Herbsleb, J. Carleton, A., Rozum, J., Siegel, J. & Zubrow, D. (1994) *Benefits of CMM–Based Software Process Improvement: Initial Results.* Technical Report CMU/SEI–94–TR–13, (August).

Humphrey, W.S. (1989). *Managing the Software Process.* Addison–Wesley, Reading, MA.

Kitson, D.H. & Masters, S.M. (1993). An Analysis of SEI Software Process Assessment Results: 1987–1991. *Proceedings of the 15th International Conference on Software Engineering.* IEEE Computer Society Press: Los Alamitos, CA, 68–77.

Jones, C.B. (1986). *Systematic Software Development Using VDM,* Prentice–Hall.

Jones, C. B. (1995). Gaps in SEI Programs. *Software Development,* (March), 41–48.

Krasner, H., Terrel, J., Lineham, A., Arnold, P. & Ett, W.H. (1992). Lessons Learned From a Software Process Modeling System. *Communications of the ACM.* 35(9) 91–100.

Linger, R.C. (1994). Cleanroom Process Model, *IEEE Software,* (March), 50–58.

Mills, H. D. (1980). Software of Certifiable Reliability. Unpublished correspondence.

Mills, H. D., Linger, R.C., & Hevner, A.R. (1986) *Information Systems Analysis and Design,* Academic Press.

Paulk, M.C., Weber, C.V., Garcia, S.M., & Chrissis, M.B. (1993). *Key Practices of the Capability Maturity Model,* Version 1.1, CMU/SEI–93–TR–25. Software Engineering Institute, Carnegie Mellon University, Pittsburgh, PA.

Paulk, M.C. (1995). How ISO 9001 Compares With The CMM. *IEEE Software,* (January) 74–83.

Pfleeger, S.L. (1991). Software Engineering: The Production of Quality Software. 2nd. Edition. New York: Macmillan.

Poore, J.H., Mutchler, D. & Mills, H.D. (1990). *Star–Cleanroom reliability, cleanroom ideas in the Starts Environment,* IBM Corporation, Systems Integration Division.

Pressman, R.S. (1994). *Software engineering: A practitioner's approach,*

Third Edition, New York:McGraw–Hill

Pressman, R.S. (1995). *A People–Centered Approach to Software Process Improvement.* Software Process Improvement Forum (March/April) 8–12.

Saiedian, H. & Kuzara, R. (1995). SEI Capability Maturity Model's Impact on Contractors. *IEEE Computer,* (January) 16–26.

Sixtensson, A. (1993). A cleanroom process profile, *Proceedings of the 1st Annual European Industrial Symposium on Cleanroom Software Engineering* (EISCE'1), Copenhagen.

Sorensen, R. A. (1995). Comparison of Software Development Methodologies, *Crosstalk,* (January) 12–18.

Spivey, M. (1987). *The Z Notation: A Reference Manual.* Oxford University Research Group.

Tate, G., Verner, J. & Jeffery, R. (1992) CASE: A Testbed for Modeling, Measurement and Management, *Communications of the ACM,* (April) 65–72.

Trammell, C.J., Hausler, P.A., & Galbraith, C.E. (1995). Incremental implementation of cleanroom practices. *Proceedings of the 2nd Annual European Industrial Symposium on Cleanroom Software Engineering* (EISCE'2), Berlin.

Whittaker, J.A. & Poore, J.H. (1993). Markov Analysis of Software Specifications. *ACM Transactions on Software Engineering and Methodology,* 2(1), 93–106.

CHAPTER 6

A Team-Based Organization Structure for Support of Cleanroom Development

Tove M. Janzon
Q-Labs, Inc. (College Park, MD)

Bengt Nilsson
Q-Labs, Inc. (Lund, Sweden)

Shirley A. Becker
American University

The complexity and size of today's systems requires the support of a team-based organization. The successful implementation of a team-based structure in an organization is achieved when four organizational improvement (OI) concepts are employed. These concepts include: organizational softskill training, formalized team processes for effective interaction within and across the organization, adherence to Cleanroom principles and concepts, and a strong commitment discipline. This chapter presents a Team Assignment Model that integrates these four OI concepts in order to develop a team-based organization focused on common goals. The Team Assignment Model uses Cleanroom as its underlying formalism for producing high-quality results from team assignments. The Model assumes that soft-skill training is integral to effective teamwork and for establishing a strong communication network within team and management structures. The Team Assignment Model is defined and recommendations for its implementation are provided. A case study has been conducted to identify and resolve barriers for the successful use of the Team Assignment Model.

There is growing recognition that team-based software engineering is an important means of addressing the complexity associated with today's systems. The current state of the software industry is such that it is one of the more labor-intensive businesses today. Despite the massive investments in automated support, a significant amount of manual effort is still required on the technical aspects of software development. Most of these manual activities are performed by groups, involving all the sociological complexities associated with group behavior. The group dynamics, communication network, and organizational aspects of software engineering all impact the software development process (Basili & Musa, 1991; White & Leifer, 1986; Constantine, 1990).

The teamwork concept is as old as work itself. In tribal primitive hunting, teamwork was essential to increase the efficiency of the hunt. Historically, in times of war, teamwork has always been obviously obligatory where mutual trust in all wartime efforts was essential. Even the manufacturing industry, which was for years oriented towards individual work, developed into team-based organizations. When the Japanese manufacturing industry started to apply the team concepts developed by Deming (1986), Juran (1951), and others, the implementation of effective teamwork and quality circles became essential. Teamwork was inherently supported by the cross-functional cooperation required by manufacturing, planning, quality inspection, and research and development. Individual workers were transformed into team members striving for continuous improvement or "Kaizen" (Imai, 1986). It was found that effective communication, a sense of belonging, and accountability were critical for successful teamwork. The organizational support of teamwork played an important role in the Japanese success story.

Yet, there has been a lag in the effective use of teamwork in the software industry. Perhaps this is an outgrowth of traditional software development efforts. Typically, assignments were given to individuals with the hope that his/her expertise, experience, or skill level would be sufficient to generate quality systems. But, due to software size and complexity, even the best developers could not resolve all of the software problems.

Another explanation for the lack of emphasis on effective teamwork is that traditional areas such as, languages, design methodologies, test strategies, software architectures, tools and metrics have been the focal point for quality improvement targeting individual development. For example, when computer-aided software engineering (CASE) technology was introduced in the 80's, it was claimed that CASE would virtually replace manual development efforts thus improving the quality of systems development (McClure, 1988). Of course this has not been realized.

However, it is becoming apparent that group aspects of the

software development process must be focused on in order to achieve significant gains in productivity and quality. Studies have suggested that developers are spending 70% of their time working in groups (DeMarco & Lister, 1987), and team activities account for 85% of the cost of large software systems (Jones, 1986). Many agree that the complexity of today's systems require collaborative efforts by individuals over time in a work group structure in order to share information, perform interdependent tasks, and create a communal product (Vessey & Sravanapudi, 1995).

Cleanroom and Teamwork

Harlan Mills developed Cleanroom to provide a practical approach to implementing the software engineering formalisms that had emerged including structured programming, correctness verification, and reliability certification. Mills defined Cleanroom as a team-based software engineering method in order to handle the complexity of today's systems (Mills et al., 1986; Mills, 1988). Yet, not much guidance has been given in terms of organizational support for Cleanroom and effective teamwork. Previous work has introduced Joint Application Development (JAD) into the Cleanroom process as a team-based approach to interacting with end-users (Becker et al., 1993). Others have discussed Cleanroom team structures and sizes, but with little guidance in the development and management of Cleanroom teams (Linger, 1994; Deck & Hausler, 1990).

The team-based approach presented in this chapter addresses the organizational need for formalizing team processes in order to use Cleanroom effectively. The project management structure, as illustrated in Figure 1, presents the organization as a "meta-team" which is composed of several layers of teams. The objective is to decompose higher level teams into smaller teams that can be managed more effectively. The underlying formalism that is used to support high quality within and across teams is Cleanroom (refer to Chapter 1 for an overview of the Cleanroom process). This team-based organizational structure can be readily applied to various organizational sizes and project complexity.

Organization Improvement Concepts

The Cleanroom process provides a foundation upon which quality projects are developed. However, what is needed to implement Cleanroom effectively in a large organization is a team-based approach that supports all team levels in the organization. A supportive team environment requires the combination of four powerful organization improvement (OI) concepts of which Cleanroom is an integral part and that fit together in a synergistic fashion. Each OI concept is addressing

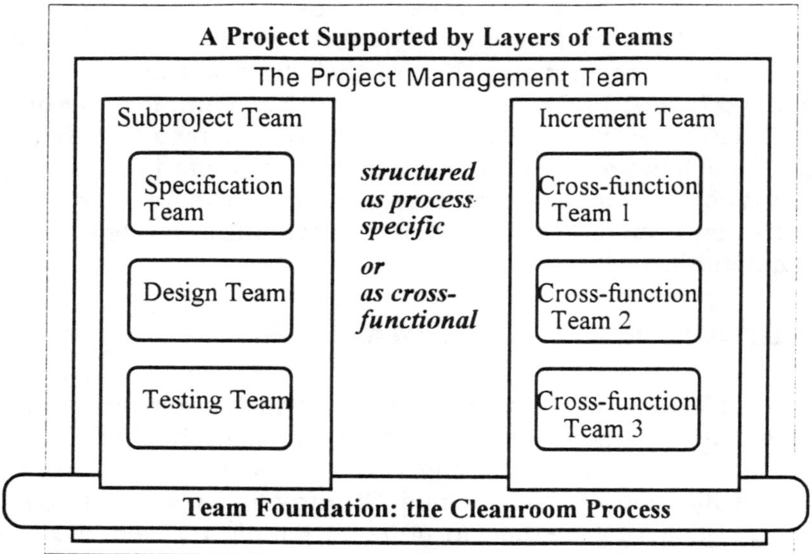

Figure 1: A Team-Based Project Organization to Support Cleanroom Development

a different aspect of the problems and opportunities characterizing complex projects that involve many teams. They are:

- Well-developed organization soft skills - Management and teams are trained in effective group dynamics including decision-making, communication, participation, and problem-solving, among others.
- Formal team process model - Teams are provided an assignment process in which team activities are performed in a predefined order. (In this chapter, a Team Assignment Model is proposed to provide teams a basis for applying the Cleanroom principles and concepts.)
- Strong commitment discipline - Both management and teams make a commitment to produce deliverables as agreed upon in terms of quality, cost, and time and to adhere to organizational processes. This provides the basis for team empowerment (Humphrey, 1989).
- Process adherence to Cleanroom - The achievement of team and organization goals depends on the proper use of Cleanroom principles and concepts during the completion of team assignments.

The soft skills training is important in ensuring that management and teams work together as effectively as possible. For management, soft skill training may include coaching teams in the use of formal processes, building high performance teams, and developing a strong sense of commitment within the organization. For teams, soft skill training may include setting common goals, identifying mechanisms for reward and recognition, understanding and defining team norms, integrating new team members, and resolving conflicts.

Soft skill development impacts the commitment discipline as

teams and management must be able to work together to achieve the organization's goals. This includes effective negotiation skills for management and teams in order to reach an agreement on shared responsibilities. For example, a team assignment may be negotiated between a team and management in terms of resources, time, functionality, and quality.

The commitment discipline provides a foundation for ensuring purpose and accountability throughout the organizational structure. The underlying concept is that teams have control over their work assignment by developing a team plan that is mutually agreed upon by management and teams. The team is responsible for providing input on the team's capabilities of meeting deadlines, producing the functionality and maintaining high-quality given its team resources. This decision-making ability also means that teams are responsible for their input, execution, and completion of the assignment. This a very different approach than management giving teams no decision-making power or flexibility in completing team assignments. This concept of teamwork is necessary for developing an organizational commitment culture from bottom-up.

To effectively apply the Cleanroom method, it is important that team members are able to problem-solve as individuals and work together to find feasible solutions. Team competence must be developed in order to apply the Cleanroom principles effectively. Team members must be able to give and receive review comments on their work. This may require soft skill training on effective communication and sharing responsibilities. The effective use of Cleanroom also requires team commitment to process adherence.

A well-functioning team will establish a Cleanroom verification

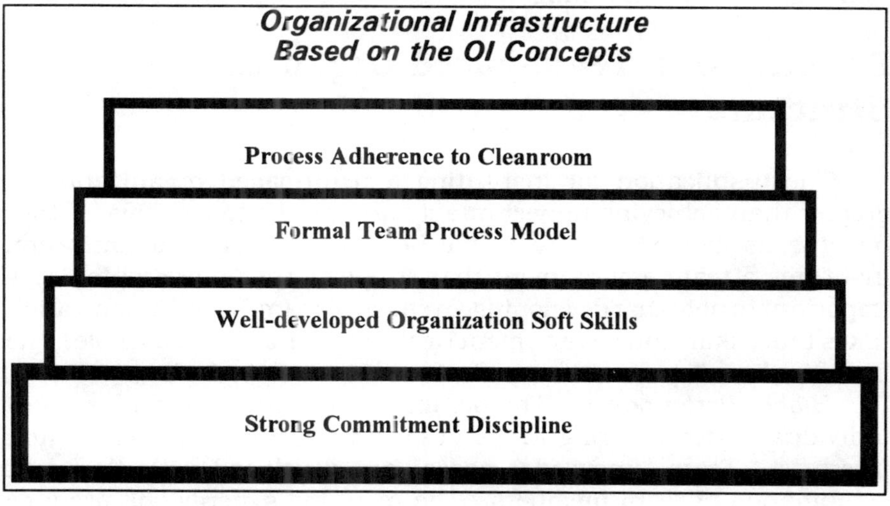

Figure 2: Organization Infrastructure for Effective Teamwork

process whereby the reviewees feel genuinely responsible for the work, share the goals of the original designer and have sufficient understanding of the application and the technical solution. In other words, high-quality components are developed and formal correctness reviews are held when teams are held accountable for their work, feel empowered to make decisions, and work interdependently to achieve common goals.

A formal team process is necessary for ensuring that the team has a standard approach for completing the team assignment. This process defines the initiation, execution, and successful conclusion phases of a team assignment for all teams within the organization structure. Organizational maturity improves when planning, tracking, assessing, and reacting activities become inherent in each team assignment phase. These four OI concepts may be viewed as organizational building blocks for successful team-based projects (as shown in Figure 2). This integrated view of OI concepts is extremely important to provide team support in achieving project goals. The organizational objectives for using such an approach include shared technical competence, improved communication network, strengthened commitment, and process ownership.

The successful use of the OI concepts requires an understanding of what constitutes a "healthy" team. What does healthy mean? Typically, teams that feel empowered, committed, and have a sense of purpose are healthy teams (Mears, 1994). There is little doubt that development efforts by dysfunctional teams impact quality even when the Cleanroom process is applied. Teams that lack motivation, don't have a sense of purpose, feel controlled with no decision-making abilities, and haven't "normed" yet won't be building zero-defect systems (refer to Tuckman, 1955 for a comprehensive discussion on forming, storming, norming, and performing stages of teamwork).

Benefits of a Team-based Organization Structure

The justification for instituting a team-based organization is greater than achieving project quality and productivity goals. Other benefits, as shown in Figure 3, may be realized when an organization institutes a team environment that supports the OI concepts. It is important to note that developing an effective team-based organization takes time, skill, and commitment by the organization as a whole. The benefits that may result from effective teamwork include:

Higher Performance - The organization is comprised of a set of individuals with differing levels of expertise, skill, experience, and interests. Team "knowledge-bases" are developed with the right combination of team members. The resulting synergy will produce high-performance teams.

Improved Competence - Individual competence is improved when teams work together to achieve a common goal. Experienced team members share their knowledge and expertise which results in more talent and technical competence within the organization.

Higher Quality - Quality is improved by organizational commitment through the use of the OI concepts. The team shares responsibility for maintaining a high-level of correctness by adhering to the team assignment process. Cleanroom adherence is inherent to the successful completion of team assignments.

Strengthened Commitment - Commitment is strengthened throughout the organization when trust has been established within and across teams and between teams and management. Trust is based on a common goal that has been established and for which all parties feel empowered to pursue.

Improved Satisfaction - An improved social atmosphere is created within the organization which breeds success. The team will give support and comfort to team members especially during times of pressure. Victorious accomplishments such as the successful completion of assignments are shared by the team. Overall, the team experience becomes a positive, motivating experience which will carry forward to the next assignment.

Higher Level of Maturity - Organizational maturity is improved when an organization has established a structured approach that can be applied within and across projects (Humphrey, 1989). The objectives of quality, performance, and satisfaction are no longer established on a project-by-project basis but become standard practices for all project development.

A Team Assignment Model has been developed to support organizations in achieving these goals. The basis of the model is

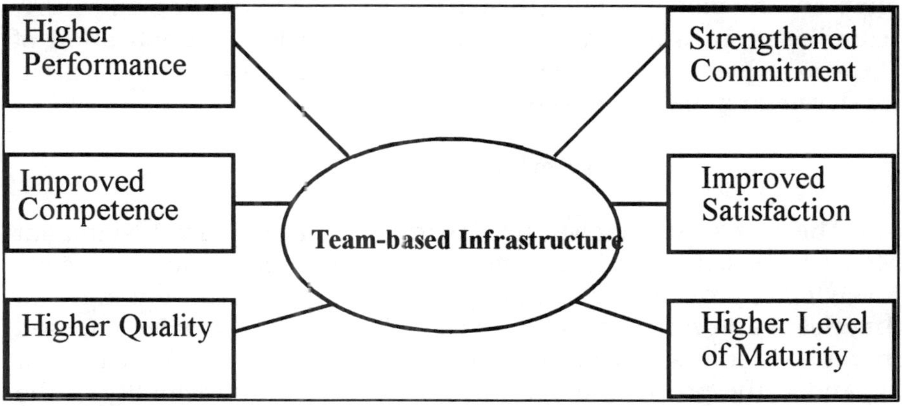

Figure 3: Benefits of a Team-based Organization

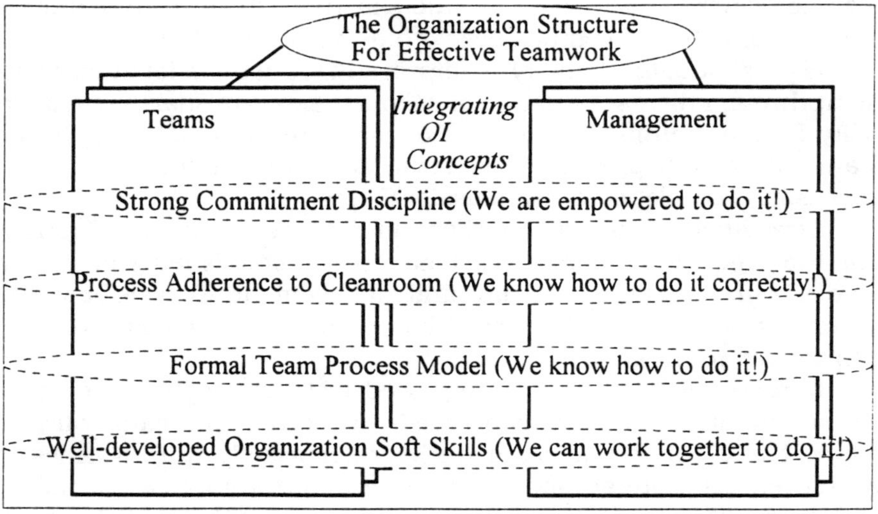

Figure 4: An Organizational Foundation for Cleanroom Development

integration of the OI concepts. The implementation of the Team Assignment Model supports effective information and work flow by:

- Stabilizing teams, projects, and organizations
- Establishing a communication network for effective top-down, bottom-up, and cross-functional information flow.
- Empowering teams, project and line managers and the organization as a whole to meet quality, performance, and productivity goals.

The Team Assignment Model has been used in a case study and the results have been incorporated into the model presented in this chapter. The motivation for the case study was to develop a healthy, team-based environment that was conducive to the application of Cleanroom principles and concepts. Figure 4 illustrates the motivation for developing the Team Assignment Model.

Overview of the Case Study

The case study that was used to implement the Team Assignment Model is based on a large, multi-site telecommunications project involving approximately 500 people. The sites were located in North America, Latin America, and Europe. The project was decomposed into increments with eight internal delivery points. Each increment expanded the previous one and as a result the functionality of the system evolved.

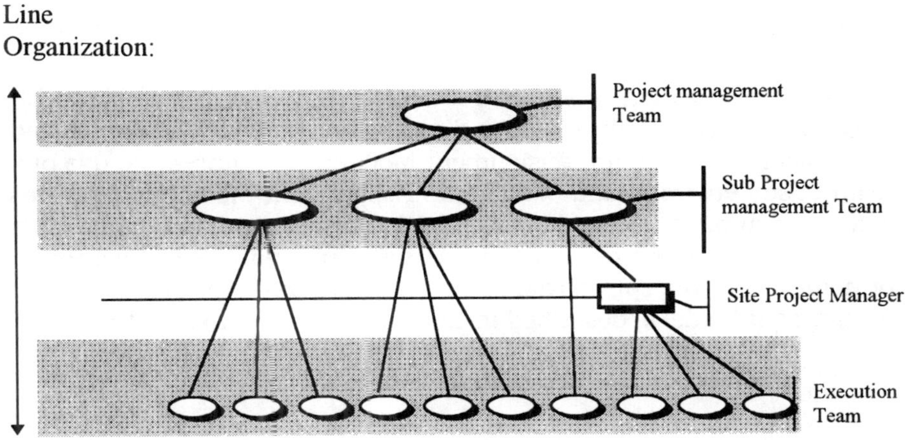

Figure 5: The Case Study Project Organization

The organization structure was project-driven as shown in Figure 5. The top level management team was comprised of representatives from functional departments such as system design, design and verification, and production. The project was decomposed into three sub-projects in order to support the three main components of the product. Each of the three sub-projects had its own project management team. These management teams were comprised of cross-functional members representing different departments within the organization. Then, these teams were decomposed further into execution teams. Each execution team was associated with one sub-project. In addition, a local project manager was required at each site due to the geographic dispersion of the teams. In other words, the assignments that were part of a sub-project were given to teams at the various sites.

Approximately 400 designers (team members) and 100 project and line managers were given the Team Assignment Model training. Most of the organization also received soft-skill training. The teams and management had access to written guidelines and support personnel. The support staff was fully trained in the OI concepts and provided a network across sites for reporting best and worst practices, issues, and problems as they occurred.

The results of the case study provide the foundation for the following discussion on teamwork. The case study provided an opportunity to assess the introduction and implementation of the Team Assignment Model in a large organization. As a result of this study, organizational building blocks and barriers were discovered. The case study also provided an opportunity to identify a means of overcoming these obstacles. The generalizations that were developed as a result of the case study are presented in the following sections.

The Organization Infrastructure: A Team Assignment Model

The organization is structured such that information flows bi-directionally between the teams and management. This is accomplished by implementing a Team Assignment Model that requires the use of a team-based environment. The Team Assignment Model incorporates soft skill components that empower both management and teams. It is based on Cleanroom development where teams adhere to Cleanroom principles and concepts (as defined in the previous chapters). The Team Assignment Model is described in the following sections.

Team Assignments

A team assignment is a project component or "unit of work" that is to be completed by a team. In the Cleanroom process, for example, each increment would be decomposed into smaller, manageable units of work. An assignment is typically given to a team based on the team's technical competence, availability, or other factors that impact the successful completion of the project. The size of the assignment is based on factors such as team composition of new/experienced members, time and cost constraints, and complexity associated with the level of reuse from existing components.

It is recommended that an assignment is limited in time and scope and assigned to a team size of 3 to 5 members. This guideline supports the concept of intellectual control as a team understands the assignment and feels comfortable proposing solutions and decomposing the assignment into tasks. The assignment must have a well-defined completion condition other than a deadline to provide the team a sense of ownership and pride in the final result.

In a software project, assignments may be:

Function-oriented - giving the team responsibility for the successful completion of an assignment from developing functional specifications through certification.

Phase-specific - giving the team responsibility for the successful completion of a phase of the assignment such as its specification.

The team assignment has a dual role in supporting teamwork. It is used by the team to determine the work flow among team members. This control flows bottom-up as teams and management become accountable for their work activities within the organization. It is also the team specification used to support the Cleanroom activities of functional and usage specification, design and verification, certification, and implementation.

Team Assignment Phases

A team will complete an assignment by performing three phases: initiation, execution, and conclusion. These phases are referred to as the *Team Assignment Model.* They are defined as:

- *Initiation* - The purpose of the initiation phase is to start work on an assignment. The team assignment activities are launched at a "kick-off" meeting at which time the team receives its assignment and supporting information required for its successful completion. The team members analyze the requirements of the assignment, define common plans and goals, and establish work methods and team routines for assignment execution. Based on the outcome of this activity, the team may need to negotiate with management the terms of assignment execution due to a lack of resources, time, expertise, or other factors. It is during this initiation phase that internal and external commitments to the team plan are made.
- *Execution* - The purpose of the execution phase is to begin work on the assignment as defined in the team plan. The execution is done according to the Team Assignment Plan and the process agreed upon, following the schedule of tasks, and using resources effectively in order to achieve the goals. The work is actively controlled by tracking and assessing task completion. Negotiation on the team plan may be initiated when management or teams cause major deviations from the agreed upon plan.
- *Conclusion*: The purpose of the conclusion phase is to compile experiences of the team effort and communicate them to management for future improvement. The assignment is brought to closure by documenting team experiences regarding the effectiveness of technical, process, and quality aspects of activities that were performed. In addition, teams can identify areas for future improvements in any of these aspects. The conclusion phase provides an effective means for communication between teams and management which is necessary for ongoing performance evaluation and improvement. This approach supports a higher-level of organizational maturity as feedback mechanisms are in place and have become part of the assessment process.

Team Assignment Roles

In the Team Assignment Model, roles have been predefined for both management and the teams (refer to Figure 6). The management roles include an Assignment Orderer and a Resource Responsible, and the team role is the Assignment Performer. Each role is defined in terms of its relationship with the other roles in the model. In a sense, the relationship is an interaction process whereby the teams and management work together to achieve the common goals of the organization. The success of this interaction is based on organizational development of soft skills, a strong sense of commitment, technical competence for use of Cleanroom principles and adherence to the Team Assignment Model. The Team Assignment roles are defined below.

Assignment Orderer: The Assignment Orderer is typically a project manager that is responsible for effective work flow within and across increments (subprojects). This is accomplished by defining team assignments and then giving the assignments to the teams. The Assignment Orderer is responsible for negotiating with the other two parties in order to reach agreement on the team plan. During execution of the assignments, the Assignment Orderer monitors the team's progress and acts on deviations from the team plan.

Resource Responsible: The Resource Responsible is typically a line manager and is responsible for assigning individuals to teams based on competence, skills, experience, interest or other factors. The Resource Responsible is also responsible for providing each team adequate resources including a sufficient number of team members, access to external expertise (i.e. technical support), work methods, and tools in order for the team to successfully complete the assignment. Effective resource allocation, use, and improvements require long-term planning by the Resource Responsible in order to ensure that future requirements are met.

Assignment Performer : The Assignment Performer is typically an execution team that has accepted an assignment and is committed to its successful completion. The team's responsibility is two-fold. The team develops a team plan that breaks down the assignment into tasks, responsibilities, and a schedule for completion. The team plan is negotiated with the other two parties in order to reach an agreement. In addition, the team completes the specification, design, certification,

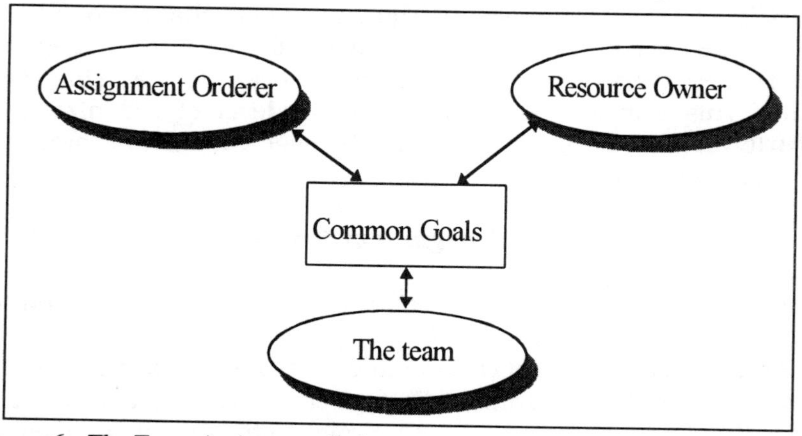

Figure 6: The Team Assignment Roles

and implementation activities required to successfully complete the assignment.

Team Size and Structure

In the Team Assignment Model a team has been defined as: *a group of 3-5 members that work interdependently to achieve a common goal. The members are jointly responsible for all results produced by the team. Each member strives for maximizing his/her performance through the use of innovative methods.*

The size of a team may vary, however, but it has been found that team size of five maximizes team performance (Hare, 1952). When team size is too small, the team synergy required for creativity, motivation, and ideation is diminished (Mears, 1994). When teams are too big, productivity may be reduced due to the number of interactions among team members. For example, team meetings lose the effectiveness because not all team members will be able to relay information within the fixed time period.

The infrastructure of an organization may not allow restricted team size. So, it is important to be aware that team size may be increased as long as team members can still communicate effectively such that each team member stills feels accountable for the results produced by the team. At times, it may be appropriate for the team to split itself into smaller teams with tasks associated with a component of the assignment. This requires management support in order to facilitate the interaction among the subteams.

High-performance teams are necessary to manage the complexity of today's systems in order to remain competitive in the market (Bradford & Cohen, 1984). In the Team Assignment Model, high performance means that teams are self-managing in terms of developing a team plan, executing it, reporting on its progress, and reacting when deviations occur. The teams are also responsible for adhering to the Cleanroom principles and obtaining external expertise when needed.

Allowing teams to be innovative in terms of decision-making, sharing of tasks, and problem-solving empowers teams to find the best solution possible, use resources effectively, and perform efficiently. An approach that works for one team may not necessarily be effective for another team.

Supporting Team Roles

In the Team Assignment Model, one of the team members is appointed the team leader. The team leader is a facilitator within the team and provides an interface to external parties. Typically, the team leader will interact with the Assignment Orderer and Resource Responsible when issues or concerns arise. The team leader is also a team member in that he/she actively participates in teamwork and maintains equal responsibility for producing the results. In order for the team to work effectively within the Team Assignment Model, it is important that the team leader does not play a supervisory or administrative role.

A team may not encompass all the expertise required to complete the assignment. External resources may be required to support certain areas including technical expertise, process support, external reviews, and others. The definition of an external resource is an individual who is not part of the team as he/she does not have responsibilities and tasks associated with the assignment. Any team member with a particular expertise may act as an external resource to other teams.

From a project perspective, it is important to identify the requirements associated with external resources to ensure adequacy as well as access to them. For teams with members new to the organization, the external resource requirements might be great. This requires timely access to external resources in order to minimize delays. For teams with significant expertise, their external commitments will impact the amount of time spent on the team assignment. For those individuals with major time commitments to other teams, it may be more effective to allow them to be full-time external resources.

Team Assignment Process

In order to describe the process that is followed to implement the Team Assignment phases, it is important to understand the interfaces of the initiation, execution, and conclusion phases. These interfaces, as summarized in Table 1, are needed to facilitate a smooth transition from one phase to another.

The Initiation Phase. The initiation phase is composed of a set of activities that must be completed before the team begins execution of the assignment. These activities are described below.

The Kick-Off:

The first activity in the initiation phase is a Kick-Off meeting where the Assignment Orderer presents the team with an assignment. This meeting provides the team and management an opportunity to come together and discuss the requirements of the assignment in terms of its technical and administrative aspects. The team can obtain clarification on any questions they may have regarding the assignment specification, process to be followed, the reporting structure, or any team-related issues.

The Kick-Off meeting is a powerful management tool from the perspective of both project and line management. The Assignment Orderer is provided an opportunity to interact directly with the teams

The Initiation Phase Begins With:	
Kick-off meeting- Assignment Orderer holds a meeting where the team is given a team assignment. The team assignment is a specification document that defines the functionality of the assignment at a very high level. It also defines the requirements on the team such as time, quality, and process.	**Team Assignment Specification** - produced by the Assignment Orderer as a means of providing teams the assignment requirements and supporting administrative information, and presented to the teams in the Kick-Off meeting.
The Initiation Phase Ends and The Execution Phase Begins With:	
Team Assignment Plan - produced by the team in order to define a work schedule including tasks, due dates, and responsibilities. The team plan is subject to negotiation and agreed upon by the Assignment Orderer and Resource Responsible.	**Negotiation meeting** - a meeting where all three parties, the Assignment Orderer, Resource Responsible, and the team, review the team plan, negotiate on changes, and reach a mutual agreement.
The Execution Phase Ends and The Conclusion Phase Begins With:	
Conclusion Report - produced by the team documenting the team's findings for future improvements.	**Activity Analysis meeting** - team presents findings of future improvements and summary of team experiences to Assignment Orderer and Resource Responsible.

Table 1: The Interfaces of the Team Assignment Model

by giving teams their assignments and explaining management expectations. The Resource Responsible is also provided direct access to the teams in order to explain how team performance will be assessed and what type of coaching support the line will provide. During the Kick-Off meeting, a date is set for negotiation of the team plan.

For teams that have assignments technically dependent on one another and that require a significant amount of coordination, the Kick-Off meetings may be combined into a common one. This will facilitate communication among the teams and provide an opportunity for all involved to ask questions and get clarification before teamwork is initiated.

The Team Assignment Plan:

Once a team has received its assignment, it develops a team plan based on the execution of the assignment. The team members are jointly responsible for decomposing the assignment into tasks, developing a schedule of task completion and responsibility, determining the resources required to maintain the schedule, and identifying assumptions, risks, and team dependencies associated with the execution of the assignment. The Team Assignment Plan provides the

Contents:	Description:
Assignment description	A brief description of the assignment as specified in the team assignment specification.
Team Composition and Skill-base	Team members and skills are made visible to the team and management.
Task List and Responsibilities	The assignment is decomposed into a set of tasks. These are presented in a task list with team members assigned responsibility for task completion. Tasks may include Cleanroom team specification, design, certification, and reviews.
Schedule of Task Completion	A team schedule is developed to establish an order of task execution necessary to complete the assignment by the delivery date. Typically, it is a weekly breakdown of task activities. It also identifies activities impacting the availability of team resources such as training, vacation, etc.
Estimated Labor Hours	The labor hours associated with each task are estimated and totaled.
Available Labor Hours	Given the team composition, the labor hours available are determined. This excludes hours that are not available due to training, vacation time, or other activities external to the assignment.
Risks	Due to a lack of information, factors that may impact the successful completion of the assignment need to be identified.

Table 2: Illustrated Contents of a Team Assignment Plan

team a means of visualizing the process to be followed in order to successfully complete the assignment. Table 2 illustrates the type of information that is found in a Team Assignment Plan. The structure and contents of the plan are organizational decisions and should be formally documented.

The Team Assignment Plan identifies whether there are sufficient team resources to successfully complete the assignment. This is accomplished by specifying the number of labor hours required to complete the set of tasks and comparing this estimate to the actual team labor hours available. A significant difference between estimated and actual hours is a basis for negotiation.

The Team Assignment Plan is a means of empowering teams to analyze their own potential for fulfilling the assignment requirements. It requires teams to evaluate their available resources, additional requirements including training and external expertise. The team as a whole must agree upon the plan before it is negotiated with management.

Negotiation:

To support a high-level of motivation within an organization, it is important to provide teams the tools necessary to develop a strong sense of commitment. The team assignment is an excellent tool for establishing a strong sense of commitment. The Team Assignment Plan may be regarded as a tender in a bid/tender situation. Formal negotiations between teams and management are held to review the team plan and reach mutual agreement. The result of the negotiation process is a formal contract on the Team Assignment Plan that provides a foundation upon which the commitment discipline is built. Negotiable factors should be established by the organization in order to come to an agreement about the resolution of differences between the team plan and the project plan.

Negotiable factors may include deliverable dates, functionality, process adherence (quality), and resources, and other factors as well. It is important to note that at least one of the factors must be modifiable in order to successfully negotiate.

Deliverable Dates - Each deliverable component in the assignment specification has a scheduled completion date. The dates may have to be extended to allow for the completion of an assignment especially when additional resources are not available.

Functionality - The assignment specification identifies the functional components that are to be completed by the team. Functionality may have to be reduced or modified if the team cannot produce all deliverables by the due date.

Process Adherence - The Team Assignment Process identifies activities, documents, meetings and Cleanroom concepts that must be followed to develop high-quality systems. If other factors are non-negotiable, then process components may have to be eliminated (i.e., reduce the number and/or rigor of team reviews or certification activities).

Resource Allocation - The size of the team may be inadequate for the completion of the assignment by the scheduled due date. Additional team members or external resources may be required to support team efforts.

The negotiation is held according to the Kick-off date established by management. The team and management review the Team Assignment Plan, make necessary changes as negotiated, and reach a mutual agreement. It may be appropriate to document the agreement by having all parties in attendance sign the plan.

The negotiation process is an integral component of the Team Assignment Model. The negotiation process is very powerful in ensuring that both management and the team are made aware of their responsibilities in the agreed upon team plan. This agreement strengthens commitment among all parties because it is based on trust and a sense of "we are all in this together". The line manager is not likely to reallocate team resources without analyzing the consequences to the agreed upon team plan. The project manager is less likely to change the requirements of the team assignment while the assignment is being completed. Team members will feel a strengthened sense of purpose and control as they have been an equal partner in the approval process.

Once the negotiation process has been completed, management and teams are not allowed to make ad hoc changes nor deviate significantly from the agreed upon Team Assignment Plan. The "freezing" of the approved plan forces management and teams to be committed to its successful completion as they are all held accountable for adhering to it. This commitment bond is strengthened for each team assignment cycle as management and teams become experienced in this working environment.

Execution Phase. The execution phase is composed of a set of activities that must be completed during the execution of the assignment. These activities are described below.

Assignment Execution:

Teams begin executing the team assignment according to the Team Assignment Plan. Each team member has been assigned tasks for which he/she is responsible. The Cleanroom process is applied by each team member in order to develop black box specifications and state box and clear box designs and perform team reviews (refer to Chapters 2, 3, and 4 for a comprehensive discussion of Cleanroom activities). A team member is responsible for scheduling and holding team reviews as well as notifying the team when problems occur (i.e., task complexity is greater than anticipated), or work-flow is interrupted (i.e., family problems, sickness, etc.).

The execution phase is comprised of a weekly cycle performed by the team. This cycle of plan, work, assess, and react is supported by established team routines in order for the team to meet its commitment as specified in the Team Assignment Plan.

Team Routines:

Team routines are established at the onset of execution activities in order to develop a high-performance team. The type of team routines that need to be addressed are illustrated in Table 3.

Team Tracking Mechanisms:

The team also needs to establish tracking mechanisms in order to

Team Routine:	**Description:**
Meetings	Meeting routines are established in terms of structure, roles, documentation, and rules of conduct.
Administration	Administrative tasks are defined and responsibilities allocated to team members. Tasks include file maintenance of weekly schedule, action lists, etc.
Decision-making	Routines are established for making decisions including when consensus is required, how decisions are documented, and team leader involvement.
Information Dissemination	The team establishes how information will be distributed among the team members. This includes file access, email use, and other forms of distribution.

Table 3: Illustration of Team Routines

keep team members informed and to ensure resolution of action items. Two commonly used reports are described below.

Action List - An action list is a document that tracks issues, problems, and concerns as they arise. The team uses an action list at all meetings to log action points and assign responsibility to their resolution. The action list is a powerful tool for bringing closure to meetings as unresolved discussions can be terminated by placing an action point on the list. An action list is presented in Figure 7. A team member is appointed to maintain the action list during a meeting. After each meeting, the action list is distributed among the team members. The action list is typically reviewed during the weekly status meetings to ensure follow-up on outstanding action points.

Weekly Schedule - The weekly schedule is a document that provides visibility to the team's performance. It is a tool that is used by the team to identify team member tasks that are to be started and completed during the upcoming week. It also may provide information about vacation, training, and other external activities that will impact the week's progress on the assignment. The weekly schedule is used during the status meeting to plan, track, and assess the team's progress. It must be made available to each team member either electronically or kept in a visible place (i.e., team leader's office).

Progress Reporting:
The team will produce periodic progress reports to management

Action Item:	Assigned:	Resolution:	Closed:
Contact Line Manager for coaching	Jones	Scheduled Meeting	open
Schedule training for next week.	Jones	Training Dpt. List	2/24/96
... ...	...	...	...

Figure 7: An Illustration of An Action List

in order to maintain project visibility of team performance. The progress report may be informal or formal depending on the organizational guidelines that have been established. The contents of a progress report are illustrated in Table 4. The progress report should be structured such that the team maintains control over the execution of the assignment as much as possible. It should not allow finger-pointing which supports a lack of team accountability.

Team Meetings:

Team meetings play an important role in maintaining control during the execution phase. The following meetings are important for obtaining timely feedback on the successful execution of the assignment.

Status Meeting - A status meeting is a structured, team meeting

Progress Report Component:	Description:
Time Period	Specifies the time period for which progress reporting is done.
Schedule Assessment	Provides a comparison of estimated and actual tasks started/completed.
Deviations	Explains deviations from the schedule. For example, an illness may have delayed the initiation of a task.
Labor Hours	Provides a comparison of estimated and actual labor hours including overtime.
Problems, Issues, Concerns	Identifies problems, issues, or concerns that the team is resolving or that require action at a higher level.
Opportunities, Highlights, Problem Resolution	Identifies opportunities, best practices, or resolutions by the team.

Table 4: An Illustration of the Contents of a Team Progress Report

that is held on a regular basis. The time, length, place, and team roles are established in order to use team resources in an efficient manner. The status meeting is an important means of assessing the progress of the team and making adjustments when necessary. Typically, a weekly schedule is developed and the action list reviewed. The status meeting supports the weekly cycle of activities necessary to keep the team on track.

The 1/3 Presentation - The 1/3 Presentation is a structured meeting that is held approximately after one-third of the team's effort has been expended in the completion of a deliverable. (For example, a 1/3 Presentation would be held on a black box specification when all stimuli and responses have been defined.) The objective of the 1/3 Presentation is to discuss the team's efforts with management, external resources, and other teams to determine whether the team is on track with its proposed solution. The 1/3 Presentation is not a review and should not be held as such.

Team Reviews:

The team review is a quality tool that is used by the team to prevent defects from occurring during execution activities. The team review is based on the Cleanroom concepts of correctness verification and validation. The objective of a team review is to identify any potential problems early during the execution of the team assignment. The team relies on the review process for maintaining a high-level of quality of team deliverables.

Team review guidelines may be developed by the organization and implemented by the team. The criteria for team reviews may be based on number of hours worked on a particular component (i.e., a review is held for every 40 hours of work), complexity (a review is held for every 100 lines of code written), or other factors. It is extremely important that a sufficient number of team reviews are held in order to minimize the size and complexity of the material being reviewed. Quality reviews are held when team members are able to maintain intellectual control over the review process. Otherwise, defects may go undetected thus impacting the quality of the assignment later in the development process.

The purpose of the team review is to convince all participants that the review component is correct based on Cleanroom correctness criteria. If consensus is not reached and there are outstanding completion conditions, another review is held. The team monitors the outstanding completion conditions to ensure that they are met. The team needs to track the number and type of completion conditions as reviews are held in order to determine whether there is a problem that needs to be addressed such as holding more frequent reviews, obtaining external resource expertise, etc. The team review process has been decomposed into a set of activities as presented in Table 5.

Step	**Description**
Scheduling and distribution of material	The author informs reviewees of the scheduled review date and provides the documentation to be reviewed. When a second review is held, the revised information may be highlighted.
Preparation by reviewers	The reviewers prepare for the review by comparing the document to its intended function or specification to ensure completeness and correctness (refer to Chapter 3 for a comprehensive discussion of Cleanroom correctness concepts).
Ensured preparedness of participants	The review is initiated when the author and reviewers are in attendance. If any member of the review team is not prepared, the review is rescheduled.
Explanation of functionality	The author explains the material to the reviewers in terms of how the document satisfies its intended functionality.
Pass/Fail and supporting documentation	The reviewees must reach an agreement on the proposed solution. If there are correctness issues, they are recorded as completion conditions.
If correctness failure then repeat step 1	If completion conditions have been recorded, a second review is scheduled and steps 1 through 5 are repeated until there are no outstanding completion conditions.

Table 5. Steps In The Team Review Process

The number of reviewers involved in a team review is established by the team. This may be done as part of the team routines or may be determined as teamwork progresses. In either case, the review work must be incorporated into the original team plan to ensure adequate resources and time are available to meet the team commitments.

The final team review may be considered a team "sign-off" of the overall correctness and completeness of the assignment. This is a commitment statement by the team as to the quality of its assignment.

Renegotiation:

During the execution phase, the team is responsible for monitoring its progress according to the Team Assignment Plan. When there is a discrepancy in the number of tasks completed compared to the assignment schedule, the team must report it to management. This may initiate a renegotiation of the Team Assignment Plan in order to keep the project on track. At any time, the Resource Responsible or

Assignment Orderer may also initiate a renegotiation especially when requirements or resource allocation change.

Organizational guidelines for effective renegotiation must be established. These guidelines are used by both teams and management to initiate changes in the Team Assignment Plan. The guidelines should be specific in terms of how, when, where, and why renegotiation takes place. These guidelines must be made available to all team structures in the organization.

The list below identifies several situations in which renegotiation should take place. It is important that management and teams feel empowered to initiate renegotiation and not "wait" for the other parties to do so.

1. The requirements of the assignment have changed causing a schedule delay, requiring additional resources, or requiring technical competence that the team does not have.
2. Team composition changes for an extended time period (typically longer than one week time period) resulting in a lack of resources. A team member may leave the team for various reasons such as providing external resources, sick leave, training, or others.
3. Complexity of the assignment is such that the original Team Assignment Plan can not be adhered to in terms of quality and/or delivery goals.
4. The risks identified in the Team Assignment Plan are impacting teamwork. Risks may include dependencies on other teams, reliance on external expertise, or technical competence of team members.

Conclusion Report:

At the end of the execution phase, the team compiles a report of findings. This Conclusion Report documents future improvements, team experiences, and any other information that the team would like to share with management and other teams to improve the Team Assignment process.

Conclusion Phase. The conclusion phase brings closure to the whole Team Assignment life cycle by presenting the team's findings as documented in the Conclusion Report.

Activity Analysis:

Once the team has documented its findings in a Conclusion Report, management schedules a follow-up meeting called Activity Analysis. During this meeting, the team reports its findings to the Assignment Orderer and the Line Manager. Other teams that have been impacted by the team assignment may also be in attendance. The Activity Analysis provides an opportunity for all parties involved to discuss problems, resolutions, issues, and concerns that the team

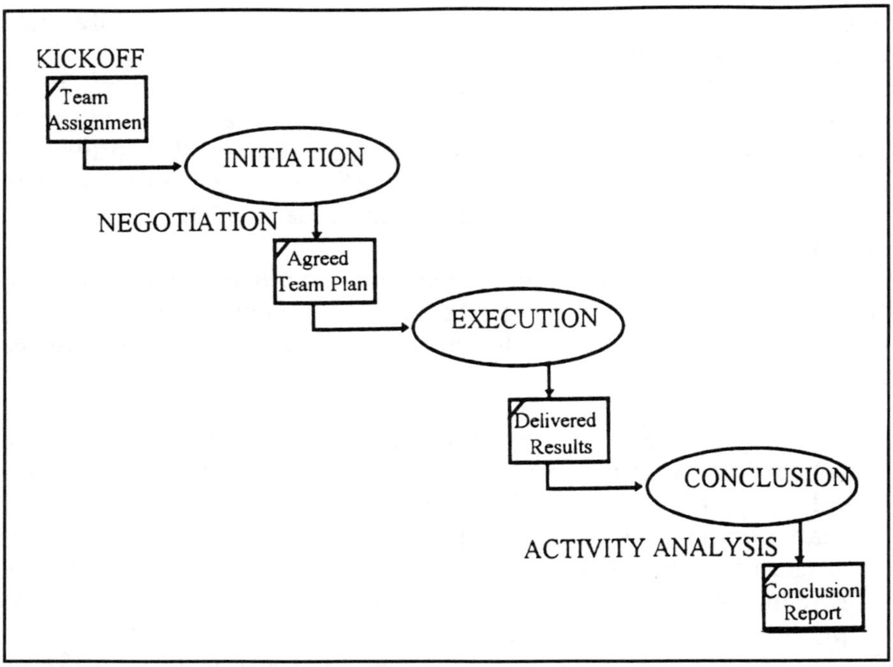

Figure 8: The Team Assignment Model

encountered during the life cycle phases. This information will be used for future improvements during the next team assignment.

The Activity Analysis meeting also may be used to discuss the requirements of the next team assignment. Thus, the groundwork is laid for the next initiation phase of a team assignment.

Summary

The successful use of the Team Assignment Model is accomplished by applying the initiation, execution, and conclusion phases as described in this section. Figure 8 shows the entry and exit points for each phase. The phases and their supporting documents, tools, and techniques form a coherent and comprehensive approach for successfully completing projects. It is important to note that the Team Assignment Model can be readily applied to any aspect of the Cleanroom process. A team would develop a Team Assignment Plan that identifies the appropriate Cleanroom activities that need to be performed. For Cleanroom development, a team plan would typically include black box specification and state and clear box design work. During execution, the specification, design, and coding activities are performed and reviewed for correctness. Then, the team summarizes its strengths and weaknesses in performing Cleanroom activities for future improvements. This is illustrated in Figure 9.

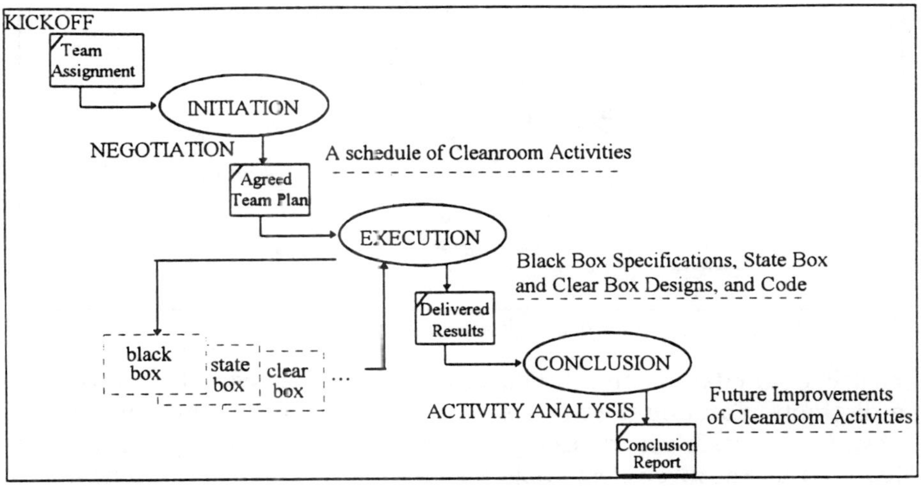

Figure 9: Illustration of Cleanroom Activities & the Team Assignment Model

Organizational Requirements for the Successful Use of the Team Assignment Model

Organizational "buy-in" is necessary from top management to the bottom tiers of management and teams. This is achieved by developing an environment that is conducive to the use of the Team Assignment Model. The following issues should be addressed by the organization in order to provide a foundation for the successful use of the Team Assignment Model.

The organizational infrastructure must be in place - The organization must be structured such that process-specific or cross-functional teams are easily formed. This requires support from both the line and project management in order to provide the teams technical support during project development and competence development over the long-run.

The project structure allows for decomposition into manageable team assignments - The organization must provide guidelines on staffing requirements and team assignment duration. Team assignments should be restricted in size and complexity to ensure the feasibility of assignment completion. Unrealistic or fuzzy assignments will reduce the performance of teams as they struggle to develop and implement a team plan.

Organization roles and responsibilities must be clearly defined - The roles and responsibilities in the Team Assignment Model must be

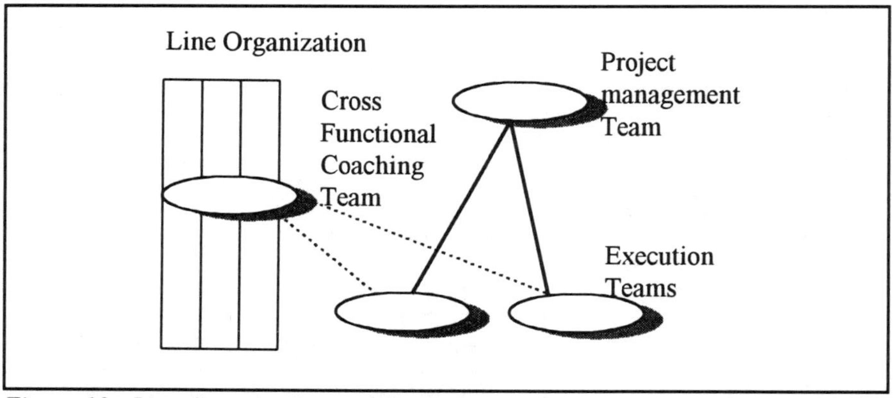

Figure 10: Line Organization and Cross-Functional Teams

clearly defined and communicated among all parties. There must be a distinction among the parties such that the Assignment Orderer is always responsible for defining the assignments and giving them to the teams, the Resource Responsible is always responsible for assigning team members to teams, and teams are always responsible for self-managing the completion of their assignments. If any party usurps the role of another, the benefits of the Team Assignment process will not be realized.

Team support functions must be established - In order for the organization to apply the Team Assignment process successfully, teams will require ongoing support from management. This support includes coaching and facilitation of team efforts to resolve soft-skill issues, ensure process adherence, and to support each phase in the Team Assignment life cycle. This is especially important for cross-functional teams as it is unlikely that there is one line manager working with the whole team (as shown in Figure 10). Management should monitor team performance via progress reporting in order to ensure that the assignment goals are met. Management should also assist the teams in making feasible commitments during initial negotiations to ensure that a realistic project schedule is maintained.

There is organizational commitment to the negotiation process - Management must understand and commit to the purpose of team negotiation. This may not be an easy task as management traditionally has had significant control over team assignments. Management must support the outcome of the negotiation process whereby the Team Assignment Plan is agreed upon by all parties.

A formal implementation plan is established - A formal implementation plan should be developed for the successful introduction of the Team Assignment Model into the organization. This includes establishing effective communication channels within and among teams, and between teams and management. In a multi-site organization, the plan should include resource requirements for local adaptation of the Team Assignment process.

Overcoming Barriers to the Team Assignment Model

Not all organizations will meet with success when implementing the Team Assignment Model. There are team and management barriers that may have to be overcome in order to attain positive results. The following team and management barriers illustrate the types of obstacles that may have to be overcome in the use of the Team Assignment Model.

Team Barriers

Team planning is done by one team member functioning as a "team leader". It is important that all team members actively participate in the planning activities and negotiation to ensure "buy-in" by each team member. It may be tempting to rely on the team leader to plan and negotiate especially when historically the team leader role included such activities. Team members that do not participate will not feel empowered nor committed to meeting the goals outlined in the team plan.

Teams are not empowered to do their planning. Teams must be allowed to develop their own Team Assignment Plans. This establishes a sense of ownership by the team and initiates trust-building in the Team Assignment process. Both motivation and commitment are impacted when teams lack a sense of control over their assignment.

Teams do not understand how the team assignment relates to the overall project. Teams will feel isolated when it is not understood how their assignment fits into the project scheme. This could impact the successful completion of the project especially when the team assignment has dependencies with other team assignments.

The team size is too large. The size of the team must be limited in order to maximize team performance. Teams that are too large may not develop a sense of "team commitment" as communication channels bog down. Management must resist the growth of teams especially during renegotiation without a mechanism in place for decomposing large teams into subteams (subassignments).

The team's plans are not respected by all parties. The involvement of all three parties in the negotiation process is absolutely essential for full commitment to the team plan. If one of the parties is absent, disagrees, or is indifferent, the outcome could be disastrous as it will be viewed as a lack of commitment. Teams will not feel empowered when team members have little or no input during negotiations or if management fails to negotiate in "good faith".

Management Barriers

Management does not follow up on the completion of assignments. Once a team assignment has been completed, it is critical that management evaluates a team's performance, and disseminates information about future improvements, best and worst practices and other information the team provided during the Analysis Activity meeting. A lack of management follow-up reduces team trust and commitment to the organization.

Management fails to perform team visits in order to track progress and evaluate motivation and team performance. Teams may feel a sense of isolation when management involvement is minimal. Teams will feel a greater sense of commitment when management takes an active interest in team activities.

Management makes decisions that impact the teams but does not facilitate renegotiation of team assignments. This points out a lack of commitment by management to allow teams to make decisions regarding their assignments. A control principle is being implemented where management does not feel accountable for the original commitment made by all parties during negotiations nor trusts the teams to complete their assignments according to the Team Assignment Plan.

Overcoming Team and Management Barriers

The teamwork and management barriers may be overcome by maintaining effective communication, establishing a training program, allowing for local adaptation, and modifying the team or assignment size. Each of these factors is described.

Communication:. The main challenge to overcoming the obstacles identified previously is to develop an effective communication network among all parties. This is particularly important for geographically dispersed projects where management and teams may not be located at the same site. Communication must be maintained bidirectionally in order for teams to feel empowered and for management to remain informed. The Team Assignment process requires a significant amount of interaction among all parties. Timely access to information means timely reaction to it.

The communication network established between management and the teams is an important aspect of prioritizing goals. A strongly-focused team may lose sight of the project goals and focus only on the team goals. For example, a team may refuse to act as external resources to other teams because of their commitment to the completion of the team assignment. Management must monitor interaction among teams and ensure that the project goals are being met. It is also important that management has communicated the project goals to the teams so that they do not perform in isolation of other teams.

A lack of communication may result in the following team perspective. "Since we are on a time-plan with no margins we do not have time to help any other teams, especially since we know that the other teams are in the same situation and will not help us in return." This is a lose/lose work mode as key players in the project will devote their effort to their assignments rather than to the good of the project.

Effective communication will result in a different team perspective. "Since we know that we are all in this together, we will do our best to provide other teams assistance and we expect that other teams will do their utmost to help us." This is a win/win situation. All team assignments will be completed according to agreed upon team plans while allowing team members to provide external support.

Training. Training plays a significant role in the successful implementation of the Team Assignment approach. It is important to provide teams and management with training on the components of the model including the life cycle activities and their interfaces, the roles of all parties, and the team planning and negotiation processes, among others. For organizations that have not established team-based development, soft-skill training is imperative to provide individuals the skills, tools, and techniques required for team-building (conflict resolution, effective communication, etc.). In addition, technical competence is developed by establishing effective Cleanroom training and coaching support.

The training of the Assignment Orderer and the Resource Responsible is also critical to the successful implementation of the process. Management may view such changes as a loss of control and especially during a time-critical project process change may be looked upon with suspicion. Management training of the process must emphasize the benefits of its use in order to promote a strong commitment to the use of the Team Assignment Model. These benefits include maintaining control throughout project development, access to timely information, improved job satisfaction for all parties because of stress-reduction and others. The training should also focus on what management by objectives means in terms of transferring control to execution teams.

Local Adaptation: Local adaptation of the process is very important in gaining support by both management and teams. The "invented here" syndrome whereby a local site adapts the Team Assignment process to suit its needs is important in promoting ownership of the process. Local adaptation may simply mean that small changes are made to improve its use in a specific cultural setting. However, it is important to note that the underlying OI concepts must be adhered to, otherwise, the model may lose its meaning in terms of achieving quality, functionality, and productivity.

Team and Assignment Size: Under some circumstances, it may be difficult to form teams that are comprised of 3-5 members. This is typically the case when the assignment cannot be successfully completed by a team of this size. It is recommended that large teams are divided into smaller subteams and then assigned components of the original assignment. The team plan would reflect this subdivision of work. Another alternative is to decompose the assignment before it is given to a team in order to reduce the complexity and size of the original assignment. Then, the newly defined assignments could be given to teams of the appropriate size. Finally, if the decomposition of the assignment results in a dependency such that one component must be completed before another is begun, the set of assignments could be given to the team. The assignment specification would define the sequence of assignments. Each assignment would be completed using the Team Assignment approach of initiation, execution, and conclusion.

Assessment: Ongoing assessment is essential for identifying barriers to the successful use of the Team Assignment Model. It is also important for the continuous improvement and adaptation of the Team Assignment Model. Frequent assessments provide an opportunity to gather information from the teams and management which can be disseminated among the sites. This includes best and worst practices, issues, concerns and their resolution, as well as project-specific about meeting goals. A healthy competition may be initiated as sites report their progress with the introduction and use of the team-based approach.

Initially, an assessment plan might simply be an evaluation of the training efforts at the management and team levels. Metrics could be established regarding the number of staff trained at each site according to the training schedule. An assessment plan should also be developed to evaluate process adherence to the Team Assignment Model. This information may be readily available via team progress reports including estimated and actual information on performance, functionality, and quality. Information may also be obtained during management visits to the teams. For example, an assessment of process adherence may be done informally by attending team reviews in accordance with the Cleanroom process.

At the management level, an assessment plan is needed to determine the level of support provided to the teams. Information can be gathered on the formation of management coaching teams at each site to facilitate teamwork, the attendance of management at kickoffs, and active participation in negotiations.

In performing assessments, it is also important to measure the benefits of the introduction of new techniques such as the Team Assignment Model. It is recommended that a baseline of productivity and quality is made prior to the introduction of the team-based approach.

Conclusion

The Team Assignment Model could rightfully be described as a common sense approach to teamwork. Yet, the underlying concept of intellectual control is basic to its success. It is important to distinguish this concept of intellectual control from automated tools and techniques that have been designed to support human problem-solving. The organization is decomposing its work-flow in units that can remain under intellectual control at all times and regardless of geographic dispersion. Intellectual control in the Team Assignment Model is achieved by decomposing a problem into smaller components that are manageable by teams. The composition of these parts is equivalent to the whole problem but without decomposition, the problem becomes unsolvable due to its complexity and size.

The success of the Team Assignment Model requires an organization to have a fundamental trust in the process and the ability of its staff to implement the process. The components of the Team Assignment Model have been developed with this in mind. The negotiation process has been established to ensure that all parties are fully informed of what is to be done, how it is to be done, and by whom. There is no hidden agenda and both the team plan and the negotiation results become part of the "knowledge-base" supporting the successful completion of the project. As a result, teams and management become fully accountable as there is no hiding from commitments and no finger-pointing when obligations are not met. Perhaps most importantly, the success of teams is highly visible. This is a change for many organizations from a fire-fighting mentality to a plan, track, and assess one where team achievements are recognized and rewarded.

References

Basili, V., & Musa, J. (1991). The Future Engineering of Software: A Management Perspective. *IEEE Computer*, September.

Becker, S., Carmel, E., & Hevner A. (1993). *Integrating Joint Application Development (JAD) into Cleanroom Development with ICASE.* The 26th International Hawaii Conference on System Sciences, Hawaii.

Bradford, & Cohen. (1984). *Managing for Excellence*, John Wiley and Sons, N.Y., N.Y.

Constantine, L. (1990). *Teamwork Paradigms and the Structured Open Team.* Proceedings of Software Development 90, San Francisco, CA.

Deck, M. & Hausler, P. (1990). *Cleanroom Software Engineering: Theory and Practice.* Proceedings of the Second International Software Engineering and Knowledge Engineering Conference, Skokie, Illinois.

DeMarco, T., & Lister, T. (1987). *Peopleware.* Dorsett House, N.Y., N.Y.

Deming, W.E. (1986). *Out of the Crisis.* MIT Center for Advanced Engineering Study, MIT Press, Cambridge, MA.

Hare, P. (1952). A Study of Interaction and Consensus in Different Sized Groups. *American Sociological Review*, 17.

Humphrey, W.S. (1989). *Managing the Software Process,* Addison-

Wesley Publishing Co., Inc.

Imai, M. (1986). Kaizen *The Key to Japan's Competitive Success,* Random House, Inc., New York.

Jones, T. (1986). *Programming Productivity,* McGraw-Hill, N.Y., N.Y.

Juran, J.M. (1951). *Quality Control Handbook,* McGraw-Hill, New York.

Linger, R. (1994). Cleanroom Process Model. *IEEE Software,* 11(2).

McClure, C. (1988). The CASE for Structured Development. *PC Tech Journal,* August.

Mears, P. (1994). *Organization Teams: Building Continuous Improvement.* St. Lucie Press, Delray Beach, FL.

Mills, H. (1988). Stepwise Refinement Verification in Box-Structured Systems. *IEEE Computer,* 21(6).

Mills, H., Linger, R., & Hevner, A. (1986). *Principles of Information Systems Analysis and Design,* N.Y., Academic Press.

Tuckman, B. (1955). Development Sequence in Small Groups. *Psychological Bulletin.*

Vessey, I., & Sravanapudi, A.P. (1995). CASE Tools as Collaborative Support Technologies. *Communications of the ACM,* 38(1).

White K., & Leifer, R. (1986). Information Systems Development Success: Perspectives from Project Team Participants, *MIS Quarterly,* September.

CHAPTER 7

Information Management For Cleanroom Support

Shirley A. Becker
American University

This chapter describes an Information Abstraction Framework (IAF) that is the basis for determining the information needs of an organization using Cleanroom. The framework identifies three levels of information requirements, technical, management, and organization. These levels support information abstraction in order to provide timely and complete information to developers, teams, and management. Once the information requirements of an organization have been identified, CASE alternatives are evaluated. These alternatives range from simple tools to sophisticated CASE environments. Three phases of CASE introduction into an organization are discussed. These include planning, tracking, and assessing the use of CASE to support the IAF. The chapter concludes with a discussion on the use of CASE to support Cleanroom.

Background

Many organizations have turned to Computer-Aided Software Engineering (CASE) technology as a means of achieving higher software quality and improved productivity. This is especially true for the development of large, complex systems where management control is difficult without automated support. In fact, CASE is becoming accepted as mainstream information technology that is used by organizations searching for effective development support, standard-

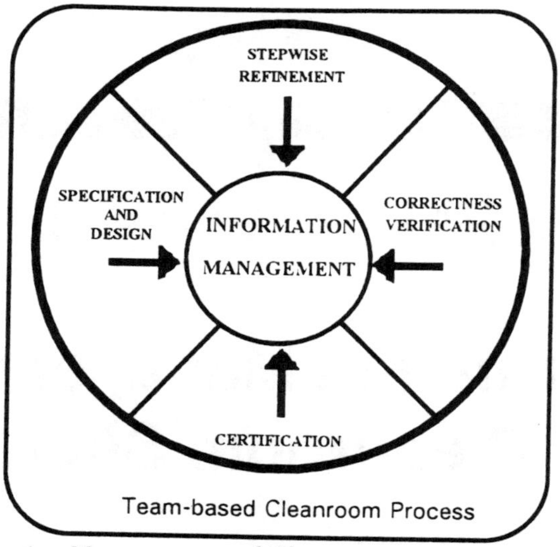

Figure 1: Information Management and Cleanroom

ization, and lower defect rates, among other improvements (Becker & Gibson, 1995).

As CASE technology matures, there has been a shift in emphasis from automated support of development activities to a broader view encompassing management and organization activities. The perspective of CASE being primarily a toolset is too restrictive as it focuses on specific features provided by the tools and not an integrated environment that supports the organization's goals. CASE should be viewed as process-driven in that it provides tool and techniques to support an engineering approach to software development at all stages of the process (Forte & Norman, 1992).

In this chapter, CASE support of the Cleanroom process is discussed. The basis for this discussion is an understanding of the information requirements of an organization using Cleanroom. An Information Abstraction Framework (IAF) is proposed for identifying information requirements at technical, management, and organization levels.

The Cleanroom techniques, when implemented properly, generate a significant amount of technical and process information that must be managed. The effective management of this information is requisite for achieving a high-level of organization maturity. An organization's risk of meeting quality and productivity standards is minimized when information is readily accessible. Figure 1 identifies information management as being an integral component of the Cleanroom process (refer to Chapter 1 for a comprehensive description of the Cleanroom process or (Mills et al., 1986; Mills, 1988)) .

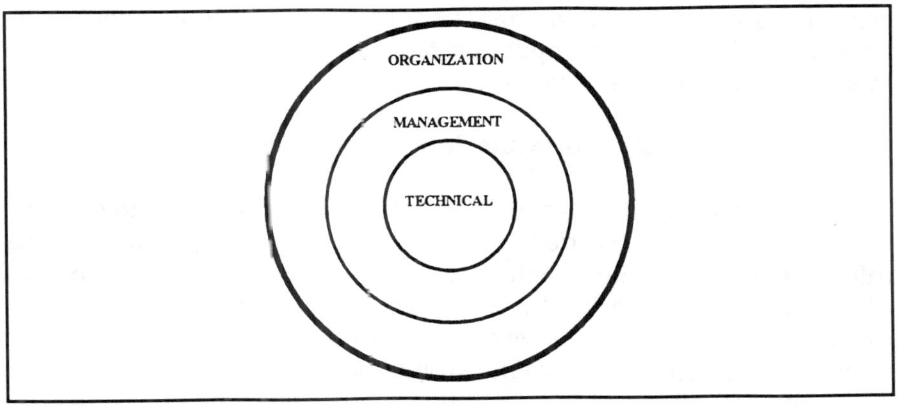

Figure 2: The IAF Layers

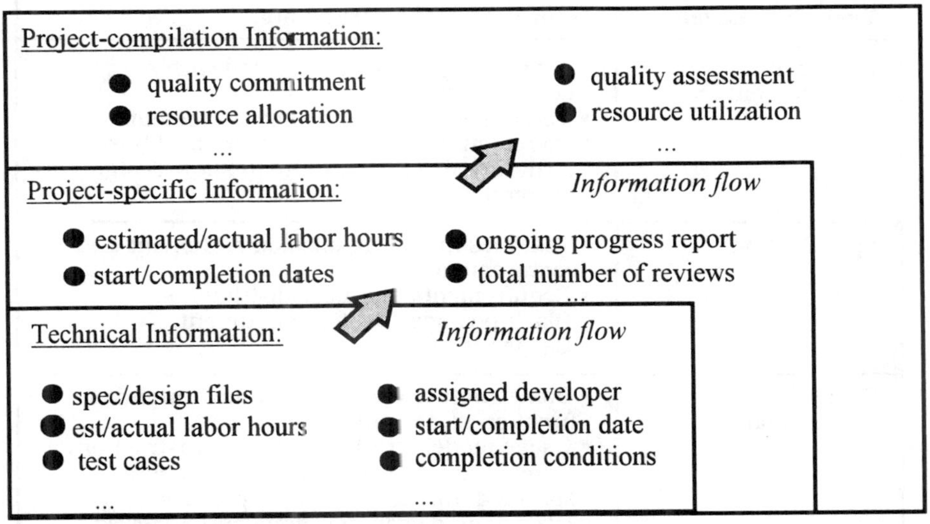

Figure 3: Information Abstraction Concept

Information Requirements

Organization objectives dictate the type of information that must be available to Cleanroom teams, team leads and management. Typically, there is a significant amount of information that is required by these three groups. In order to support their information needs, an Information Abstraction Framework (IAF) is presented in Figure 2 whereby information is categorized as technical (software engineering), management, or organizational. This framework provides a basis for identifying information within and across these levels.

Information abstraction capabilities are necessary to hide low-level details and provide access to meaningful data. This concept is illustrated in Figure 3 where technical information is summarized to generate project-specific data. Then, project-specific information is abstracted for project-compilation data in order to provide management feedback across projects and over time.

Technical Information Requirements

The technical information that is typically required to support Cleanroom team-based development is presented in Table 1. This information is associated with the technical level in the Information Abstraction Framework. Note that the list is not meant to be all-inclusive but is representative of the type of information that must be managed. Each organization would identify specific information requirements for effective project development.

Technical Level:	**Information Requirements:**
Incremental Development	• Team assignments associated with a design increment. • Version control over design increments. • Incremental development plan and box structure usage hierarchy to show design decomposition.
Specification	• Text files including mission statement and requirements list. • Requirements and user documents. • Black box specification document. • Usage model.
Design and Verification	• Box structure designs including intended function statements. • Usage model stratification and abstraction. • Completion and correctness conditions specified during the review process. • History of design decisions and reviewed material. • Conceptual and physical designs of data. • Code generation.
Statistical Certification	• Markov usage modeling, stratification, and abstraction. • Statistical test generation. • Experimental statistics.
All techniques	• Cleanroom documentation and guidebooks. • Action lists.
Team-based development support	• Shared files for reviews and design work. •Team member performance plan & evaluation. • Team member skills, expertise, and training needs. • Team schedules (planned, actual, and deviations).

Table 1: Technical Information Requirements

Technical information resulting from Cleanroom activities may be managed in a common (CASE) repository. For specification activities, technical information includes the mission statement and its validation argument and functional and usage specifications. For design activities, technical information includes box structure designs, a usage hierarchy of box structures, data usage matrices for defining uses of state, and conceptual and physical designs of state data (ERDs, normalized tables, etc.). Lower level designs typically are translated directly into code before or during implementation.

Management Information Requirements

The management level in the IAF identifies information requirements to support project management. Typical information requirements for managing a project are listed in Table 2. It is important to note that much of this information is abstracted from the technical information generated by Cleanroom process adherence. Technical information is abstracted and then summarized to provide individuals,

Management Level	**Information Requirements:**
Incremental Development	• Construction plan identifying planned tasks and assignments. • Progress reports on task and assignment completion and deviations from the construction plan. • Quality, productivity, and performance goals.
Specification	• Status reports on quality and productivity. • Status on completion conditions, action items,etc. • Management issues arising from specification process.
Design and Verification	• Status reports on quality and productivity. • Number and type of completion items. • Management issues arising from design and verification process.
Statistical Certification	• Summary of test results. • Statistical analysis of problem areas to measure quality.
Team-based development support	• Increment schedule and team assignments. • Team composition and performance. • Training reports and list of tool requirements.
All Techniques	• Reports on quality, productivity, and resource utilization.

Table 2: Management Information Requirements

Organizational Level:	Information Requirements:
Process	• Acceptable process adherence. • Assessment of effective teamwork. • Evaluation of effective training and tool use.
Project	• On-going assessment of: - quality - productivity - resource utilization.
Personnel	• Performance assessment - Individual - Team • Skill base - Experience - Training requirements - Expertise and skills.

Table 3: Organization Information Requirements

teams, team leads, and management feedback on the successful completion of tasks and assignments. Abstracted information may include planning (estimations on time, resources, functionality), tracking (actual time, resources, and functionality), and assessment (comparison of estimations and actual data) information for project evaluation on quality, productivity, and resource utilization.

Organization Information Requirements

The organization level in the IAF identifies information regarding all projects over time in order to assess organization maturity as measured by quality, productivity, and resource utilization. Typical information requirements for Cleanroom projects are listed in Table 3. Much of this information is abstracted from the other two levels in the IAF. Project-compiled information is important for achieving organizational goals.

IAF and Its Conceptual Schema

A conceptual model of the IAF provides insight into an organization's needs for automated support to manage its information. A conceptual model can be used to identify information requirements at each level in the IAF. The intellectual control gained by modeling this information is significant as information requirements for developers, teams, and managers are included.

A powerful means of conceptualizing information requirements is an entity-relationship diagram (ERD) such as provided by Chen (Chen, 1981) and automated via CASE tools (Barker, 1994). The ERD notation, illustrated in Figures 4a and 4b, can be used to model the hierarchical relationships that exist between a project and its increments; an increment and its team assignments; and an assignment and its tasks. It also supports the modeling of complex relationships such as employees working on more than one project at a given time. Another important consideration is the ability to include Cleanroom constraints whereby one activity must be completed before another is initiated. The ERD may identify resource requirements specific to a task or assignment and more general information such as personnel

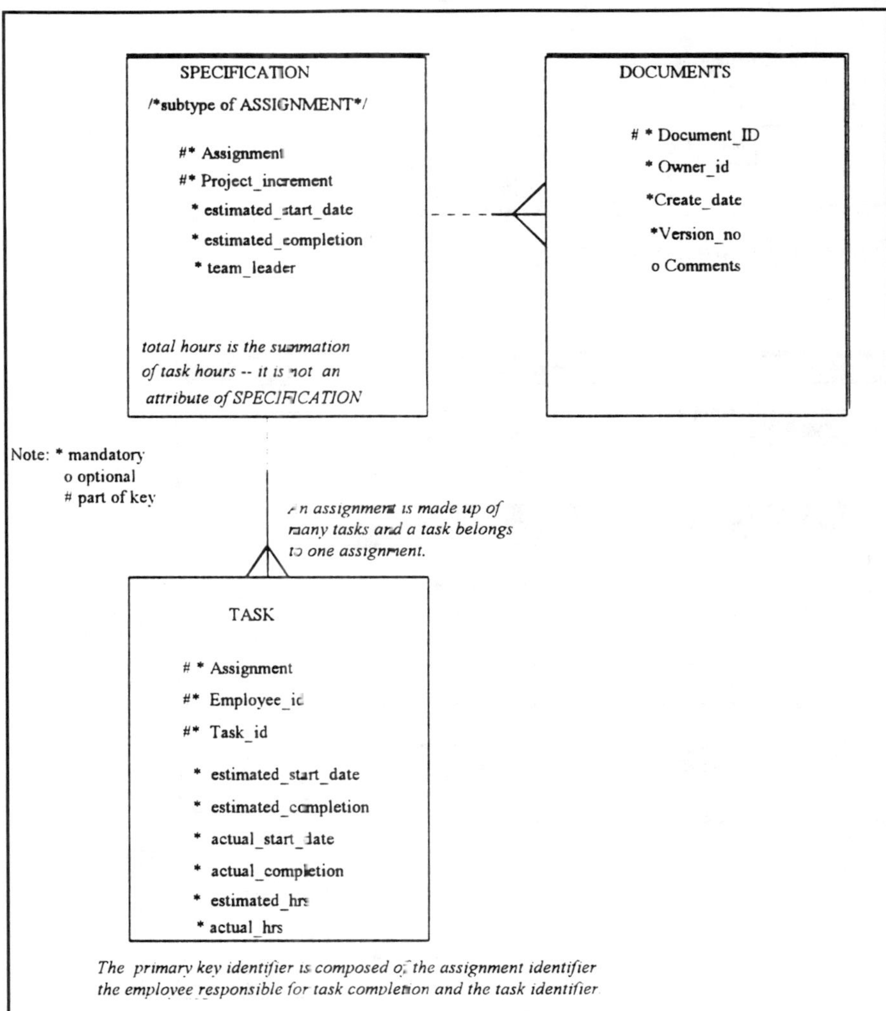

Figure 4a: An Illustration of Entities and Their Attributes

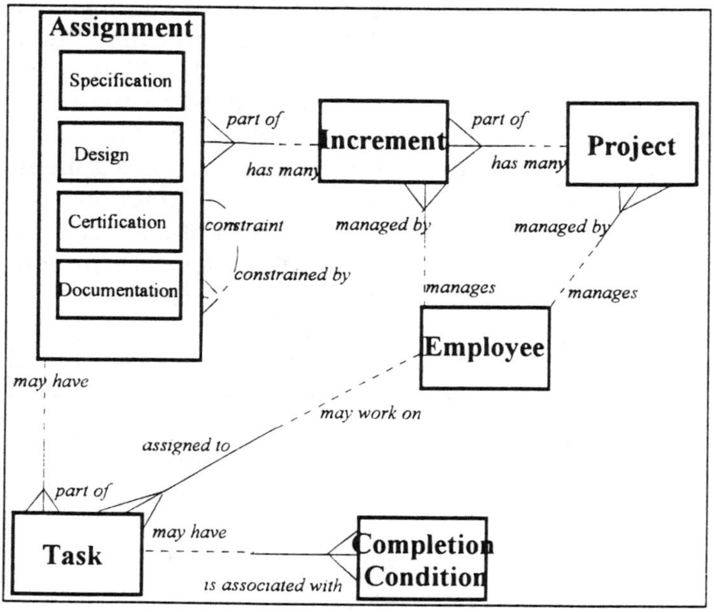

Figure 4b: Illustration of ERD Support of IAF

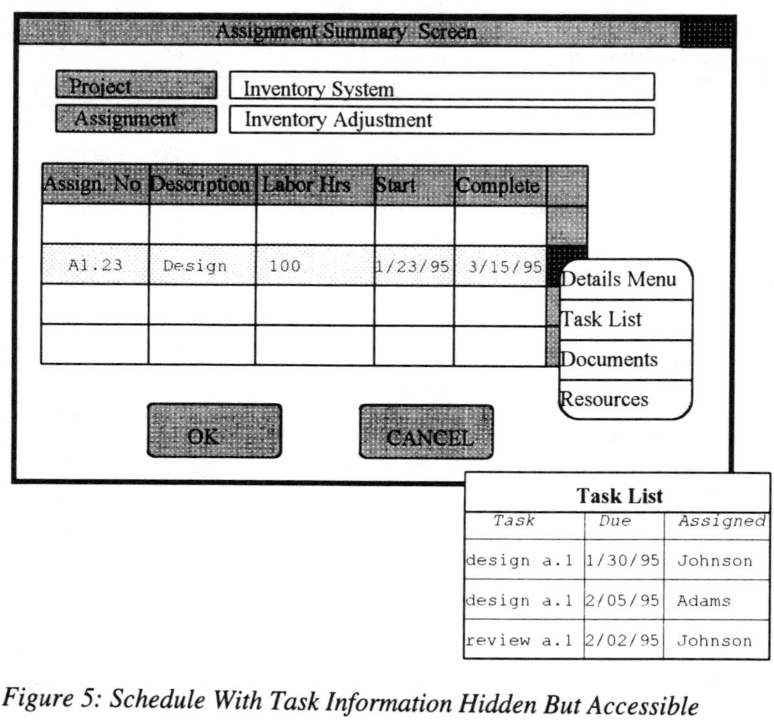

Figure 5: Schedule With Task Information Hidden But Accessible

data, userids, team composition, and other pertinent information.

At the management level, the ERD captures planned and actual events as they occur (i.e., start/stop dates and labor hours for a particular task). Assessment information is not represented in the ERD as it is typically not stored in a common repository. Such information is produced on an "as needed" basis by retrieving planned and actual events and calculating their differences.

The conceptual schema (ERD) supports information abstraction by allowing information hiding of task/assignment details that can be summarized in management and organization reports. These details, however, are essential for team member and team use. Information abstraction is illustrated in Figure 5 where only labor costs and start and completion dates for an assignment are presented to the manager. The task-specific information is hidden from view but is readily accessible.

The Effective Use of CASE Technology

Once the information needs of the organization have been identified, how does an organization select a CASE product to meet its needs? There are many CASE toolsets that provide various levels of support of an organization's IAF including technical information generated by the use of Cleanroom. Effective information management is achieved by planning, tracking, and assessing the use of CASE technology in meeting the objectives of the organization. By implementing these phases, the risk associated with using CASE technology is minimized. Each of the three phases is described.

Planning Phase: Selecting the CASE environment that is right for your organization

Ideally, a CASE environment must be adaptable, flexible, and dynamic in order to effectively manage an organization, its personnel, and its processes (Chen & Norman, 1992). Of course, the level of CASE automation depends on the information needs and objectives of the organization. To determine the appropriateness of CASE use, an organization must first understand what CASE technology is available.

According to Fuggetta (1993), there are three classifications of CASE support: tools, workbenches, and environments. A tool is typically used to support a specific Cleanroom task. A workbench would support in a generic sense a set of the Cleanroom development activities. Its main feature is its common repository where information generated during Cleanroom activities can be stored and shared. An environment supports the whole software process and allows for a level of process customization. As a result, environments offer more features to support aspects of Cleanroom development than the other classifications.

CASE Tools - There are many CASE tools that can be used to support various aspects of Cleanroom software engineering. Hevner et al. (1992) have categorized these tools as:

• Textual and graphic support
• Code generators/compilers (and other programming related tools)
• Testing/debugging
• Data modelers
• Configuration management
• Metrics
• Project management
• Databases/spreadsheet capabilities
• Design/architecture modelers.

CASE tools are used primarily for the technical activities in the IAF as their support is limited. These tools provide specific features used during the execution of a Cleanroom task or assignment but often provide little support for the management and organization levels in the IAF.

CASE Workbenches - The use of specific tools becomes more powerful when integrated into the workbench toolset. The workbench provides for tools that may be used to support various development tasks and activities. It also has a common repository for sharing information primarily within and across the software engineering and management IAF layers.

CASE Environments - Environments include a suite of tools and an underlying workbench for supporting tool integration. In addition, CASE environments are process-driven in that they are capable of supporting an organization's process model such that information requirements for all three levels in the IAF are met. This is accomplished by providing automated capabilities for supporting methodologies, lifecycle activities, forward and reverse engineering, and allowing for process customization to meet the needs of an organization. This flexibility is essential for ongoing support of project development.

Considerations When Selecting a CASE Product

Table 4 identifies the trade-offs to be considered when evaluating CASE products. This table should be used in conjunction with the organization's objectives in order to determine the needs of the organization and how they could be satisfied by CASE products.

For a tool, workbench, or environment that is selected to satisfy

Type	Benefits	Drawbacks
Tool	• Provides automated support of specific tasks. • Typically less expensive. • Minimal learning curve and training requirements.	• Use limited to specific function(s). • Minimal support of Cleanroom process. • No guarantee that tool integrates with existing tools, platforms or environment. • Little support of higher levels in the IAF.
Work-bench	• Supports many/all of the technical aspects of Cleanroom development. • Provides support within and across the layers in the IAF. • Provides access to a repository for information sharing.	• Longer learning curve increasing training requirements. • Greater hardware and software requirements. • May need to deal with integration issues. • Typically more expensive. • Complexity of toolset may impact intellectual control over development process.
Environ-ment	• Provides support within and across IAF levels. • Supports a higher level of organizational maturity. • Supports standardization and information sharing across projects. • Allows for process customization.	• Longer learning curve increasing training requirements at all levels in the organization. • Greater hardware and software requirements. • May need to deal with integration issues. • Typically more expensive. • Complexity of toolset may impact intellectual control over development process. • Complexity of software may require technical and process expertise.

Table 4: CASE Trade-offs

the information requirements of the organization, it is important to determine the extent to which it can support Cleanroom activities. This is essential for maintaining a high level of process adherence necessary for implementing the Cleanroom principles. Strict adherence to the process will result in a higher quality design.

For example, a word processor may be used to support Cleanroom specification, design, and implementation activities. This is accomplished by enforcing a use of the tool whereby all designs are written in box structure specification/design language. Once a design component has been reviewed for correctness, the design can be expanded to include application code. By commenting out the box structure statements, the code becomes compilable. The file now contains a documentation trail of intended functionality, expanded design statements, and implementable code.

Table 5 illustrates an organization's list of objectives that has been developed as an outgrowth of its information requirements. The prioritization is typically done with management support. Once the list has been developed, cost/benefit analysis is performed to assess CASE options before a product decision is made. This is important as CASE selections too often result from the successful marketing efforts of the CASE producer and not as a result of a proper needs assessment by the organization. It should be noted that these objectives are considered "second-order" or derived objectives as they are project-specific as ways to achieve higher quality and reduced cost.

Analyzing the Costs and Benefits of CASE

Cost/benefit analysis minimizes the risk associated with choosing inappropriate CASE technology to satisfy information requirements. In the past, CASE technology was introduced into an organization as a means of improving quality and productivity. Quality and productivity gains were often not realized because of obstacles that the organization failed to overcome. As a result, many organizations have become disillusioned with the use of CASE (Fuggetta, 1993).

A lack of planning when choosing or enhancing CASE support often results in the following:

- A mismatch of tools, environments, and platforms.
- Information requirements not met.
- Lack of process support (such as defined in the Cleanroom method).
- CASE assessment becomes difficult after it has been implemented.
- Productivity and quality are negatively impacted.

Priority Scale:
4 - mandatory requirement
3 - highly recommended requirement
2 - recommended requirement
1 - not a requirement

Priority	**Applicable Objective:**
4	Organization support for achieving and maintaining a level of maturity.
3	Management support at a project level.
3	Project-based support including reusability and standardization.
2	Teamwork support via information sharing.
2	User, system, and developer documentation support.
4	Technical support of Cleanroom techniques.
3	Graphical and text support of formal notation of specification and design activities.
2	Common repository for storing and accessing information within and across projects.
3	Integrating capabilities in an existing platform/ suite of tools.
2	Communication mechanism across all layers of IAF including management, developer, testers, and users.
2	Specific features such as testing capabilities, data integrity and/or consistency checks, normalization support, and code generation.

Table 5: Objectives List

Cost Factor#	Cost Description:
1	Training and learning curve
2	Flexibility and customization
3	Hardware and software support (platform,etc.)
4	Accessibility (geographic dispersion)
5	Technological advances
6	Integration with existing systems (proprietary)
7	Application support across projects
(Note: The Cost Factor# is a unique identifier for the cost description used in Table 7)	

Table 6 Costs Assessment

A Costs Assessment table as illustrated in Table 6 provides visibility to the costs associated with introducing CASE technology in the organization.

The benefits associated with the introduction of CASE are also identified. A table similar to a Cost table is developed and each benefit is rated in terms of its importance in meeting the objectives of the organization. This becomes important in deciding upon a particular CASE toolset, workbench, and/or environment. It is critical to match costs and benefits in the tables as much as possible to assess the overall impact on the organization.

Table 7 illustrates a Benefits table. Each benefit in the table is rated according to its level of support in meeting the information needs of the organization. The Cost Factor# column is used as a link between the Cost and Benefits tables.

Azani and Khorramshahgol (1993) compiled a list of barriers to the introduction and implementation of CASE technology. This list includes:

- Lack of in-house CASE support.
- Lack of top management support and commitment.
- Lack of participation in decisions.
- Employee's resistance to change.
- Existing organization culture.
- Lack of a cost justification.
- Rapid obsolescence of the technology.
- Short-term perspective.
- Absence of a structured methodology.
- Insufficient training.
- Lack of teamwork and collaboration.

These barriers can be eliminated or minimized by performing cost/benefit analysis and then applying a review process to the resulting documents (refer to Chapter 6 for a discussion on team reviews). The review process will generate support and reduce resistance to the introduction of CASE in an organization. Reviews

Benefit Rating	Cost Factor#	CASE Benefit
3	2,4,7	Improved quality - built-in consistency checks, supports normalization of database systems, allows for process customization, transparent access to shared information, records events as they occur, design translation into code.
2	1,3	Performance satisfaction - learning curve is minimal, supports existing technology, automates daily tasks or assists in their completion.
1	3,4	Skill base and expertise - developers learn or share skills, provides automated expertise not available in the organization.
2	2,6,7	Traceability and accountability - information is easily accessible in a common repository. Documentation is automatically generated from existing information. History files are supported providing documentation trails.
2	4,6,7	Reusability - easily recognizable and accessible in a common repository.
0	2	Process adherence - customizable environment allows for high-level of process adherence. Provides a level of support for one or more Cleanroom processes.
1	2,6	Communication link - Improved communication among developers, users, testers, and managers.
3	5,6,7	Project Management - supports management and organization layers in the IAF.

Table 7: Benefits Table (Benefits of CASE Usage)

also ensure the correctness and completeness of the assessment process.

A team review allows developers and managers to validate the information requirements, costs, benefits, and objectives associated with the use of CASE. The review process not only ensures a correct assessment of information needs, but also provides an opportunity for involvement in CASE decisions by personnel associated with all three levels in the IAF. Figure 6 illustrates this review process.

Common Repository Considerations

In order to support the IAF, an important consideration is a common repository for providing access to information within and across the three layers. The accessibility of information is related to

CASE Assessment

Review of:

Information Requirements

Are requirements met at all three levels in the IAF?
Are requirements consistent with organization objectives?

Costs and Benefits

Is it feasible to meet all of the information requirements?
What are alternative solutions to satisfy organization objectives?

Organization, Management, and Developer Objectives

Are the objectives of developers, managers, and the organization supported by the alternative solutions?

Review Results:

Action Item	Action Description	Tentative Solution	Due Date	Assigned To
1. Training	Training needs have not been assessed for testers.	Identify CASE needs and options for testing support	02/4/95	S. Jackson

Figure 6: A Formal Review of CASE Information

the level of support of the characteristics associated with a common repository as identified by Hevner & Becker (1992). These characteristics are summarized as:

Repository Architecture - Front-end tools; such as VisualBasic, Powerbuilder, PowerObjects and Oracle Forms/Reports application generators and other GUI (Graphic User Interface) tools provide accessibility to detailed and abstracted information. As a result, information becomes available at appropriate levels for effective process management.

Repository Platform - Ideally, CASE tool support includes execution in a distributed environment and may require linking various client/server platforms. Distributed support would provide transparent links among data objects such that information is easily accessible locally or remotely.

Information Content - Conceptual modeling capabilities provide visual and textual descriptions of data and relationships. Information typically is stored in a relational data format for flexibility, efficiency, and ease of use.

Repository Services - The repository would maintain version control as tasks are performed iteratively and would support import/ export capabilities required for accessibility to external files.

A common repository may already exist in the organization or may be part of the CASE technology that is implemented. In either case, a common repository is essential for maintaining information within and across the levels of the IAF. This concept of repository support is illustrated in Figure 7.

Tracking Phase: Ensuring the Successful Use of CASE

After the initial planning phase has been successfully completed, mechanisms for CASE use must be in place. This includes integration of existing and selected CASE tools, proper training, user documentation and technical support. It also includes an ongoing assessment of the "good use" of CASE in developing complete and correct system components and management information.

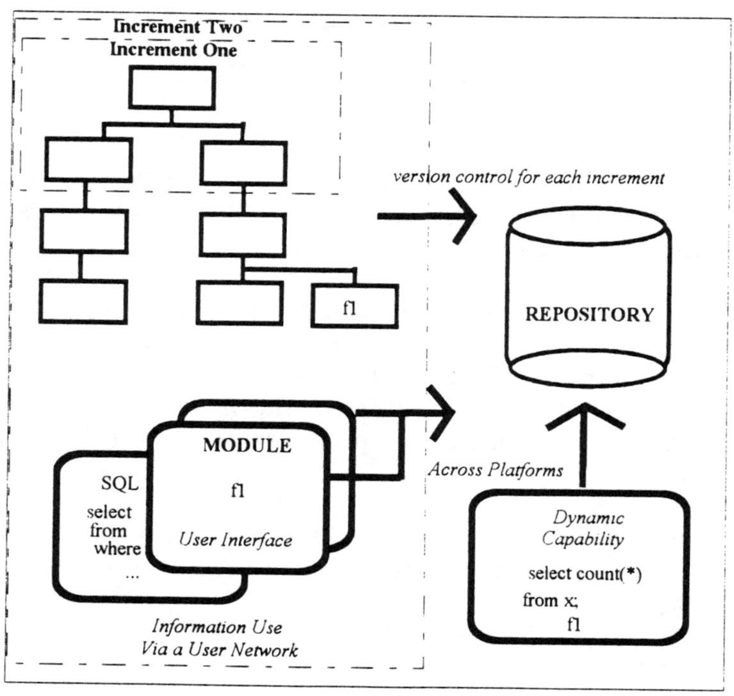

Figure 7: Repository Support of Cleanroom Process

The Successful Integration of CASE Support

A framework for CASE integration as presented by Thomas and Nejmeh (1992) has been modified as shown in Figure 8 in order to apply it to the proposed CASE support. The three components in the framework represent the different conceptual and physical levels at which integration should be supported: the presentation level (i.e., appearance, behavior, and overall interaction paradigm presented by the user interface); the control and process levels (activities and functions of the various tools themselves); and the data level (the extent to which interoperability, nonredundancy, data consistency, data exchange, and synchronization are supported by the common repository (Becker et al., 1993)).

Data integration - All information gathered during Cleanroom activities is managed as a whole, regardless of how the parts are used and transformed. This is important for supporting the abstraction capabilities as outlined in the IAF.

Control integration - Provides flexibility for customizing CASE to support the Cleanroom techniques. Control integration allows for the combination of an environment's functions according to project preferences and underlying processes.

Process integration - Ensures that tools interact effectively in support of Cleanroom activities.

Presentation integration - Improves user interaction with environ-

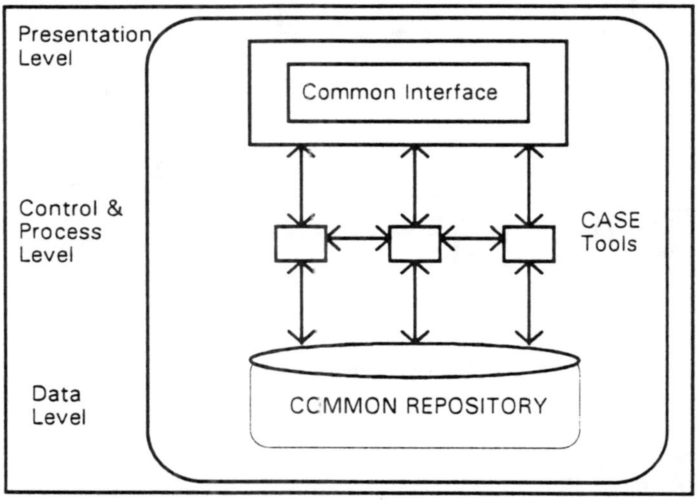

Figure 8: A Framework for CASE Integration

ment by reducing user's cognitive load. This is important for supporting the three levels in the IAF. Information is abstracted and displayed appropriately to support developers, team leaders, and managers in Cleanroom activities. It is essential for hiding detailed information until the user requests it.

Use of Quality and Completeness Checks

An important feature of CASE is its automated support of completeness and design consistency at the technical level. These features are not meant to usurp Cleanroom reviews, but to support intellectual control during task completion. Many of the workbench and environment CASE toolsets provide quality checks. Correctness and consistency features should be considered integral components for supporting the Cleanroom process and its emphasis on error prevention. The CRUD matrix and consistency checks presented in Figures 9 and 10 illustrate common correctness features that are part of CASE environments.

A CRUD (Create, Read, Update, Delete) matrix is a powerful tool in checking the sufficient and necessary use of data in supporting all of the functions. The functions and datatypes (typically represented as entities) are the columns and rows; respectively, in the matrix. The cells are filled with a blank (no relationship) or a CRUD for data use. The matrix supports the Cleanroom correctness concept of closure as it validates whether all datatypes are used in the system functions (the necessary condition) and whether they are used appropriately (the sufficiency condition) (Mills et al., 1987). Lower level data usage

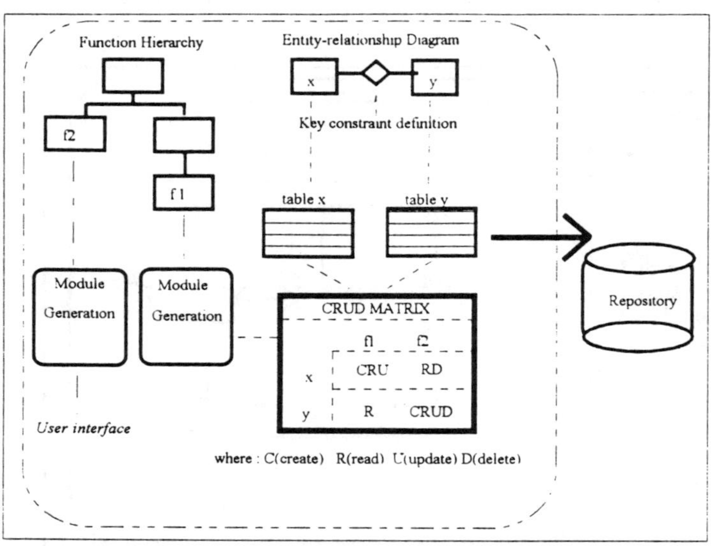

Figure 9: CASE CRUD Matrix and Its Relationship to Other Tools (Becker, 1995)

matrices may also be supported by CASE in order to validate the use of attributes in each entity. The relationship of the CRUD matrix to other supporting tool components is illustrated in Figure 9.

The correctness and consistency evaluation illustrated in Figure 10 provides automated feedback on consistency of data definitions, data use, and other supporting checks. These checks are useful in validating consistent use and definition of data at various levels of design.

Assessment Phase: Evaluating the Successful Use of CASE

The assessment of CASE technology should be done on an ongoing basis in order to evaluate its impact on the organization. How is the successful use of CASE measured? There are several factors that can be evaluated depending on the organization's objectives. Azani and Khorramshagol (1993) identified them as:

- Integration into existing suite of tools was done successfully.
- Quality and productivity standards have been met.
- Employee performance and morale has been improved.
- Accessible documentation, designs, reviews and their completion conditions, code generation, and other shared technical information.
- Improved customer service.

At a technical level, the CASE toolset allows for a number of consistency checks on information provided by a developer. Example errors and conflict feedback include:

1. Inherited attribute name conflicts.
2. Inherited relationship name conflicts.
3. Standalone entities with no attributes or relationships.
4. Attributes without information types.
5. Illegal key definitions (optional instead of mandatory).
6. No or invalid resolution on complex relationship.

CASE may also provide for exception analysis where feedback includes:

1. Missing definitions for all objects.
2. Missing comments.
3. Missing minimum and maximum values.

An illustration of a Data Modeling Analysis Report provides the following information:

Source Diagram: The Entity-Relationship Schema
The following errors were found while analyzing the ERD. Error messages should be checked as they can result in an incomplete or incorrect physical schema.

Figure 10: Illustration of Correctness and Consistency Evaluation Using CASE

- Improved interface between technology and users.
- Increased flexibility in developing existing and future projects.
- Information requirements met for each level in the IAF.
- Management reports can be created dynamically as well as on a scheduled basis.

What is needed is a management checklist that allows for assessment of CASE technology use and its successful acculturation in the organization (Chmura & Crockett, 1995). An example checklist that has been compiled from the organization's objectives and expected CASE benefits is presented in Table 8. If expectations have not been met, then the organization can take appropriate action.

The three phases of effective introduction and use of CASE in an organization are repeated as often as necessary to ensure that employee resistance is overcome, communication channels remain open, and the objectives of the organization are met. This iterative process will minimize the risk that in the past has been associated with the introduction of CASE in organizations.

Status	**Checklist Item**	**Objective**
Pass	Proper Tool Selection	Improved quality of documentation, designs,etc.
Fail	Sufficient Training	Personnel has been trained in the proper use of CASE technology to support the Cleanroom process.
Improve	Information Requirements Met	Minimal support for Cleanroom project management.
Pass	Process Adherence	Cleanroom procedures have been established and are adhered to.
Pass	Integration of Tools	Transparent integration of CASE into existing platform.
Pass	Budgeted Costs	Training, technology upgrades, learning curve, and other cost factors are within budget.
Pass	Learning Curve	Employee performance and satisfaction are within goals established for successful use of CASE.
Pass	Acceptance Factor	CASE technology is accepted as an integral component to the successful use of Cleanroom.

Table 8: CASE Assessment Checklist

A Summary of the Use of CASE

It is important to involve developers and managers during all three phases to ensure successful acceptance and use of CASE. The successful use of CASE technology in an organization may force a change in the existing development paradigm. Development control is transferred at least in part from "human knowledge-bases" to a shared common repository. This shift from individual development efforts to a team approach improves the maturity of an organization especially when information is available via a shared repository. This approach is consistent with the Team Assignment Model in Chapter 6 where development teams are held responsible for the successful completion of project tasks and assignments.

Another important issue in the successful use of CASE is establishing procedures on the "good use" of CASE technology to support Cleanroom. CASE technology, as in past development environments, can be used to "hack" out documents, designs and code. It is important that CASE procedures be established at the initiation of project development to ensure that the Cleanroom techniques are adhered to. This is especially critical for ensuring team reviews of CASE generated documents, designs, code, and other components are held on a regular

Several key areas have been identified that require formal procedures for the effective use of CASE:

- **Design Consistency** — Design changes in CASE may not automatically cascade to higher/lower level designs resulting in design inconsistencies. All modifications to technical information including specification, design, or implementation must be team reviewed and documented.

- **Data and Domain Definitions** - CASE promotes reuse by providing for the design of shared data domains. Once defined, domains become common data types that may be used to maintain system integrity. Developers must be made aware of this capability and encouraged to use it. Otherwise, duplicate domains will be defined which may result in a loss of intellectual control over data definitions.

- **Integrity Constraints** - CASE allows for the definition of integrity constraints including UNIQUE, NOT NULL, CHECK (validation), and PRIMARY/FOREIGN constraints. Good use of constraint definitions supports data integrity as the implementation of the constraints is hidden from the use of the data.

- **Design Generation** - CASE has a capability of translating designs into user forms and application code. Form and code generation should be performed only after the design has passed team reviews, completion conditions have been met, and certification has been done. Otherwise, debugging is promoted as system components are compiled without proper Cleanroom quality checks thus compromising system quality.

Table 9: Procedures for the Good Use of CASE

basis. Any completion conditions that are specified during a review must be met. Table 9 illustrates a set of procedures that have been established to support a structured approach to using CASE.

At the technical level, a drawback of most CASE environments is a lack of support of semantic correctness. Many CASE products provide various consistency and data integrity checks but these cannot replace a formal verification of correctness and completeness as provided by Cleanroom. In fact, CASE tools may actually increase the need for correctness verification. Errors that are introduced into the design when using CASE may be the result of improper use or due to inexperience. CASE generated errors may be the consequence of incorrect data manipulation and the resulting interpretation by the CASE tools. These defects will proliferate throughout the system design because they typically become part of shared information stored in the common repository. Cleanroom reviews should be held on all output generated by CASE to eliminate the potential for undetected defects.

References

Azani C.H., & Khorramshahgol, R. (1993). The Adoption and Implementation of CASE Technology. *Computer-Aided Software Engineering: Issues and Trends for the 1990s and Beyond,* Idea Group Publishing, Harrisburg PA.

Barker, R. (1994). *CASE*Method Entity Relationship Modeling,* Addison-Wesley Publishing Company, 1994.

Becker, S. (1995). *The Use of CASE for Effective Process Management, Information Technology Management and Organizational Innovations,* 1996 IRMA Conference Proceedings, Washington, D.C.

Becker, S., & Gibson, R. (1995). Integrated CASE Support for an Information Abstraction Framework. *Managing Social and Economic Change With Information Technology,* 1995 IRMA Conference Proceedings, Atlanta, Georgia, 321-326.

Becker S., Gleason B.J., & La Salle A. (1993). An Integrated CASE Model for Forward and Reverse Software Engineering. *Computer-Aided Software Engineering: Issues and Trends for the 1990s and Beyond,* Idea Group Publishing, Harrisburg PA.

Chen M., & Norman R.J. (1992). A Framework for Integrated CASE. *IEEE Software,* 9(2).

Chen P. (1981). *A Preliminary Framework for Entity-Relationship Models. Entity-Relationship Approach to Information Modeling and Analysis,* ER Institute, PO Box 617, Saugus, CA 91350.

Chmura A., & Crockett H.D. (1995). Point-Counterpoint: What's the Proper Role for CASE Tools? *IEEE Software,* 12(2).

Forte G., & Norman R.J., (1992). A self-assessment by the Software Engineering Community. *Communications of the ACM,* 35(4).

Fuggetta A. (1993). A Classification of CASE Technology. *IEEE Computer,* (26)12.

Gutierrez, O. (1993). A Contingency View on Prototyping Practice, *Journal of Information Technology,* 8(2).

Hevner A., & Becker S. (1992). *Central Repository Design For Cleanroom*

Systems Development. Proceedings of the 25th Hawaii International Conference on Systems Sciences, Hawaii, January 1992.

Hevner A., Becker S., & Pedowitz L. (1992). Integrated CASE for Cleanroom Development. *IEEE Software,* 9(2).

Mills H. (1988). Stepwise Refinement and Verification in Box-Structured Systems. *IEEE Computer,* 21(6).

Mills H., Dyer M., & Linger R. (1987). Cleanroom Software Engineering. *IEEE Software,* 4(5).

Mills H., Linger R., & Hevner A. (1986). *Principles of Information Systems Analysis and Design,* Academic Press, San Diego.

Thomas I., & Nejmeh B. A. (1992). Definitions of Tool Integration for Environments. *IEEE Software,* 9(2).

GLOSSARY OF TERMS

abstract model The user's view of data encapsulated by a system, used in the definition of a black box specification. May be any collection of abstract data types, except in classic box structures where only stimulus history is permitted.

abstraction The act of recovering a specification from existing design materials.

black box One of three views of any system, object, or part. This view hides both data implementation (if any) and process implementation.

box structures An approach to information systems analysis and design, using three box views: black box, state box, and clear box.

case explosion Results from the composition of functions during abstraction of a sequence or alternation clear box. The initial number of cases is the product of the number of cases of each sub-specification.

clear box One of three views of any system, object, or part. This view exposes process implementation.

common service A black box specification that appears in multiple places in the development hierarchy.

complete correctness The design and the specification have the same domain of definition, and produce the same output on every domain element.

composition A way of combining two mappings, in which the output (range) of one becomes the input (domain) of the next.

concrete model The designer's view of data, used in the definition of a state box design. May be any collection of instances of data specifications.

control structure One of the organizing structures of a clear box. Typical control structures are sequence, if-then, and while-do.

correct A design is correct with respect to a specification if it sufficiently meets the behavior defined by the specification.

data space The set of all possible values of a concrete or abstract data model.

data specification A black box that defines a data-encapsulating entity.

design A step, or series of steps, towards implementation of a specification.

design quality A collection of project-dependent design characteristics, usually including performance, simplicity, manageability, robustness, reusability, and so forth.

inheritance A characteristic of the object-oriented paradigm, in which properties of one class are inherited by its subclass.

local data Data objects that are visible only to the clear box where they are defined and have the duration of that clear box. Named instances of data specifications.

machine The collection of process specifications that are part of the state box.

partial function A mapping that is undefined on some of its possible inputs but gives only one value for each argument in the domain of definition.

primitive A specification that is already implemented, either by the team (and placed in a library) or by another agent (such as the compiler).

process specification A black box that does not encapsulate data.

relation A mapping that gives a set of values for each argument.

representation mapping A mapping between the concrete and the abstract data spaces of the state box and black box respectively.

specification The black box definition or description of the behavior of software.

specification function A single-valued functional abstraction that names a specification concept.

state box One of three views of any system, object, or part. This view partially exposes data implementation but hides process implementation.

state data The concrete data storage defined by a state box.

state migration The act of hiding data implementations via a hierarchy of data specifications.

sufficient correctness For inputs that are in the domain of the specification, the design produces the same outputs (or a subset) as the specification. For inputs that are outside of the domain of the specification, the design may produce any output.

total function A function that is defined on all possible inputs.

validation Informally arguing or testing to demonstrate the adequacy of a specification or design.

verification Demonstrating, based on correctness theory, the correctness of a design with respect to a specification.

INDEX

AUTHORS' BIOGRAPHIES

EDITORS OF THIS BOOK

Shirley Becker is an Associate Professor of Computer Science and Information Systems at American University. Her research interests include innovations in teamwork, process management, CASE, and Cleanroom software engineering. She has published many articles in these areas. Dr. Becker received her Ph.D. and M.S. in Information Systems from the University of Maryland at College Park. She is a member of IEEE Computer Society, IRMA, and ACM.

James A. Whittaker is an Assistant Professor of Computer Science at the Florida Institute of Technology in Melbourne, Florida. He specializes in statistical testing of software and software-intensive systems. He has publications in IEEE and ACM technical journals on software testing and reliability and is a regular speaker at software conferences worldwide. He has largely industry experience and has lead a number of testing projects at his former employer Software Engineering Technology of Knoxville, Tennessee. Dr. Whittaker has also participated as a consultant to various organizations, including the DoD, Ericsson, IBM and Microsoft. Dr. Whittaker received his BA from Bellarmine College, Louisville, Kentucky and the MS and Ph.D. degrees from the University of Tennessee in 1990 and 1992, respectively.

CONTRIBUTORS TO THIS BOOK

Michael Deck is a software quality consultant specializing in the application of Cleanroom software engineering. From 1982 to 1993 he held a number of positions at IBM, including software developer, project manager, and technology consultant. In 1993 he formed Cleanroom Software Engineering, Inc., to help companies solve software process and quality problems through the application of advanced software engineering techniques. He has taught hundreds of software developers and managers how to apply Cleanroom practices, across the US and in Japan. His current work focuses on tailoring Cleanroom techniques for unique projects and environments. These include, but are not limited to, CMM Level 1-3 environments, projects using object-orientated techniques, and embedded applications. He has a BA (Mathematics) from Kalamazoo College and an MS (Computer Science) from the University of Maryland, and has taught at both institutions. He is presently chair of the Boulder, Colorado, Chapter of the ACM, and is a member of the IEEE and ASQC. Michael Deck can be reached at Cleanroom Software Engineering, Inc., 303-494-3152 (voice), 303-494-3026 (fax), deckm@cleansoft.com, http://www.csn.net/~deckm.

Rick Gibson received his Ph.D. in Information Systems from the University of Maryland in 1992. It was there, while under the influence of Al Hevner, that he was first introduced to the Cleanroom approach. Several years of teaching computer science and business management in Italy, Germany, Belgium, Korea, Japan, and the Philippines provided the impetus for adopting multidisciplinary perspectives regarding information systems. International and domestic consulting assignments in the area of software engineering provided the opportunity to investigate applications of the Software Engineering Institute's Capability Maturity Model. Concurrent research interests include the evolutionary internationalization of the information systems curriculum and the revolutionary application of complex theory to information systems development.

Tove Janzon is the Operating Manager for Q-Labs, Inc. in College Park, Maryland. She is also a consultant in the software engineering field with special emphasis on human factors, project management, and organizational structures. Ms. Janzon has received a MSc. in Computer Science from Lund Institute of Technology in Sweden.

Bengt Nilsson has 10 years of experience as a software engineering consultant. He has worked as a practitioner with focus on Project Management for several years before specializing in process improvement. He has worked with large scale process change involving the introduction of teamwork, Cleanroom and Object-Oriented methodologies. He is currently working for Kipling Information Technology but was previously employed by Q-Labs, Inc. He received a M.Sc in Electrical Engineering from Lund Institute of Technology in Sweden.

Stacy Prowell is a member of the professional staff of Software Engineering Technology, Inc., where he provides consultation and training in the use of software engineering techiques, conducts research on rigorous software specification and development techniques, and advises on the construction of tools to support specification and development. He received his Ph.D. in Computer Science from the University of Tennessee in 1996. He is a member of the ACM, AAAS, and Sigma Xi.